COMMUNICATIVE PLANNING THEORY

Communicative Planning Theory

TORE SAGER
Department of Transportation Engineering
Norwegian Institute of Technology
University of Trondheim

Avebury

Aldershot · Brookfield USA · Hong Kong · Singapore · Sydney

© Tore Sager 1994

Published by
Avebury
Ashgate Publishing Limited
Gower House
Croft Road
Aldershot
Hants GU11 3HR
England

Ashgate Publishing Company
Old Post Road
Brookfield
Vermont 05036
USA

British Library Cataloguing in Publication Data

Tore, Sager
Communicative Planning Theory
I. Title
303.3

ISBN 1 85628 543 X

Printed and Bound in Great Britain by
Athenaeum Press Ltd, Newcastle upon Tyne.

Contents

v

Figures and tables

Preface

This book is based on the belief that the critical theory of communicative action holds great potential for the renewal of planning theory. One reason is that the function of public planning in society is not only to prepare the implementation of physical projects and social policies. Planning has an integrating function as well, and it nurtures and enlightens the public debate over collective action. In this perspective it is clear that planning problems can be solved in two contrasting yet complementary ways: one can trust expert judgement based on analytic technique or discuss the matter and reach a group decision. These modes of problem-solving are reflected in the dichotomy of calculation vs communication. The planners have to balance efficient goal achievement and democratic procedure. On the abstract level it is a question of bounding the domains of instrumental and communicative rationality in public planning.

A conceptual scheme comprising the various functions of planning is needed. This scheme should also make clear that different types of rationality are required to guide reasoning within the competing modes of problem-solving used when attacking the various tasks of planning in society. The critical theory of Jürgen Habermas provides this conceptual framework and helps me do the following: (1) reformulate central themes of mainstream planning theory and give new answers to old questions, (2) examine how the main planning theories relate to the concepts of power and conflict, and (3) analyse the mechanisms causing irrationality or flexibility to be the outcome of clashes between the planning system and threatening impulses.

The book is divided into three parts following a simple logic: Part one presents a dialogical and 'ideal type' planning theory and discusses the rationale and paradigm of planning in light of it. Part two is a conceptual analysis of some important obstacles to dialogical planning in society, namely conflicts and power relations. Part three inquires into the very different ways planners react to the difficulties encountered in the attempt to promote instrumental and communicative rationality in unfavourable political and social contexts.

Three discourses or perspectives permeate the entire exposition and justify the title *Communicative Planning Theory*. Firstly, all themes are explored by employing concepts from the critical theory of communicative action. Secondly, I focus on the tension between communicative and calculative practice in public planning. Thirdly, the book is kept in close contact with mainstream planning theory by contrasting the features of synoptic and incremental approaches. This theme may seem exhausted, but with the acknowledgement of communicative rationality, the dichotomy can be analysed in a dialogue/technique perspective with considerable novelty. The discussion strengthens the textbook qualities and serves my aim of making the book a natural companion to elementary texts in planning theory.

I conclude the book by considering how to retain some of the dialogical ideal in a society more preoccupied with instrumental rationality than with integration and mutual understanding. It is a fascinating challenge to make planning an active instrument for critical analysis and simultaneously a responsive servant to democratic politics and administration.

*

I am indebted to a number of colleagues who took time from their own work to read individual chapters, giving me the frank and careful criticism that is a writer's greatest need. Ragnvald Sagen has read the first version of each chapter. Though always on the alert against inconsistencies and sloppy formulations, he was always very supportive.

Andreas Faludi and John Forester encouraged me at an early stage to write a book on the basis of my 1990-dissertation *Communicate or Calculate* from the Nordic Institute for Studies in Urban and Regional Planning. I doubt that the project would have got off the ground without their inspiring comments. John has given me more encouragement and advice than anyone has the right to hope for, and I wish to express my gratitude.

It is appropriate to acknowledge the prior publication of some of the ideas in this book in earlier papers. Chapter 2 draws heavily on 'Why plan? A multi-rationality foundation for planning' published by the *Scandinavian Housing and Planning Research* (1992), and 'Paradigms for planning: a rationality-based classification' published by the *Planning Theory Newsletter* (1993).

My working place, the Department of Transportation Engineering at the Norwegian Institute of Technology, gave me the opportunity to work continuously on this book throughout the first half of 1993. I greatly appreciate the flexibility and tolerance exercised by my colleagues.

Part one   Communicative rationality in planning theory

Part one revives some central themes of mainstream planning theory by applying the critical theory of communicative action set forth by Jürgen Habermas. I work out contrasting 'ideal types' of incrementalism and synoptic planning that are antipodes regarding the use of dialogue and analytic technique. Based on this revised dichotomy, a typology of planning paradigms is set up.

My aim is to solve two problems marring most mainstream planning theories. Firstly, they lack sufficiently clear assumptions concerning information, communication, and analytic technique. This makes it difficult to assess, e.g., whether notions of legitimation, power, conflict management, and responsiveness are consistent with the main planning theories. Secondly, the theories prescribe no way that the goals can be rationally determined. Therefore, they have to take goals as externally given, which is unrealistic in many cases. It would often be preferable that evaluations of plans and planning processes include an assessment of the goals and the way they are decided on. This problem can be solved by explicitly acknowledging Habermas's communicative rationality.

As indicated above, 'dialogical incrementalism' is not a practical mode of planning but rather a theoretical model and an analytic tool. This tool is needed when discussing planning theories and assessing planning in a communicative perspective. That is why the chapter on dialogical incrementalism opens the book. Towards the end of the exposition, the 'ideal type' will be modified to account for difficulties faced by real life planning.

Several dilemmas are due to the unfairness and irrationality manifest in power relations and conflict. Time and again planners feel the pulse of injustice and unreasonableness, since their professional field has so close ties to politics. There seems to be an almost unlimited number of definitions of both 'politics' and 'planning'. A fairly conventional view is to see poli-

1

tics as an attempt to influence the collective and practical efforts aiming at determining and achieving the societal goals. Of course the various terms of this definition can be specified in a number of ways. However, the point is that most of the work taking place in public planning agencies would be part of politics according to this definition. Commonplace conceptualizations of planning confirm my impression. Planning is seen to be

- a set of procedures for finding out and assuring appropriate future action (Davidoff and Reiner 1962:103);
- 'foresight in formulating and implementing programs and policies' (Hudson 1979:387);
- 'the application of scientific method - however crude - to policy-making' Faludi 1973:1); or
- the bridge from ideology and knowledge to collective action (Friedmann and Hudson 1974:2).

The above is all in accordance with the view of planning as closely related to politics. Despite this closeness, I begin the analysis by defining planning in a way that does not explicitly refer to politics: one can think of public planning as technique and communication aiming at organizing knowledge to provide a basis for decision-making on future collective action.

1 Dialogical incrementalism

The contrast between the central types of planning theory should be based on opposing assumptions concerning key concepts. A profound distinction is achieved when the synoptic and incremental theories are founded on different types of nearly unbounded rationality. The reformulation of incrementalism requires the introduction of dialogue and the communicative rationality of Jürgen Habermas. Disjointed incrementalism is not a perfect theoretical opposite to the synoptic ideal because (1) its conceptualization of communication is too vague and narrow, and (2) it only modifies instrumental reason without introducing an alternative type of rationality. Further criticism is derived from this. The traditional synoptic/incremental dichotomy (3) does not permit fully rational combinations of the two central planning modes, and (4) it does not give due attention to the design of planning processes with intrinsic qualities. My purpose is to reformulate incrementalism to arrive at a main dichotomy answering to this criticism. Moreover, I want to show that incrementalism founded on dialogue can better avoid lack of direction and systematic support of the powerful. The planning modes of the synoptic/dialogical-incremental distinction are theoretical opposites regarding the rationality types, the use of the means-end scheme, and the application of dialogue and analytic technique.

Introduction on dialogue in planning theory

The synoptic-versus-incremental debate rapidly grew to be the most important one in the theory of planning after Charles Lindblom had published his paper on 'muddling through' in 1959.[1] More than thirty years later, the dichotomy is still central, and usually it is the principal distinction made when helping students of planning structure the theoretical landscape.

3

While I am not strongly opposed to this situation, I want to show that the dichotomy can be improved upon from a theoretical point of view. The present chapter does not imply a criticism of Lindblom, as the construction of an 'ideal type' (Burger 1987) was not his aim. The pragmatic and dis-jointed type of incrementalism is admittedly useful for describing planning practice, and it even holds some normative merit. The purely theoretical type of incrementalism developed here may nevertheless display some strong features in classificatory work and in normative planning discourse. It offers a new and theoretically grounded fixed point for students trying to survey the field of planning theory.

I specify two theoretical modes of planning guided by different types of rationality. Modifications and combinations of such contrasting theories[2] will have the potential to describe a larger part of the preparation for future collective action; not only instrumental and strategic action to reach stated goals, but also non-teleological action. This is action to improve integration, mutual understanding, democracy, etc. - i.e., action laudable in itself. An incremental process that is a purer expression of Jürgen Habermas's communicative rationality, makes the contrast between synoptic and incremental planning more deep-rooted. The reformulation also brings a richer concept of communication into the core of planning theory. While the synoptic 'ideal type' specified here gives room only for communication as one-way transmission of information, the restated incremental mode incorporates the ritual view of communication which accentuates mutual understanding and commonality (Carey 1975). The reformulated incrementalism advances un-dominated communication which is here called dialogue.

The point of departure in this chapter is the presupposition that a few fundamentally diverging types of rationality guide the profoundly dissimilar kinds of human action.[3] The communicative rationality analysed by Habermas is appropriate in situations where mutual understanding and unforced agreement are desired. Such rationality is proposed here as the foundation of a dialogical incrementalism.

John Forester connects the concept of communicative rationality to planning theory in another way. He shows how dialogue can be used to overcome repressive political bounds on planning. Such bounds are formed by socially ad hoc interpersonal manipulation and by systematic structural misinformation (Forester 1981). Forester argues that making processes communicatively rational and thus dialogical is a worthwhile strategy for emancipative planning. Facilitating dialogue is the answer to his question 'If political-economic inequalities threaten to make our political life only formally democratic, democratic "on paper" but not actually so, what are planners and public administrators to do? How may they respond *practically?*' (Forester 1982a:68). The contributions of Forester demonstrate how

4

a critical theory of communicative action can be related to planning practice. In this chapter I point out some advantages of founding an 'ideal type' planning theory on the same theory of communication. A planning theory explicitly based on communication was developed by John Friedmann more than two decades ago. He does not refer to Habermas in the book presenting transactive planning (Friedmann 1973). Even so, their analyses have a common trait: Friedmann, too, goes beyond instrumental reason and accepts the possibility that ends may be rationally determined. The idea is adopted from Karl Mannheim's 'substantial rationality'.[4] Friedmann applies the notion when relating rationality to the process of societal guidance.[5] The transactive mode of planning is essentially a response to the communicative gulf between planner and client. The planning process transforms knowledge into action through an unbroken sequence of interpersonal relations (ibid.171). The term 'transactive' itself indicates that planning is conducted in face-to-face contexts by exchanging the planner's processed knowledge for the personal knowledge of the client. In other words, 'transactive' indicates the salience of dialogue and mutual learning.[6] Friedmann emphasizes that dialogue is a relation of equality between two persons, and that it must not be perverted into an instrumental relationship.

The transactive planning model has utopian features, as it is closely coupled with a reorganization of society in task-oriented working groups and a hierarchy of assemblies. The utopian character of the dialogical incrementalism outlined here springs more directly from the Habermasian notion of 'dialogue', which is more demanding than Friedmann's. In the critical theory of communicative action, dialogue takes place only in ideal speech situations where all interlocutors have the same possibility of forming and setting forth arguments and equal possibilities for having them accepted, as domination is not present in any form. Only in these circumstances can generalized interests and thus the goals of society be rationally derived, according to Habermas.

I propose working with Habermas's concept of dialogue instead of Friedmann's, in order to profit from grounding the antipode to synoptic planning in an unbounded and noninstrumental rationality type. Still, roughly speaking, what is done here is twofold:

(1)   Recasting the communicative core element of transactive planning in the theoretically more elaborate terminology of Habermas.
(2)   Inserting the norm of dialogue into disjointed incrementalism, which is the planning theory most easily developed into the opposite pole of the synoptic ideal.

The themes of the ensuing sections are arranged as follows. I start by giving a short account of the rationality types on which synoptic and dialogical incremental planning theory are founded. These rationality types are applied to specify the two modes. Synoptic and incremental planning are distinguished in terms of communication and analytic technique. Then, it is argued that disjointed incrementalism is an imperfect theoretical contrast to synoptic planning. This implies a critique of the synoptic/incremental dichotomy regarded as the main distinction of planning theory. 'Dialogical incrementalism' is described, and I suggest that it is a fruitful theoretical opposite to the synoptic planning ideal (or 'strategical rationalism' in more Habermasian terminology). It is admitted, though, that communicative rationality cannot function perfectly within an incremental framework. Some concluding remarks are offered in the last section.

The rationality concepts

The principal dividing line between types of rationality in planning distinguishes the type appropriate for goal-oriented behaviour within a means-end structured problem area, and models of consistent reasoning when means and ends are not distinct categories. The first kind has been recognized for a long time (Brubaker 1984), and is discussed by Habermas (1971b) as 'instrumental reason'. It tells us how to combine the means and use them to achieve given ends. Applications of analytic techniques in planning are examples of the use of instrumental reason. However, there is more to planning, as is evident from (e.g.) Forester's (1989:Ch.5) view of planning organizations as 'instrumentally productive and sociopolitically reproductive'.

The identification and analysis of noninstrumental types of rationality have mainly gathered headway after the Second World War. Paul Diesing (1950, 1955, 1958, 1962) and Jürgen Habermas (1984, 1987, 1990, 1991) are among those giving significant contributions. Habermas (1987:137) distinguishes three aspects of communicative action:

> Under the functional aspect of *mutual understanding*, communicative action serves to transmit and renew cultural knowledge; under the aspect of *coordinating action*, it serves social integration and the establishment of solidarity; finally, under the aspect of *socialization*, communicative action serves the formation of personal identities.

Communicative rationality guides communicative action. It is found in speech meeting the validity claims of comprehensibility, truth, rightness, and sincerity, and at the same time aiming at mutual understanding and agreement. Within a speech situation thus defined, a community can rationally derive the goals to be collectively pursued. Values and norms, which could not be seen to have any rational founding under instrumental reason, may come into existence in a communicatively rational manner.

The co-ordination and socialization aspects of communicative action come close to what Diesing (1962) denotes 'social rationality'. I shall be referring to this kind of reason as the integrative aspect of communicative rationality. Put in Habermas's phrases, the integrative aspect serves to avoid that the resources 'social solidarity' and 'ego strength' become scarce. It guides the part of communicative action aiming at integration on the personal and the small-group level. That is, it leads to integration which furthers personal growth and community.[7]

In one way or another, a purpose or a goal can be formulated for any action. The means-end scheme is invalid in communicative rationality not so much because goals are too unclear and ambiguous to inform action - which they often are. It is more to the crux of the matter that the ulterior end is embedded in the activity itself. Dialogue, close ego-confirming relationships, and the experience of being able to make a difference when issues are discussed (democracy) are important to the development of mature personalities. Hence, they have intrinsic value independent of any goal-oriented strategy. Potential advantages in terms of goal achievement are by-products. The activity in question might even deteriorate if the by-products were announced as goals (Elster 1983). For instance, dialogue in Habermas's sense should be motivated by no compulsion but the force of the argument itself. An argument concerning values or norms is valid or invalid without reference to operational ends. The introduction of objectives would simultaneously induce an irrelevant compulsion on the discourse and transform the dialogue to technique. It is, however, the decisive criterion of a dialogue - as of integration - that it is *not* technique; and this is what invalidates the means-end scheme.

The concept of 'relational goods' was recently introduced in the literature on rational choice (Uhlaner 1989). Relational goods cannot be acquired by an isolated individual; they are the fruits of relationships with others. Examples are social approval, solidarity, friendship, the desire to maintain an identity, and the desire to experience one's history (ibid.255). The pursuit of relational goods is guided for a large part by the integrative aspect of communicative rationality, although one may have instrumental motives too. It is unsatisfactory to deal with relational goods within the traditional means-end scheme, especially when ends are changed in the process of consuming such goods.

Planners draw on communicative rationality for example when preparing controversial projects. It guides them when making the contending parties co-operate and when designing a conflict management procedure. The integrative aspect is also appropriate when building new towns and new residential areas. One task is then to choose symbols and designs facilitating the construction of social networks and giving the inhabitants a sense of belonging. Suggesting that planners apply essentially different types of rationality throughout a conflictful process begs the question of how one is to know when to shift from one type of rationality to another. Seel (1991: 46) holds 'that the normative thrust of the concept of the interplay of the forms of rationality pertains to a special performance of the *faculty of judgement'*. Reasonable action requires a capacity for inter-rational judgement provided by a flexibility of mind (Sager 1990a:Ch.8.2, Habermas 1991: 226).

Synoptic and incremental planning theory

Since the characteristics of synoptic and incremental planning are common knowledge among planners, I will only emphasize the features having particular bearing on my exposition. An epistemological clarification is important; knowledge is not seen as objective, as something given and external to man. Instead, knowledge is regarded as constructed in discourse. True knowledge is that on which a consensus is formed among informed people discussing the matter in undistorted communication. This is a starting point for the following formulation of both the synoptic and the incrementalistic planning models.

Synoptic planning is usually defined in a way presupposing perfect information. Unbounded instrumental rationality implies full knowledge of all possibilities; i.e., of the consequences of all the alternatives. With perfect and objective knowledge, synoptic planning is an almost self-negating term. There is little need for planning, in any common sense of the word, when 'everything' is already known (Masuch 1986). When assuming that knowledge is inter-subjective rather than objective, 'everything' takes on a less absolute meaning. Nevertheless, synoptic planning should not correspond to some sort of bounded rationality. Reason can be limited in any number of ways. Making synoptic planning a manifestation of bounded instrumental rationality would open for numerous variants and damage the synoptic mode as a clear theoretical point of reference. I therefore propose to accept only the most modest limitation on knowledge.

Perfect information is here taken to mean that the planners are informed of all planning relevant issues that would (hypothetically) gain consensus, were the matter to be discussed in a perfect speech situation. Assuming that consensus would not be obtained on all consequences of all the planning alternatives, this implies a modification of the traditional conception of perfect knowledge and thus a modification of instrumental rationality.

In the synoptic planning model it is assumed that all other actors have inferior knowledge compared to the planners (the experts). It is nevertheless presumed that not only the planners but even the other actors maximize despite uncertainty and imperfect knowledge. As pointed out by van Witte-loostuijn (1988), maximizing is compatible with considerable deviations from ideal conditions. The strategy of politicians and laymen implies the acquisition of information from the planners. Dissemination of knowledge to the deficiently informed laymen and elected officials will be part of the maximizing strategy of the planners, as it helps them persuade the others to support their proposals.

In synoptic planning computation takes time but is otherwise free. The calculative capacity is sufficient to identify the best alternative and survey the effects of any action under consideration. When all information neces-sary to carry out a certain task is either available already or can be calculated while solving the task, there is nothing to gain from returning to that task later on. The assumption of intersubjective knowledge opens for relaxation of this linearity condition. The planners may now increase their knowledge as time goes by; that is, the number of issues agreed upon may expand. Then one can imagine situations in which the improved insight is important enough to warrant reconsideration of previous work.

Synoptic planning is thus established as a process of communication and calculation. However, the communication is one-way and has a purely informative purpose. The concept of communicative rationality is used only to define the data base available to synoptic planners. This type of rationality does not at all guide the way information is applied. Synoptic planning is instrumental rationality at work; i.e., it is purely strategic action and may be referred to as 'strategical rationalism' to accentuate this point. My intention is not to compare an 'ideal type' of synoptic planning with incremental planning as it is found in practice. Rather, I aim to delimit two stylized forms of planning which are both theoretically clear-cut. There is a need for theoretical tools that are honed to judge in questions of consistency when applying - as planners often do - notions and theories from other branches of social science. Furthermore, a foundation is needed for analysing mixed planning models, bounded not by irrationality but by tensions between the behavioural implications of competing rationality types.

Synoptic planning theory is normative. It tells you how to go about tackling a planning problem if you want to behave rationally - as you ought to. Lindblom launched disjointed incrementalism as both a descriptive and a normative theory. I compare the synoptic and the incremental modes as two prescriptions for rational planning, i.e., as normative analysis. Below are reproduced some points from Hirschman and Lindblom (1962), which

9

are needed for a comparison with dialogical incrementalism later on. The points reveal clearly that the conception of the means-end scheme differs from that of synoptic planning. This is the most fundamental difference between the planning theories. The crucial point is that the ends are not taken as given throughout the incremental process; they are not even fully known:

- Instead of simply adjusting means to ends, ends are chosen that are appropriate to available or nearly available means.
- Instead of comparing alternative means or policies in the light of postulated ends or objectives, alternative ends or objectives are also compared in the light of postulated means or policies and their consequences.
- Ends and means are chosen simultaneously; the choice of means does not follow the choice of ends.
- Ends are indefinitely explored, reconsidered, discovered, rather than relatively fixed.
- Analysis and policy-making are remedial; they move away from ills rather than toward known objectives.

Synoptic and incremental planning are opposites when it comes to the assumptions concerning information and communication:

Synoptic planning: The data base for acquiring perfect information exists at the outset, little need for external communication during the planning process, little learning with bearing on decisions already made, and consequently only sporadic feedbacks.

Incremental planning: Incomplete initial data base, need for external communication during the process to improve information, understanding and agreement; learning and feedback loops are essential.

Stating the communicative characteristics this squarely also helps to highlight the differences with regard to technique.

The ambitions of the synoptic planner to be instrumentally rational encourages the application of technology. Analytic techniques ensure that the knowledge is systematized and put to use efficiently. Perfect information means lots of information, which would simply cause a mess without suitable techniques for handling the data. Due to the perfect information, the synoptic planners hold the ambition of embarking on the grand optimization right from the start. The synoptic approach to planning is weak on participation but strong on technical issues. There is no gap between an agent's competence and the difficulty of the decision problem to be solved.

Incremental planners have scant initial information, and the level of aspiration is lower than in synoptic planning. The defective information does not warrant ambitions of finding 'best' solutions to problems. Instead,

10

one goes for the first solution that is found 'good enough' when the degree of support and agreement is taken into account. There is little point in a formal impact analysis when the impacts are supposed to be incremental. Formal search techniques are superfluous when a few somewhat familiar policy alternatives will do. Long range forecasts seem a waste of time and money in a sequence of trials, errors, and revised trials. To some extent, disjointed incrementalism implies a substitution of politics for analysis (Lindblom 1977:317):

> Insofar as policy makers care about public opinion, as they must in a ... society in which broadly willed rather than correct policies are sought, they will turn their limited analytical energies in some large part and sometimes exclusively to the analysis of citizen volitions rather than the substance of the policy problem at hand.

This notwithstanding, the difficulties of incomplete information create the need for other techniques in incremental planning: techniques for decision-making under uncertainty, for conducting experiments, procedures for letting new information improve previous analysis, and techniques for communication and learning.

In this section, the differences between the main planning modes are briefly stated. Synoptic planning accepts the means-end scheme and relies strongly on analytic technique. Incremental planning rejects the means-end scheme and depends heavily on communication. The intention has been to show that it would be misconceived trying to combine dialogue with synoptic planning, while the idea of striving for dialogue and communicative rationality in the less instrumentally rational incrementalistic process is not injudicious. After all, two reasons for the small-steps procedure are the wish to enhance agreement and the need to understand and survey the implications of proposed changes. Disjointed incrementalists are not unconcerned with regard to the political system. The planning mode is designed to function within a pluralistic democracy where political pressure will come from many sides. The presupposition is that no particular agency or interest has a monopoly on the production of information and analysis concerning a proposed plan or policy. Somehow a workable agreement must be built.

Critique of disjointed incrementalism as the theoretical opposite to synoptic planning

The four interrelated critical points I am going to make are not directed at disjointed incrementalism as a practical mode of planning. They affect

11

incrementalism only in its capacity of being regarded as the most fruitful theoretical contrast to synoptic planning. The task is to show that the contrast between the two planning modes is not as striking as it could - and should - be. The essence of the matter is that disjointed incrementalism implies bounds on the instrumental type of rationality (which is nearly unbounded in synoptic planning) without being based on an alternative form of unbounded noninstrumental rationality. The application of such an essentially different kind of rationality would

(1)   provide a clearer synoptic/incremental contrast, which might give pedagogical advantages, and

(2)   make the synoptic/incremental dichotomy cover a larger part of planning behaviour, by establishing a theoretical foundation for the integrating aims of conflict management.

An additional benefit will become clear in the third subsection below.

The conceptualization of communication is too narrow

Incrementalism was designed for pluralistic settings and thus has a built-in need for communication. Fragmentation of analytic work to many (partisan) participants in policy-making requires subsequent coordination. Furthermore, as 'the test of a "good" policy is typically that various analysts find themselves directly agreeing on a policy' (Lindblom 1959:81), communication is necessary to negotiate agreement. This is different from the calculative process and the one-way transmission of information included in synoptic planning.

The above difference shows that the synoptic/incremental dichotomy is well suited to separate non-communicative and communicative planning processes. However, there is nothing in Lindblom's incrementalism to prescribe communication approaching dialogue. The primary function of communication in disjointed incrementalism is to maintain a reasonable degree of means-end rationality under difficult conditions precluding complete accomplishment of the instrumental ideal. To solve this task, communication approaching dialogue does not have to be resorted to. Consequently, the synoptic/disjointed incremental distinction does not invoke the different types and functions of communication. Neither does it embrace the two opposite ways of solving a public planning problem, namely by dialogue and by analytic technique. This is my first criticism of the traditional synoptic/incremental dichotomy when it is regarded as the principal one in planning theory.

Instrumental rationality is only modified, not replaced or supplemented

A comparison of the communicatively rational, integrative process (Note 7) with Hirschman and Lindblom's (1962) point by point exposition of disjointed incrementalism shows that the two have important properties in common. These include the piecemeal problem-solving, the scepticism towards pronounced goals, the willingness to reformulate both problems and ends, and the inclination to move away from ills rather than towards known objectives. And most important, the means-end scheme is considered invalid in both processes.

In communicative action for coordination and socialization, the integration itself is the purpose. In disjointed incrementalism the main purpose is to implement collective action on which there is sufficient agreement. Integration as consciousness-raising and conflict management is only strived for insofar as it is required to become aware of preferences and mitigate the resistance against the next small change. The planner does not aim at a state of harmony or equilibrium like Diesing's social rationality. Conflicting interests and opposed points of view on collective actions are seen as a permanent state in disjointed incrementalism. Tension reduction in individual, group, and society is not regarded as processes which will transform that situation, but enable us to act collectively in a searching, piecemeal fashion *despite* persistent conflict of interest. The rational integrative process consists of continuing adjustment and mutual modification of forces. On the individual level this process promotes personal growth, and on the collective level it builds community. But neither personal growth not community is the aim of incremental planners. Their mutual adjustment process is primarily designed to maintain the capacity to produce incremental changes in a pluralistic democracy.

The introduction of the satisficing criterion in the strategy of decision does not result in an alternative to instrumental rationality. In fact, Herbert A. Simon does not acknowledge any unbounded type of reason implying that goals are set rationally (Miller 1990:168). Nevertheless, in disjointed incrementalism instrumental rationality is stretched in such a direction and to such an extent that the conceptual differences from communicatively rational integration are not large. However, the decisive step is not taken. What is lacking is a clear statement of the integrative value of the process itself. Disjointed incrementalism is mainly meant to increase the likelihood for a satisfactory output, while rational integration is process-oriented. To the extent that the disjointed incremental process itself is asserted to have intrinsic value, it is as part of The Intelligence of Democracy (Lindblom 1965).

A similar line of reasoning can be developed for the relationship between incrementalism and the mutual understanding aspect of communicative action. It is not required that conflict management in incremental planning is conducted in a manner approaching or aspiring to dialogue. Strategic action for seeking compromise - like bargaining and negotiation - will do. The process is not arranged to initiate communicative rationality and a mediated consensus. Thus, disjointed incrementalism does not fully incorporate any (unbounded) type of rationality which can compete with instrumental reason in guiding planning. This is my second criticism of the traditional synoptic/incremental dichotomy being regarded as the principal one in planning theory.

Fully rational combinations of synoptic and incremental planning are impossible

Inspired by Herbert Simon's (1957) theory of satisficing, Lindblom stressed the restricted ability of man to optimize and maximize; that is, the impossibility of being fully instrumentally rational in planning matters. Elster (1984) identifies two kinds of bounding processes. 'The first is defined by the set of structural constraints which cuts down the set of abstractly possible courses of action and reduces it to the vastly smaller subset of feasible actions ... The second ... is the mechanism that singles out which member of the feasible set shall be realized' (ibid.113). Incrementalism is bounded by both processes. Being confined to incremental steps partly caused by the fragmentation of analytic work to many (partisan) participants in policy-making is an example of the first kind. The strategy of satisficing is an example of the second kind, recommending choice of the first alternative that is found to be good enough - also with regard to the degree of support - compared to a predetermined aspiration level. Hence, satisficing explicitly breaks with maximization.

Bounds may have to be reinterpreted when more than one kind of un-bounded rationality is acknowledged. Several kinds of bounded rationality have been identified. I focus on 'posterior rationality' because it points beyond instrumental reason and is affiliated with the incrementalist view of the ordinary means-end scheme as invalid. In fact, it is intrinsic to the incrementalists' way of thinking. March (1978:593) gives a brief outline of the thought process:

Ideas of posterior rationality emphasize the discovery of intentions as an interpretation of action rather than as a prior position ... Actions are seen as being exogenous and as producing experiences that are orga-nized into an evaluation after the fact. The valuation is in terms of

14

preferences generated by the action and its consequences, and choices are justified by virtue of their posterior consistency with goals that have themselves been developed through a critical interpretation of the choice. Posterior rationality models maintain the idea that action should be consistent with preferences, but they conceive action as being antecedent to goals.

If communicative rationality is accepted as having equal status with instrumental reason, it seems inexpedient to regard posterior rationality as a phenomenon bounding reason in general. It certainly represents a bound when the ideal is instrumental rationality. However, within rational integration it would be more appropriate to regard the posterior formulation of goals and ex post assessment of actions as natural parts of the process.

What is considered a bound may change when the perspective is shifted from one type of unbounded rationality to another. Critique of disjointed incrementalism for failing to broaden any bounds (Taylor 1975) is misconceived when communicative rationality is recognized:

- Confinement to incremental steps is a bound on instrumental reason but furthers rational integration.
- A lack of preconceived ends and objectives is detrimental to instrumental reason, but the comparison of alternative ends in the light of available means and likely consequences promotes communicative rationality.
  Moving away from ills rather than towards known objectives reveals a lack of instrumental reason but may be rational from an integration point of view.
- A causal scheme in which values are attached to the 'means' as well as to the ends makes instrumental efficiency inappropriate but is fertile ground for communicatively rational problem-solving.

Thus, bounds on one type of rationality may be integral parts of another type. This suggests that we might conceptualize certain kinds of action as compromises or syntheses of two or more unbounded types of rationality, rather than think of them as outcomes of insufficient rationality. That is, bounds are not set only by irrationality, power relations, constraints on various kinds of resources, or other imperfection. Human action may be the outcome of competing types of rationality bounding one another.

As long as noninstrumental reason is not acknowledged, one cannot consider combinations of synoptic and incremental planning as completely rational strategies offering the best possible compromises between types of unbounded reason. Instead, such combinations will have to be interpreted as mixtures of irrationality and instrumental reason - i.e., as bounded instrumental rationality. This is my third criticism of the traditional synoptic/incremental dichotomy being considered the main distinction of planning theory.

Bias towards product-oriented planning

The focus in this subsection is on procedural planning theory, which describes and explains procedure and method, saying which tasks have to be accomplished during the process, and how to go about tackling the problems attached to them. Procedural theory can be process-oriented or product-oriented. Process-oriented theory tells you how to design a planning process with intrinsic values. Product-oriented theory tells you how to design a planning process leading, with high probability, to a preferred plan. The product and the process are different references for the evaluation of planning. The difference is crucial because it reflects opposing views on what is essential to a good life: how you do things or which things you possess. Product-orientation implies planning as technology, while process-orientation tends to accentuate the dialogical qualities of planning.

Synoptic planning with perfect information cannot be process-oriented. It takes time only to the degree that computation takes time. Even if some learning and communication take place, synoptic planning is not arranged so as to improve the interlocutors in any way and thus to have intrinsic value. The only purpose of the process is to increase the probability of identifying and implementing a better product.

Incrementalists recommend a different process - more piecemeal and groping - not mainly because it is believed to have a value of its own. Rather, they find it necessary to proceed in a stepwise trial-and-error manner to be able to correct failures and guide projects through all the partial decisions of a pluralistic democracy. I hasten to add that disjointed incrementalism is not *purely* product-oriented:

> It reduces the stakes in each political controversy, thus encouraging losers to bear their losses without disrupting the political system. It helps maintain the vague general consensus on basic values (because no specific policy issue ever centrally poses a challenge to them) that many people believe is necessary for widespread voluntary acceptance of democratic government.   (Lindblom 1979:520)

In spite of this quotation the main impression is one of product-orientation. Incrementalists put much emphasis on simple implementation, on getting *something* done. Synoptic planners emphasize that what is done, should be the best possible. In neither approach is prominence given to the process, and three conclusions follow from this:

16

- Synoptic and incremental planning theories do not stand out as the clear contrasts they might have been, were the incremental process infused with qualities of intrinsic value.
- A significant part of procedural planning theory is not affected by the central dichotomy; the problem of creating an intrinsically valuable process is not properly addressed in synoptic and incremental theory.
- No combination of synoptic and disjointed incremental planning can result in a planning mode balancing the advantages of a process conducive to personal growth and the advantages of a process increasing the chances of a satisfactory product.

Hence, it is unsatisfactory that planners are able to address only the product-oriented and not the process-oriented type of procedural planning when working with the main distinction of planning theory. This is my fourth criticism of the traditional synoptic/incremental dichotomy.

Dialogical incrementalism

The four weaknesses specified in the former section are remedied with the requirement that communication in the incremental planning process be in accordance with the dialogical ideal. The aim of the planners would be the ideal speech situation 'in which only the compulsion of argumentation exists and in which genuine symmetry among all participants permits them to interchange role-taking completely' (Albrecht and Lim 1986:126). In theory, integration and mutual understanding result from this 'dialogical incrementalism'. One gets an idea of how the planning mode would work by allowing for undistorted communication in Hirschman and Lindblom's (1962:215-16) point by point description of disjointed incrementalism:

A. Attempt at mutual understanding is limited to policies that differ only incrementally from those previously agreed upon.
B. The number of alternative means or policies is thus restricted, but the directions considered should grant all participants a possibility for gradually approaching a situation acceptable to them.
C. Instead of simply adjusting means to given ends, ends are dialogically chosen from the set appropriate to available and unanimously accepted means.
D. Instead of comparing alternative means and policies in the light of postulated ends or objectives, alternative ends and objectives are compared in the light of their accordance with generalizable interests.
E. Ends and means are chosen simultaneously; the choice of means does not follow the choice of ends.

F. Ends are reconsidered whenever necessary to maintain consent; they are not regarded as relatively fixed.

G. Planning is a dialogical process aiming at mutual understanding and agreement on future-directed collective action. Each actor responds with new analyses, arguments, or judgements as other actors present their points of view. Thus, for any actor, analysis and policy-making are serial or successive; that is, problems are not 'solved' but are repeatedly attacked.

H. Analysis and policy-making are remedial; they move away from ills rather than toward known objectives.

I. The analysis of consequences carried out by each actor is quite incomplete. The actors are aware of this and counteract by exchanging knowledge of calculations and impact assessments. Hence, each actor has the information base for judging what change represents generalizable interests.

J. Analysis and policy-making are socially fragmented; they are carried out by many separate actors simultaneously. Plans emerge through a mutual exchange of views where nobody yields to other pressure than that inherent in a valid argument.

As indicated by the preceding section, the following four advantages result from the revised main distinction. The 'strategical rationalism/dialogical incrementalism' dichotomy

(1) spans the communicative forms from the verbal expressions of force in strategic action (e.g., threats, propaganda, and persuasion) to the dialogical argumentation free from group influence and entirely devoted to the identification of generalizable interests;

(2) prescribes rational processes both for situations when a means-end scheme is valid and when it is not;

(3) accounts for the possibility that a planning effort can be fully rational even when neither reaching maximum goal achievement nor using all resources for integrative purposes (Diesing 1958); and

(4) opens for hybrid planning modes that are both process-oriented and product-oriented.

The background for point (4) is the strong process-orientation of dialogical incrementalism, which lets the inter-human aspect come out strongly. Personal growth is enhanced by dialogue and interaction on equal terms. Bowles and Gintis (1986:138) hold that preferences 'are as much formed as revealed in the exercise of choice. Individuals choose in order to become, and the nature of the opportunities given for the expression of choice affects the formation of the will'. The self-transformation thesis, maintaining that democratic experience will transform individuals in demo-cratic ways, is discussed by Warren (1992, 1993).

In addition to the gains just listed, obligatory dialogue answers to criticism raised against disjointed incrementalism already decades ago: it may easily lack direction, and it is apt to serve those already in power. Etzioni (1967:388) states that in the absence of fundamental decisions, 'incremental decision-making amounts to drifting - action without direction'. Forester (1981) concurs in this criticism when he describes disjointed incrementalism as pragmatics without principles and says it 'offers no protection from opportunism' (ibid.183). In institutional economics and the institutional approach to policy analysis (Williamson 1981, Bryson and Smith Ring 1990), opportunism is seen as self-interest seeking with guile. It characte-rizes the behaviour of agents disguising intentions or preferences, distorting data, obfuscating issues, and otherwise confusing transactions. Disjointed incrementalism does not imply guile, but it may be liable to opportunism in a weaker sense, namely the habit of adapting one's actions, thoughts, and utterances to circumstances. The point here is that dialogical incrementalism cannot be criticized for this. Changing a collective decision under com-municative rationality requires arguments that are comprehensible, true, right, and sincere. Furthermore, policy change must be shown to serve what Habermas calls 'generalizable interests' - what is agreed to by everybody in an ideal speech situation. Referring to group interests will not do.

The second critical point was also raised by Etzioni (1967:387): disjointed incrementalism will 'reflect the interests of the most powerful ...; demands of the underprivileged and politically unorganized would be underrepre-sented'. Forester (1989) subscribes to this criticism. Under severe structural distortion and inequality, the consent-seeking behaviour of incrementalists 'may avoid unpleasantries, but social justice is likely to be the price of such convenience' (ibid.60). Again, dialogical incrementalism comes a long way in mending the weakness. Surely, one is still restricted by the small-steps-procedure, giving radicals a handicap. But when it comes to choosing *direction* of policy change, economic resources and political power have no effect. Under the rule of communicative rationality everyone is perfectly capable of assessing each argument as if behind a 'veil of ignorance' (Rawls 1972:Ch.3). That is, they judge as if unaware of their own capa-cities, resources, power, and general standing in society. The 'original position' formulated by Rawls specifies the conditions under which individuals would behave as if they were equals, and under which they would therefore be able to communicatively agree on a fair procedure.

I have now commented upon a number of benefits following from dialo-gical incrementalism. They will never be fully realized, because commu-nicative rationality is a theoretical ideal to be completely fulfilled neither in practice nor in the proposed dialogical planning theory. I am not primarily referring to the modest capacity of human beings for empathy, and our lack of will to reason behind a 'veil of ignorance'. However important this may be, there is a more interesting point from the perspective of theoretical consistency: the core ideas of incrementalism are logically incompatible with unbounded communicative rationality. Communicative distortions should not be found in perfect, dialogical incrementalism, yet this is inevitable. Distortions emerge from

- restricting the choice set to a few familiar alternatives;
- considering goals as restricted by (nearly) available means;
- neglecting some values and consequences; and
- fragmentation limiting the number of people making each decision.

Hence, to uphold the incrementalist procedure one has to accept modification of communicative rationality. There is a parallel to the modification of instrumental reason in synoptic planning, resulting from dismissing the notion of perfect objective knowledge. Theoretical inconsistencies are caused by insisting on unboundedness in both cases. Nevertheless, unbounded communicative rationality is important as a standard against which existing discourses and strategic behaviour can be judged (Kemp 1985:188).

When assessing the seriousness of the last couple of bounding mechanisms listed above, one should distinguish the entire incremental process from each of the partial incremental decisions. Even if a limited number of people are involved in each partial decision, the participation in the entire process may be considerable. And although some values and consequences are ignored in each of the small and fragmented decisions, it is usually not the same ones that are excluded throughout the entire process. In the incremental decision-making routine all values and consequences will eventually be taken into account if every interest has its watch-dog. When they have, however, there is still nothing in disjointed incrementalism to secure a clean fight between them. This is corrected by accepting the demand for dialogue in Habermas's sense.

An additional guideline should be observed in order to avoid fundamental conflict between incrementalism and the demands of communicative rationality. One should not apply some kind of non-dialogical strategy to decide on an incremental process, and advance the claims of dialogue only afterwards. When the incremental procedure itself is dialogically chosen by those affected, restrictions on the choice set are accepted from the outset. Then the communicative distortions embedded even in dialogical incrementalism may not be felt so hard.

One may ask if there is no problem in transforming disjointed incrementalism into an 'ideal type' comprising dialogue and communicative rationality.

Some might regard the reformulation as a retrograde step because dialogical incrementalism is just as utopian as synoptic planning. Lindblom's disjointed incrementalism, on the other hand, is applicable in practice, and even meant to be an adequate description of typical real life planning. The intention here is not to *replace* this very useful practice-oriented approach by a purely theoretical construct. My aim is to inquire which additional theoretical benefits can be gained from an ideal type formulation of incrementalism, in which communication is uninfluenced by power relations. The reformulation places the categories of the synoptic/incremental dichotomy on an equal footing. The dichotomy is changed from signifying the contrast between a theoretical 'ideal' and a practical, implementable procedure, to distinguishing two equally unobtainable, but theoretically useful, ideal types. Planning modes applicable in real life situations are easily obtained by relaxing the extreme assumptions of the ideal types. For instance, a practical planning strategy would not require 'dialogue' in the utopian sense I have used this term. Instead it would require that communication in the citizen participation process is arranged so that one *tries to live up to* the ideal of communicative rationality. This claim may be specified for example by encouraging the negotiating parties to follow the procedure for 'getting to yes' suggested by Fisher and Ury (1981). Alternatively, one may recommend mediation with emphasis on self-determination (Cormick 1982).

Concluding remarks

The purpose of this chapter is to assist both teaching and research. A more systematic map of the field of planning theory can be drawn for the students by using categories on the same level of abstraction, which are also antipodes. Basing synoptic and incremental planning theories on essentially different types of rationality, distinguishes clearly between them and provides unambiguous reference points for the analysis of planning behaviour. Research advantages are derived mainly in conceptual discourse. Numerous ideas and notions in (e.g.) sociology and social psychology concern interpersonal relations with significant noninstrumental elements - like friendship, autonomy, and integration. Such notions can be more fruitfully merged with a planning theory explicitly acknowledging non-instrumental rationality - as dialogical incrementalism does.

The strategical rationalism/dialogical incrementalism dichotomy is used for:
a) Charting the main contours of planning theory, establishing fixed reference points for discussing what planning can be and ought to be.

b) Identifying maximum and minimum requirements for analytic technique and method in planning.
c) Characterizing practical planning modes by modifying and combining the theoretical extremes.
d) Providing clear-cut theories ('ideal types') facilitating investigations of consistency between planning theories and theoretical elements from adjacent disciplines.

Dialogical incrementalism (a) brings the widely discussed communicative ethics of Habermas into mainstream planning theory, without implying the cellular structure of society that is a corollary of Friedmann's transactive planning. The revised dichotomy can (b) specify maximum and minimum requirements not only for technique, but for participation and communication as well. From the new dichotomy, one can also (c) 'derive' practical planning modes relying on communication as a distinct feature, like advocacy planning and Forester's 'planning as questioning and shaping attention'. The revised main distinction of planning theory is (d) helpful when
- considering if and how definitions of central social science concepts - like legitimation, power, conflict, and collective choice - are consistent with the prominent planning theories (Sager 1990a);
- analysing the functions and forms of flexibility and rigidity in plans and planning, and
- studying how the competing problem-solving procedures - communication and calculation - set their mark on public planning processes.

In general then, when using the current dichotomy, the spectre of planning modes appears to be limited to instrumental rationality and strategic action. The introduction of communicative rationality sets the antipodes further apart, and thus new and interesting combinations of theoretical elements and practical solutions come into view.

Practical combinations of synoptic and incremental procedural elements display bounds on rationality for at least three main reasons:
1. There are imperfections in human capabilities and social organization.
2. Logical inconsistencies would follow from unbounded rationality, whether instrumental or communicative.
3. Instrumental and communicative rationality bound one another, because increasing goal achievement does not always enhance integration and reciprocal understanding - and vice versa.

The present exposition stresses the last two points.

Synoptic planning has been reformulated by introducing the epistemological assumption that knowledge is established by intersubjective agreement. The rejection of perfect objective knowledge makes the logic of the synoptic planning process intelligible and motivates a simple, one-way form of communication. Incremental planning has been reformulated by basing it on communicative rationality, which requires that dialogue is aimed for throughout the planning process. This means communication between the involved parties in a manner as free from domination and discursive restrictions as can be obtained within the incremental framework. The reformulated modes are opposites in a communicate-or-calculate perspective. The planners in the synoptic process have nearly unlimited calculative capacity, and the planners in the dialogical incremental process possess nearly unlimited communicative capacity.

Notes

1   The term 'muddling through' was not launched by Lindblom. It was used by Mannheim (1940) when pleading for large-scale comprehensive planning, and it was there meant to denote an inferior practice:

> At the present stage of development the successful organization of society cannot be left to chance. Prevailing trends cannot be successfully influenced or even deflected in the spirit of 'muddling through'. (Mannheim 1940:7)

In his critique of Mannheim's holistic approach, Karl Popper makes use of the phrase. But to Popper (1986) 'muddling through' gives positive associations. In fact what Popper argues for in his critique of historicism is precisely a science of muddling through. (Popper's critique was first published as three articles in *Economica* in 1944-45.) In Popper's defence of 'piecemeal social engineering' against 'collectivist planning' one recognizes topics from the synoptic/incremental debate.

2   The mixed scanning proposed by Etzioni (1967, 1986) is probably the most well-known of the planning theories combining synoptic and incremental features. Etzioni brings together elements of unbounded and bounded instrumental reason. When there is a type of incrementalism founded on communicative rationality, it is possible to reformulate mixed scanning. The reformulated strategy consists of planning elements based on nearly unbounded instrumental reason and nearly unbounded communicative rationality. Diesing (1958) describes decision processes of a closely affiliated kind, mixing elements of what he calls economic and social rationality.

3   There are several parallel and partly intertwined discourses of rationality with implications for planning theory. Examples are:
    -   The discussion of the extent to which human rationality is bounded, and whether the behavioural models of social science should be

based on bounded or unbounded (instrumental) rationality (March 1978, Cherniak 1986, Forester 1985a, 1989:Part 2, Simon et al. 1992);

- The debate, most notably between economists and psychologists, on the criteria for rational choice (Hogarth and Reder 1987);
- The psychological and social anthropological theories explaining the observed systematic deviations from the rationality paradigm of maximal expected utility (Kartez 1989); and
- The controversy in planning theory concerning the emphasis on procedural and substantive rationality, respectively (Faludi 1987).

Several other aspects of the rationality debate are treated in Breheny and Hooper (1985).

4 Mannheim (1940:Chs V and VI) believed in a 'substantial rationality' defined as 'the capacity to act intelligently in a given situation on the basis of one's own insight into the inter-relations of events' (ibid.58). The core of the notion is 'the capacity for independent judgment'. Judgement and thus substantial rationality include the assessment of goals, not taking them for given. Mannheim does not say *how* goals can be rationally formulated.

One of Max Weber's main dichotomies is formal vs substantive rationality (Brubaker 1984). Formal rationality guides the maximization of the calculability of action, means and procedures. Substantive rationality means rationality from the point of view of some particular substantive end. This rationality is a matter of value or belief, because one must accept the end to regard the striving for its fulfilment as rational. Weber does not aim at describing a rational way of establishing the goals. To him, social life is marked by perennial conflict over ends and beliefs, conflict that cannot be resolved through any neutral procedure. He believes in the irreconcilability of conflicting judgement of rationality, and therefore in the limits of rationality as an organizing principle of social life (ibid.4-5). Thus, communicative rationality is not a subtype of substantive rationality.

5 'Societal guidance' is among Friedmann's key concepts, denoting the planners' efforts to make society adaptable to external changes, responsive to internal demands, and more able to carry out large-scale projects. The idea of societal guidance and several other key elements of transactive planning were already developed - if not yet fully - in Friedmann (1969). He there uses the term 'action-planning' and sketches the new role of the planner that makes dialogue fundamental: 'In action-planning ... the planner moves to the foreground as a person and autonomous agent. His success will in large measure depend on his skill in managing interpersonal relations' (ibid.317). Empathy, readiness to

24

listen, and ability to successfully communicate his thoughts to others are among the qualifications required from the action-planner. These abilities are also premises for dialogue.

6 'Social learning' is another central concept in Friedmann's thinking. It is one of the main traditions of planning theory identified by Friedmann (1987). Only part of the contributions to the tradition is closely related to communicative rationality. There is a connection between planning and social learning, since 'it is through transactive planning that social practice discovers how to deal with a specific problem' (Friedmann and Abonyi 1976:938). Friedmann regards transactive planning as corresponding to a social learning paradigm. However, he also recommends transactive planning as part of the strategy for 'radical planning', which is synonymous with social mobilization in his terminology (Friedmann 1987:402-3).

7 Social rationality is described clearly by Diesing (1962) as a way of thinking which forms a striking and easily understood contrast to the reasoning embedded in synoptic planning. Besides, the integration process works in much the same way as the incremental planning process. The integrating process consists of the adjustment and mutual modification of forces. It reconciles elements that are in opposition, but also separates irreconcilable forces and excludes disruptive elements. In an integrative approach human action and inclinations, for instance habits and stated desires, are treated as symptoms of a social system or personality in conflict. In this case the conflicts are resolved by an integrative process in which the desires are changed rather that satisfied. Action alternatives are chosen according to their contribution to this process. Adequate integrative decisions are not possible unless one is in a position to acquire an understanding of the hidden aspects of a problem. Integration as an inner reality cannot be forced on people. In integrative decision-making there must be preferences attached to the means themselves. The means-end scheme collapses when the means are also the ends.

2 Rationale and paradigms for planning in light of communicative rationality

The traditional economic rationale for planning as correction of the deficiencies of the market mechanism goes well with instrumental rationality. When even noninstrumental types of rationality are acknowledged in planning theory, the rationale for planning should be based on them as well. Hence, a compound rationale is suggested. The idea of market correction is combined with the personal growth rationale and the aid-for-undistorted-communication rationale. The latter shows that the communicative rationality of Jürgen Habermas is reflected in the fundamental reason for planning.

The idea that there are more than one type of rationality is employed to construct a rationality-based classification scheme for planning paradigms. By applying only one fundamental criterion, namely the rationality type with which a planning theory is most closely associated, I aim to minimize the subjective and arbitrary element of categorization. The scheme accommodates John Forester's approach to planning as questioning and shaping attention as well as the SITAR package of planning traditions. By anchoring synoptic, incremental, transactive, advocacy, and radical (or rather recalcitrant) planning in distinct types of rationality, profound differences between the paradigms are brought to the fore. The revised rationality-based conception of the SITAR is a powerful pedagogical tool for mapping the field of planning theory.

The functions of rationale and paradigm

My first aim in this chapter is to present a compound rationale for planning. It is a composition of three rationales already proposed in the planning literature. The need for such a rationale follows from the acceptance of different types of rationality. A rationale does not state what is intended by a certain kind of plan, by planning a particular project, or by planning in a specific sector. The planning rationale is for general use and is independent of the situation at hand. It identifies the fundamental reason for and the logical basis of planning. I proceed from the basic premise that when contrasting types of rationality are indispensable in the planning process, they should leave their marks on the fundamental reason for the effort. For instance, a rationale focusing strictly on goal achievement cannot form the logical basis of efforts to design a planning process with intrinsic value.

A rationale for planning is needed for at least three reasons:

(1) Planners are criticized because many of their recommendations are unpopular. Part of the task is to protect the interests of groups outside the decision process against strong and directly involved actors. The vulnerable position of the planners necessitates a solid theoretical foundation pointing out why their work is important. The rationale allows the planners to direct energy towards debating issues of the plan in question instead of repeatedly having to legitimize their profession.

(2) The rationale shows planning novices their function in society and helps them understand what is expected of them. A clearly expressed core of their professional activities serves to uphold conviction despite adversity.

(3) The rationale is an ideological compass for the planner. Practical planning is replete with conflicting interests. The rationale sustains principled choice of direction when a workable compromise is hard to find.

The second purpose of the chapter is to classify paradigmatic theories of planning. Planning paradigms function as the framework for 'normal science' in the field; that is, as exemplary procedures for solving the countless technical, economical, political, etc problems of varying planning contexts.[1] Paradigms have to be stable over several years in order to serve this function, and so frequent paradigm change is not necessarily an advantage. Hence, one should not proclaim stagnation in the field of planning theory if contemporary theories can be demonstrated to fit well with a twenty-five years old classification of paradigms. I shall argue that the situation is as follows: The paradigms constituting the SITAR package introduced by Barclay Hudson in 1979 are still useful for guiding puzzle-solving in planning when sufficiently broadly interpreted. However, the SITAR needs tuning, and the classification into synoptic, incremental, transactive, advocacy, and radical planning theory can be given a more solid foundation. When I turn to this task, radical planning will be seen to belong to a wider set of 'recalcitrant' planning theories, emphasizing rationality types different from, but overlapping, those guiding the four other SITAR traditions.

27

Public planning - which is the object of this study - is commonly seen as preparation for making decisions on public matters. But it is not a homogeneous discipline in the sense that one common theoretical paradigm guides the planners of the differing professional traditions. Nevertheless, planners of most convictions feel an obligation to rationality: 'If there is one theme that runs through all the discussions and debates on planning, it is that of rationality' (Friedmann 1987:97). I start from the assumption that normative theories earning the status of paradigms for planning, presuppose some kind of rationality. However, there are different opinions on what qualifies as rational behaviour, and this is an important reason for the diversity of normative planning theories. Acceptance of Habermas's communicative rationality allows one to detect intelligence in action that is noninstrumental and an end in itself. A planning process may be designed in a particular way because the resulting interaction is considered right or democratic in itself or believed to promote personal growth. These qualities are not stated ends in planning but rather essentially by-products (Elster 1983).

The themes of the chapter are outlined below. Previously proposed planning rationales are briefly surveyed. Some problematic features of the personal growth rationale and the aid-for-undistorted-communication rationale are discussed. Then, some concepts are explained before a tripartite rationale for planning is presented. Following that, the exposition turns from rationale to paradigm, and a rationality-based classification scheme is introduced. I outline paradigms related to instrumental and communicative rationality, respectively. The SITAR classification of paradigmatic planning theories is reconstructed, and some conclusions are drawn.

Previously proposed planning rationales

Planning is seen here as the preparation for collective decisions and for their implementation. There is no clear borderline distinguishing planning from politics in such preparatory work. I cannot eliminate this conceptual diffuseness, but the following sentence may improve clarity sufficiently to make it meaningful to carry on the analysis of rationales. By planning I think of professional analysis aiming at predicting future impacts and bringing them in line with goals by co-ordinating efforts and by studying causal relationships before selecting means to influence the consequences.

The question 'why plan?' recurs occasionally as the general political climate changes and disturbs the balance between regulations and market forces. The planning profession's reassessments of its own function in society have resulted in several proposed rationales. No matter what the decision is about, information is required in the preparation. Thus, collecting information relevant for deciding on future collective action has been suggested as a rationale for planning (Skjei 1976, Klosterman 1985). The focus here is not on information gathering as education and enlightenment, but on the operative knowledge needed to make immediate decisions. However, most authors in the field prefer to link planning more closely to the economic or the political subsystem of society. I refer to them as market and nonmarket systems, respectively.

The market produces and distributes goods and services. The political system has a number of functions, but the important thing here is that it produces and distributes power and decision-making authority. The two systems are not mutually independent. Political power may have a material basis established in the market - and vice versa. There will be both market and nonmarket imperfections, and these can cause malfunctioning in distribution as well as in production. Accordingly, there are four main types of correction, and each of them has been proposed as the basis of the rationale for planning (Sager 1992).

The four 'correction rationales' imply that planners hold visions of how society ought to be organized. The perspective may be abstract, like the idea of how an efficacious market should function, of what would be a just society, or what would constitute a real democracy. Or the planner's vision might be concrete and physical, picturing well organized new towns, green belts, pedestrianized and preserved town centres, or well protected rural environments and national parks. In any case, the correction rationales establish the planners as interventionists and not as mere advisors (Kaufman 1978).

There is a close connection between answers to the question 'why plan?' and concepts used to legitimize planning. For example, the information gathering rationale can be linked to the public interest, which is a legitimizing concept. Information processing will not take place in an entirely disinterested manner. A collective decision is to be made, and therefore the aim of the information gathering may be to disclose a public interest. For the other rationales mentioned above, the following legitimizing concepts are identified:

Correcting market production: Efficacy
Correcting market distribution: Equity
Correcting nonmarket production: Community and the public interest
Correcting nonmarket distribution: Emancipation

Efficacy means to produce the goods or to implement the projects that have the highest priority among the users (within a given budget). An equitable situation is one in which no individual envies another. A community is here a group of people with a certain common identity and a considerable amount of shared values and norms. Something is in the public interest if it is everyone's interest and if the serving of this interest is social in nature.[2] Emancipation in this context points to political liberation giving more equal regards and more equal opportunities.

Important tasks are brought to the fore by each of the five rationales treated in this section. Nevertheless, I lay aside the information gathering rationale in the following. There is always an element of preferences and political will in planning. There is also a process and a substance. It seems unsatisfactory that nothing of this is reflected in the rationale, beyond a self-evident preference for informed decision-making. The information gathering rationale implies a commitment to rationality, but no more than that. Even when correction of the production and distribution of benefits from market and nonmarket systems is proclaimed rationale, information gathering is an important part of planning. But as a *rationale* it does not combine easily with the other. The fundamental reason for planning cannot simultaneously be correction and pure, disinterested information processing.

The information gathering rationale is based on an unrealistic view of the contrast between planning and politics. It reflects Max Weber's idea of a clear difference between ends and means, with preferences only attached to the ends. These are determined by the politicians, while the planners analyse the use of means on objective criteria. By choosing the information rationale, one neglects that the economic and political systems admit deficiencies which might have been put right by planning. The central idea is that there are no structural or systemic mechanisms preventing optimal decisions, provided the decision-makers receive enough information. The information rationale cultivates the research function of planning and ignores the political function. The question is if participatory planning is possible when the role offered involved citizens limits their influence to that of informants.

However, each of the four 'correction rationales' is too narrow seen in isolation. I see no reason why one of them should be preferred at the expense of the others. My intention is therefore to construct a compound rationale including all the correction rationales mentioned above. The remainder of the section identifies the three partial, although fundamental, reasons for planning from which the compound rationale will be composed. The partial rationales reflect three planning functions: planning as production, integration, and politics. They also correspond to particular types of rationality. Planners usually look at their professional practice as a contribution to rational decision-making. If planning is rational, there should be close and explicit relations between the fundamental reasons for planning and the types of rationality required to manage and learn from the process and to produce the plan.

The correction-of-market-production rationale concurs with the quest for economic efficiency, and it reflects instrumental rationality. Planning is seen as the means for optimal production of public goods. The correction-of-nonmarket-production rationale focuses on planning as integration. It draws attention to the formation of the individual in the community. Diesing's (1962) social rationality explains the logic of individual and interpersonal integration (see Note 7 to Chapter 1).

The two distributive correction rationales are united in the following exposition. The aid-for-undistorted-communication rationale embraces both the market and the nonmarket elements of distribution. Both equalization and liberation are processes kept up by a mix of economic and political distribution. The end states are equity and autonomy - but they are never fully achieved. The distribution rationales focus on planning as politics. Processes of equalization and liberation may be guided by instrumental and by communicative rationality. Redistribution by means of instrumental power may be politically preferable to status quo, but power strategy is here regarded as an emergency 'solution'. The ideal is that political goals and collective actions should be determined in dialogue, i.e., communication free from deception, self-deception, strategic deliberation, and domination through the exercise of power (Dryzek 1990). This is exactly the content of the aid-for-undistorted-communication rationale: planning practice should foster open and authentic political debate by questioning possibilities and shaping responses in the face of societal values and norms restricting openness (participation in decision-making), power relations maintaining domination, and conflict repressing legitimate interests (Forester 1981, 1982b, 1989).

The above simplification of the categorization of planning rationales leaves us with three fundamental reasons for planning. They are correction of market production, personal growth, and aid for undistorted communication. The main reason for the subsequent focus on the rationality types is that they provide the modes of thinking underpinning the three rationales and the corresponding productive, integrative, and political aspects of public planning.

Paradox of the personal growth rationale

This section explains first what is meant by personal growth. Then it is suggested that personal growth may be a by-product of planning. Finally, it is shown that this characteristic gives rise to a paradox when personal growth is proclaimed the rationale for communicative and participative planning.

The idea of deliberately promoting the betterment of man is not at all novel in the planning literature. The conception of rationality improving man himself is an inheritance from the Enlightenment. Half a century ago Karl Mannheim (1940:223) was bold enough to pose the following question: 'Is mass transformation of external behaviour the right way to begin, or must we start with the complete transformation of the individual?' More recently, the ideal of personal growth has become a central idea in humanistic planning. Although Friedmann (1973) does not use the word 'growth', his ambitions are the same, namely to transform man through dialogue from object to subject, to the protagonist of history. His 'life of dialogue' engenders a process of mutual self-discovery. One tries to integrate these discoveries into the already existing structure of the personality, thereby changing and expanding it (ibid.178).

The idea of personal growth as an essential ideal for planning was probably nourished by 'the third force' in psychological theory, namely humanistic psychology. This professional movement and theoretical approach drew its ideas largely from the same sources of social criticism in the USA during the second half of the 1960s as did humanistic planning. A part of humanistic psychology is the human potential movement which starts where psychotherapy concludes: with a normally functioning human being. The roles of patient and therapist are foreign to the approach of this movement. One can think of the relationship as one between a guide and his fellow seekers, both pursuing inner growth and a richer outer existence. This is similar to the societal guidance role shaped by humanistic planners.

Diesing argues that social rationality is the kind of thought promoting personal growth. Such growth is the abstract ideal of socializing, as welfare is when economizing. Personal growth is seen as an endless process of integration and increase in integrative ability and creativity (Diesing 1955:34). The result is an expansion of the problem area that can be mastered. In social relations, growth consists of increase in mutual understanding, undominated communication, and trust; it implies increased mutual security, and increased ability to resolve differences and to tolerate differences that cannot be resolved.

The idea of personal growth is elaborated upon in the contributions of Carl Rogers and Abraham Maslow.[3] Rogers (1961, 1977) is convinced that tendencies towards health and personal growth are facilitated by any interpersonal relationship in which at least one of the involved is free enough from incongruence to be in touch with his or her own self-correcting centre. Congruence means accuracy between communication experience and awareness. The major task in therapy, and in citizen participation aiming at personal growth, is to establish such genuine relationships. Acceptance of one's self is a prerequisite to an easier and more genuine acceptance of others. In turn, being accepted by another leads to a greater willingness to accept one's self. This self-correcting and self-enhancing cycle is the major way one minimizes obstacles to personal growth (Fadiman and Frager 1976:289).

A difficulty is created for the personal growth rationale if some effects cannot be realized by intended or planned action. Elster (1983:43) maintains that 'some mental and social states appear to have the property that they can only come about as the by-product of actions undertaken for other ends'. Although personal growth is crucial, it may be attainable only if it is not sought. The planners may secretly have this side effect of the participative process in mind, but they cannot coherently invoke it in public. The pursuit of personal growth may even be self-defeating. Revealing that personal growth is the superior goal can make the planning endeavour lose credibility and would probably make it seem meaningless to most potential participants. Paradoxically, this would preclude the state one is trying to bring about.

Social relations are patterns of shared actions and feelings. Shared experience comes from active participation in a system of relationships. Social rationality, in making social relations serve integrative purposes, leans heavily on communication. It is also a frequently stated ideal that public planning should be communicative and support democratic virtues. A paradox arises here because the democratic ideal is best served by a dialogue free from domination, while the personal growth rationale for planning seems to require constraints on the communication. If Elster is right, which is disputed by Hubin (1986-87) and Chan and Miller (1991), planners have to manipulate in the sense of holding back the information that promoting personal growth is the ultimate end of the planning process. It seems dubious to recommend as a basis for social organization a principle that could succeed only if members of the social system remained ignorant of it.

Planning needs to pursue concrete ends. Nobody starts a planning process primarily to achieve personal growth, and few would presumably invest time and energy in a process with this pronounced main goal. People get involved to obtain far more tangible products, like a new road, a better school, better protection from traffic accidents, and so forth. The instrumentally rational planning process guides the selection of means to achieve the concrete ends of the plan, not the unintended consequences. If personal growth results and is not arbitrary, some other kind of rationality has to be at work in the planning process alongside instrumental reason. As long as we think within the frame of instrumentality, the personal growth appears to be accomplished in spite of the rationality of the process.[4]

The aid-for-undistorted-communication rationale for planning: ideal and practice

Most planning theoretical contributions inspired by Habermas examine the requirements and possibilities of social action cast not simply as instrumental problem-solving but as emancipatory political practice. The aid-for-undistorted-communication rationale is developed in the theory of planning as questioning and organizing attention. In this section a virtual 'paradox' arising from an unclear distinction between ideal and reality is identified and discussed. The problem is that planning means the mobilization of bias, while it is simultaneously holding out prospects of emancipation through unbiased, undistorted communication.

The fruitfulness of expanding the notion of rationality beyond the instrumental concept is confirmed by Forester's analysis of planning as communicative action. His ideas of planning as organizing attention contain important elements of a theory of planning as social critique. Forester recognizes that the instrumental and communicative aspects of planning practice are inseparable and not mutually exclusive. As instrumental actions 'get things done', they also necessarily set up expectations, affect meanings, influence political relations, and shape understandings. Forester (1982b:64) contends that:

> In the communicative dialogue, conversation, and play of power that constitute the planning process, the evolution of the questioning of selective possibilities and the shaping of equally selective responses, planners' communicative actions work to organize (or disorganize) citizens' attention, their engagement, investment, and participation. ... (P)lanners open or foreclose possibilities, alert or ignore others, call forth or disregard particular concerns, and spread or narrow the bases of design, criticism, participation, and thus decision-making.

The planner is not seen as a processor of facts, but a practical organizer of attention. Regarded as organizing, planning implies advancing some views and issues and holding back others. As Schattschneider (1975) declared, organization is the mobilization of bias.[5] Planning is a political activity furthering some interests and weakening others. Real world social systems are certainly not characterized by communication free from coercion. There is no reason to believe that public plans are implemented only when they gain universal support or when they can be claimed to represent generalizable interests in Habermas's sense. Thus, organizations - including planning agencies - may be understood as structures of systematically (non-accidentally and sometimes unnecessarily) distorted communication (Forester 1982b:65).

At first glance, Forester's communicative theory of planning seems to point at a paradox of participatory planning. The ideal is that planning should contribute to emancipation by arranging for dialogical practice throughout the decision-making process, but the plan itself, as all products of organized activity, is the outcome of a mobilized bias, and thus of distorted communication. The theoretical dilemma emerges when planners propose to educate for emancipation and personal growth through undistorted communication by inviting lay people to participate in a process which serves to mobilize bias. How can communication be free when attention is at the same time directed? In the perspective of planning as organizing, planning is seen to involve power; if not in the form of manipulation - e.g., caused by the choice of personal growth as the planning rationale - then at least in the form of persuasion and authority necessary to shape attention.

Comparing the result of the former section with this one, the problems are seen to be affiliated:

1) In the first case (personal growth rationale) planners want to educate by dialogue in a process guided by an incommunicable superior ideal - and hence the communication is distorted.
2) In the second case (aid-for-undistorted-communication rationale) planners want to emancipate through undominated communication in a process that itself implies attentional bias - and hence the communication is distorted.

However, the second problem turns out to be a pseudo-paradox. Planners do *not* invite people to participate in communication that is undistorted in Habermas's sense. In practice such 'ideal speech situations' do not exist. Accordingly, the planners encourage participation in efforts to counteract major distortions (transportation plans ignoring the interests of non-motorists, one-sided entrepreneurial information neglecting environmental issues, etc.), well aware that the planning process will be selectively attentive, and that the eventual implementation of a plan will inevitably be a partial act. The utopian dialogical ideal should not be allowed to prevent us from 'organizing to make democratic politics a reality' (Forester 1985b:xv).

A compound rationale for planning

The basis of the compound rationale

The purpose here is to explain some terms applied to outline the compound rationale for planning in the next subsection. The starting point is a decomposition of the social system in subsystems that are the domains of different forms of rationality. Moreover, in each subsystem a special paradigm for emancipatory practice takes precedence.

In accordance with Parsons (1977) I use 'social system' as a general term. Parsons sees the social system as composed by the integrative, the political, the economic, and the pattern-maintaining subsystems. I only make use of the three first of these subsystem designations. They correspond most directly to the main functional aspects of planning: integration, politics, and production, respectively. They also match the social, communicative, and instrumental types of rationality. The subsystem of pattern-maintenance is the locus of cultural and motivational commitments, as for instance solidarity and value-based claims to loyalty. The integrating subsystem contains legal institutions and injunctions and rites ensuring co-operation among individual and collective actors. Integration takes place on all levels from self to society. Here, stress is put on the mutual adjustment process converging opposites by applying social rationality on the personal level and in close interpersonal relationships.

Three ways to promote emancipation are briefly dealt with. Psychoanalysis is the paradigm of practice in the integrative subsystem. Conflict-analysis is the analogous paradigm of the political subsystem, and the applied science component of technology - engineering science - is the paradigm for practice in the economic subsystem.

Psychoanalysis may be seen as a technique for emancipation on the individual level. The treatment requires a 'depth hermeneutics' in which interpretation is directed to the various ways in which the patient fundamentally and systematically misunderstands himself, and fails to grasp the significance of the symptoms from which he suffers. The experience of self-reflection by the patient is the criterion for the correctness of the depth interpretation of his condition. To Habermas (1971a:266) 'the interpretation of a case is corroborated only by the successful continuation of a self-formative process, that is by the completion of self-reflection, and not in any unmistakable way by what the patient says, or how he behaves'. He aims to make modern critical theory emancipating in line with Freud's psychoanalysis and Marx's critique of ideology. Psychoanalysis is to Habermas a paradigm for theory with an emancipatory interest. The emancipation aimed for in psychoanalysis is the relaxation of mental obstacles to personal growth.

Conflict-analysis studies interpersonal (intergroup, etc.) relationships and is a critical examination of what structures and sustains social power relations. The aim is to uncover domination causing illegitimate social inequalities. Conflict-analysis comprises both the study of (1) manifest controversies between individuals or collectives, and (2) cases in which there is virtual agreement despite objective conflict of interest. In the first case, conflict-analysis studies the genesis of controversies, how and why they escalate and contract, and what hampers conflict resolution. Examples are Marx's analysis of the intrinsic antagonism between classes under capitalism (Fay 1987:Ch.2.3) and Castells's (1983) analysis of urban social movements. Some examples referring directly to planning practice are Benyon (1978), Fainstein (1987), Feiveson et al. (1976), and Kemp (1980). In the second case, an important task is to question any de facto consensus as potentially ideological. When emancipation is conceived as escape from the influence of dogmatic prejudice, as in the communicative theory of Habermas, one must try to disclose any domination in the alleged demo-cratic procedures leading to the consensus. One has to focus on the legitimacy of political decisions that have been made through formal democratic channels.

Analysis of conflict is a theoretical and critical undertaking different from the practical art of conflict management. The critical analysis of conflict can have a politically liberating effect for several reasons:
- It reveals and criticizes illegitimate use of force, coercion, etc.
- It seeks to disclose the real motives of the contenders in contrast to their published statements, making manipulation more difficult.
- It reveals the underlying and possibly system-determined causes of conflict which might not be clearly perceived by any of the disputing parties.
- Critical conflict-analysis in planning is a questioning process inquiring how political processes deviate from dialogue.

In short, not only the observable but the hidden structure of conflict is analysed.

Engineering science is, roughly, research resulting in new technology, or in more efficient application of known technology, and hence it increases productivity. This is the paradigmatic kind of analysis for improving the material conditions and alleviating economic scarcity. In other words, the analysis promotes the relief aspect of emancipation. Engineering science is paradigmatic to the instrumental analysis of the economic subsystem because it has the clearest division between ends and means, and because the correctness of its predictions are largely unaffected by human expectations.

Planning based on a personal growth rationale tries to build community and to identify and realize the public interest. The planners hold a consensus view emphasizing the maintenance of shared values and norms as the fundamental characteristic of societies. Conflict is regarded as a social anomaly caused by factors such as bad will, exaggerated egoism or inability to see the common good. Planning based on the promotion of undistorted communication is legitimized by appeal to social equality. This corresponds to a conflict view of society regarding conflicts between groups as a normal and inevitable form of interaction, which might even have positive functions in the society (Coser 1956). Planning based on the correction-of-market-production rationale does not presuppose a particular standpoint in the sociological consensus-conflict debate.

The distinction between process-orientation and product-orientation says from where we expect the most fundamental results of planning to emanate. Product-orientation implies the view of planning as technology and analytic technique, while process-orientation tends to accentuate the dialogical qualities of planning.

The tripartite rationale for planning

The purpose here is to give a schematic presentation of the fundamental reasons for planning. It has to be a composite construction as it is meant to cover the logical basis of planning relying on social and communicative rationality as well as on instrumental reason. The rationale comprises three basic functional aspects of planning, viz., integration, politics, and production - corresponding directly to the three rationality types, respectively. The three aspects of planning are connected to emancipation as relaxing mental constraints, liberation, and relief, in that order. Other functions of planning - like innovation, control, change, giving long-term direction - are regarded as derived from the three basic aspects.

The compound rationale for planning includes the personal growth rationale (integration), the aid-for-undistorted-communication rationale (politics), and the market correction rationale (production). A rationale for planning should make explicit the fundamental reasons why planning ought to be undertaken. It should identify the underlying ideals strived for. Thus, the concepts used to legitimize public planning are reflected in the rationale. A schematic survey of the compound planning rationale is given in Table 2.1. As far as I can see, all well known theories of planning can find their place inside a framework erected on integration, politics, and production.

Table 2.1
A compound rationale for planning

Main aspects of planning	Planning as integration	Planning as politics	Planning as production
Features defining the planning aspects	*1*	*2*	*3*
1 Elements of the planning rationale	Personal growth	Aid for undistorted communication	Correction of market production
2 Legitimizing bases	Community and the public interest	Overcoming illegitimate social inequalities	Efficacy in meeting material needs
3 Kinds of emancipation primarily aimed at	Relaxation of mental bounds	Liberation	Relief
4 Target areas for the planned action	Integrative system, i.e., self and close interpersonal relations	Political system, i.e., collective decision-making	Economic system, i.e., material conditions
5 Main types of rationality	Social rationality, stress on ego strength and solidarity	Communicative rationality, stress on mutual understanding	Instrumental reason, stress on goal achievement
6 Paradigms for practice	Psychoanalysis	Conflict-analysis	Engineering science
7 Paradigmatic planning theories	Transactive, dia-logical incremental	Advocacy	Synoptic
8 Sociological perspective	Consensus-view	Conflict-view	Neutral[6]
9 Foci of planning interest	Process-orientation, e.g., citizen parti-cipation for con-sciousness-raising and empathy-training	Primarily process-orientation, e.g., citizen participation as direct democracy[7]	Product-orientation, e.g., citizen participation for information and smooth implementation

Environmental planning might be grouped under the production aspect when this is defined to include protection and preservation of nature and man-made objects. My specification of the three aspects of planning does not fit all theories, however. For example, radical planning in the Marxist tradition strives to overcome illegitimate social inequalities but does not necessarily show strong commitment to communicative rationality. Redistribution by means of power (manipulation or force) is not part of the tripartite rationale sketched in the table.

The three first lines of Table 2.1 list the legitimizing concepts, the next three are concerned with the rationality models, and the last three lines show some important planning perspectives. Before turning to more comprehensive remarks on the composite rationale, the lines of Table 2.1 treating emancipation and rationality merit comments.

It is quite common among planners to regard emancipation (line 3) as a legitimizing concept along with the notions on line 2. It is seen to be close connections between the forms of emancipation and the elements of the planning rationale on line 1. Haworth (1984) suggests autonomy as the rationale for planning, but it is a somewhat problematic proposal. It idealizes an end-state instead of a process: an aspect of freedom instead of an aspect of emancipation. However, as a degree of control is inherent to planning, freedom is problematic as a planning rationale. Planning can contribute to emancipation but may not go along with freedom, as discussed in Chapter 5.

Under planning as politics it might appear sensible to apply Diesing's (1962) category of 'political rationality' on line 5 of the table. This concept designates a mode of reasoning directed to the maintenance of the capacity for making collective decisions. However, such maintenance is not what I have in mind as the task of planning as politics. I rather think of the kind of rationality required to solve 'practical' problems in a philosophic sense, i.e., to clarify normative questions concerning goals, values, and conflicting interests. This is the kind of reason Habermas aims to identify with his concepts of the 'ideal speech situation' and 'communicative rationality'. One might argue that politics is so much more than attempts to reach mutual understanding, yet this narrow meaning is indicated by the focus on communicative rationality. Politics, with a catch-phrase, is the process of deciding who gets what when. However, simply politicizing does not bring legitimacy to planning, while striving to overcome illegitimate social inequalities by a commitment to communicative rationality may do just that. In the first section of Chapter 3, I criticize Faludi's human growth rationale for largely ignoring the political facet of planning.

My line of reasoning started with a typology of the rationales already referred to in the planning literature. After evaluating and regrouping the previous proposals, I was left with three basic arguments for planning. These candidates to a planning rationale refer back to different types of rationality. I do not rank the importance of the rationality types in public planning, so a ranking of the arguments would have to draw support from other criteria. For instance, arguments pointing to effects that are regarded as by-products of planning could be assigned a lower rank. However, instead of choosing between the candidates and ending up with a rationale suitable only for a subgroup of planning efforts, they are united in a compound rationale for planning.

The composite rationale of Table 2.1 mitigates the detrimental effects of the problems attached to the personal growth rationale and the aid-for-undistorted-communication rationale. First, personal growth cannot con-stitute the entire rationale of participatory planning, but is nevertheless retained in Table 2.1. When economic and political redistribution and the implementation of a desired product are announced as the basic reasons for the planning effort in addition to personal growth, the consequences of openly admitting this last mentioned aim will not be so harmful. People are not likely to lose the motivation to participate, because they will see after all that their intentions have much in common with the planners'. Thus, part of the compound rationale may be a by-product of planning if the other parts are not, and if they give strong enough motivation for participation even if the by-product part is made public. Second, in a planning process only directed at undistorted communication, it is serious if some interests are pushed into the background. Attentional bias is more likely to be tolerated with a compound rationale. Propaganda for a particular viewpoint may be required to build sufficient agreement to implement a plan satisfying material needs or improving equity.

It might be objected that market correction, personal growth, and redistribution can all be obtained by other means than public planning.[8] In my opinion, these three arguments for planning can nevertheless be parts of the rationale. The crucial question here is not whether planning is indispensable. Planning does not even have to be the most effective means. A combination of public planning and other collective action might still be the preferable way to pursue a number of collective goals and objectives. All that is needed to defend the rationale against the objection that the positive effects it ascribes to planning can also come about by other means, is to show that the results of planning in accordance with the rationale are valued above the resources spent on the effort.

Planning paradigms: a rationality-based scheme

There are a number of alternative distinctions between rationality types. One has to choose among them, which means that only a few of the well-known concepts appear in the classification scheme for planning paradigms proposed here. Table 2.2 is based on the important distinction drawn by Habermas between instrumental and communicative rationality. The other central differentiation is between bounded and unbounded rationality. The instrumental/communicative distinction was selected among several alternatives because (1) Habermas's theory of communicative action is

Table 2.2
A rationality-based classification scheme for normative planning theories

	Rationality type	Paradigmatic core	Corresponding planning theories
1	Instrumental rationality	Search for the best possible combination of means for given ends	Synoptic planning, Public sector strategic planning
2	Bounded instrumental rationality	Search for satisfactory alternative, given an unclear and partly collapsed means-end scheme	Incrementalism (disjointed), Strategic choice approach
3	Communicative rationality	Organize dialogue to promote democracy and personal growth and search for a solution agreed upon in undistorted communication	Transactive planning, Dialogical incrementalism
4	Bounded communicative rationality	Counteract structural communicative distortions to promote equal opportunities and build support for a reasonably effective and fair alternative	Advocacy planning, Planning as questioning and shaping attention
5	Other types of rationality, e.g., system-maintaining types, like political and ecological rationality	E.g.: Political rationality preserves and improves decision structures to prevent indecisiveness and internal conflict	Recalcitrant planning, i.e., planning emphasizing other rationality types than those above. E.g., radical planning and ecological planning

widely discussed in contemporary social science and philosophy, (2) communicative rationality has been ably introduced to planners through John Forester's approach to planning as questioning and organizing attention, (3) it is a theoretically well underpinned differentiation between the rational use of means to achieve given ends and the rational deduction of the goals themselves, and (4) the resulting systematization is able to classify most well-known planning theories.

The contrasting rationality types applied here are well suited for establishing a taxonomy of planning theories, because they are in accordance with some important distinctions in planning. The instrumental and communicative rationalities are associated with
- product-oriented/process-oriented theory
- accomplishment-oriented/fairness-oriented theory and
- technocratic/democratic theory.
Unbounded and bounded rationality accord with
- normative/descriptive theory and
- idealistic/realistic theory.
Table 2.2 shows that very different planning theories correspond to the types of rationality and to the assumptions of boundedness stemming from high uncertainty, ignorance, distorted communication, and generally deficient human competence.[9]

One should resist the temptation to imagine a time axis from top to bottom of the table. It would only apply to the four first lines of the two first columns, for at least three reasons. Firstly, the fifth line of the table accommodates rationality types specified before communicative rationality. Examples are social and political rationality analysed in Diesing (1950, 1955, 1958) and Diesing (1962), respectively. Secondly, there are both new and 'old' theories of planning linked to each of the rationality types, and, among the 'old' theories, advocacy planning preceded transactive planning. Thirdly, a planning theory may be fully developed before the corresponding rationality type is explicitly formulated. Transactive planning and advocacy planning were launched before the corresponding rationality concepts were established. One might object that this contradicts my contention that planners aim at rationality. However, intuition and experience told scholars that the maximization of given ends is not all there is to socially intelligent behaviour, long before any alternative to 'economic man' appeared in the social sciences. This is a caveat not to apply Table 2.2 mechanically to predict future theoretical evolution.

There is no reason to believe that every planning theory can be placed on one single line in Table 2.2 without violating or ignoring some of its important features. For instance, Quinn (1980) combines incrementalism and strategic planning. His 'logical incrementalism' seems to imply that managers shift between views of planning as expressions of bounded and unbounded instrumental reason. A couple of additional examples will show that the need to adapt technic-economic skills to political and participatory processes has encouraged planners to develop procedures combining different types of rationality. Firstly, Faludi (1984:Ch.3) combines instrumental reason with Diesing's social rationality to establish a human growth rationale for planning theory. Human growth, implying a continuing enrichment of human life and the widening of the range of goals which human beings are capable of pursuing, is not obtained by instrumental reason alone. Secondly, Saaty and Kearns (1985:90) define rationality as '(a) process of using reason to defend the selection of goals, the specification of alternative ways to achieve them, and formulation and implementation of plans.' That is, their 'analytical planning' is founded on 'substantial' as well as instrumental rationality.

The existence of borderline cases does not detract much from the usefulness of the classification scheme. Attempts to prevent such cases would imply oversimplification of reality, giving the impression of clear borders where in fact the real phenomena overlap and fade into each other. The point is to facilitate survey of the planning field by placing each planning theory in relation to other theories by applying one basic criterion. A number of rationality concepts can be interpreted as belonging to one of the four rationality-categories produced by the instrumental/communicative and unbounded/bounded distinctions. There are nevertheless reasons for introducing a rest category:

1) There may be forms of rationality not comprised by the instrumental/communicative distinction. For example, some authors specify rationality on more than one level. The instrumental and communicative types characterize actors, but a systemic rationality may also be defined (Habermas 1987:333). Elster (1983) distinguishes individual and collective rationality.

2) Some concepts of rationality cut across the instrumental/communicative distinction; for instance the 'common sense rationality' of Geertz (1975) and Slote (1989). Other notions, like aesthetic rationality, are only partly covered by the categories of the distinction (Habermas 1984:238-40, Ingram 1987:180-86). Such concepts of rationality may have other paradigmatic cores than listed in Table 2.2.

The introduction of an unspecified rest category like 'other types of rationality' will alert critical readers. There would be reason to question the fruitfulness of the classification scheme, were several important planning theories guided by types of rationality belonging to this 'catch all' category. In my opinion this is not the case in the first half of the 1990s, even if some forms of radical and environmental planning theory come under the 'recalcitrant' rubric in Table 2.2.

44

Political rationality is an example of 'other types of rationality' which cuts across the instrumental/communicative distinction. It is outlined by Diesing (1962), Grauhan and Strubelt (1971), and Elkin (1985). Political rationality designates a mode of reasoning directed at the maintenance of the capacity for making collective decisions. Diesing considers political rationality to be more fundamental than the other types. 'This means that any suggested course of action must be evaluated first by its effects on the political structure' (Diesing 1962:228). Nothing is basically solved until the political problems (in this narrow sense) of an organization or society are solved. The reason is that without a well-functioning decision-making structure the system is unable to deal with its other problems in a continuing fashion. Theories of planning are concerned with political rationality when discussing the function of planning in society. Such analyses are most often found in urban and regional planning. The central problem is whether planning can achieve something beyond reinforcing the political-economic 'regime' of which it is a part. Elkin (1985) describes a regime as a political way of life defined by the political institutions of the society.

Other planning theories could have been added to those in Table 2.2. I have not aimed to be exhaustive on this point. The theories constituting the SITAR are supplemented with some recent planning modes, each with a clear connection to a particular rationality type - bounded or unbounded. The table indicates that several contemporary planning theories can be classified in accordance with the rationality-based scheme, and this will be confirmed in the succeeding discussion. I repeat no more about each planning theory than necessary to appreciate the correspondence with a particular type of rationality.

Main features of the planning paradigms

Paradigms related to instrumental rationality

The well known synoptic (or rationalistic) planning model is instrumental reason at work. Its essence is a means-end analysis. As it has been the prime planning paradigm for many years (Banfield 1959), there is no need to describe this planning mode here. Its foremost challenger, Lindblom's (1959) disjointed incrementalism, contains a critical view of the means-end scheme, as outlined in Chapter 1. The crucial point is that the ends are not taken as given throughout the incremental process; they are not even fully known. The consequence is remediality, stating that people move away from ills rather than towards known objectives. It seems difficult to modify instrumental reason much further without discarding it. Lindblom's model was a radical break with the presupposition of exogenously determined preferences which economic theory is still struggling to dispense with.

The synoptic and incremental paradigms are both more than thirty years old, but theoretical work is still done to apply their principles for solving problems created by the ever changing societal context of planning. Recent theory formation along synoptic lines seems to take place primarily under the heading of strategic planning. The bulk of the literature deals with corporate planning in the private sector. Especially during the 1980s, however, public sector variants emerged (Eadie 1983, Smith 1984, Bloom 1986, Kaufman and Jacobs 1987). Public sector strategic planning systems typically focus on a few areas of concern, rely on a decision process in which politics plays a major role, and control something other than pro-gramme outcomes - budget expenditures, for instance (Bryson 1988:32).

At its best, strategic planning is a reasonably orderly, participative, and effective approach for determining what is best for an organization. Bryson (1988:5) defines 'strategic planning as a disciplined effort to produce fundamental decisions and actions that shape and guide what an organi-zation (or other entity) is, what it does, and why it does it'. Bloom (1986: 254) mentions five basic steps: (1) Formulation of overall mission and goals; (2) environmental scan and analysis to identify factors that affect the organization; (3) resource audit of the managerial, operational, and fiscal resources; (4) formulation, evaluation, and selection of strategies; and (5) implementation and control. Here is little to distinguish strategic planning from other types of synoptic planning. Bloom concludes that 'in examining some of the literature on comprehensive planning, ... it becomes evident that most of the steps of the two planning techniques appear to be the same' (ibid.256). Bryson lists some differences between strategic planning, long-range planning, and comprehensive planning, but without focusing on features indicating that they are not all synoptic modes. Strategic planning searches for ways in which to maximize an organization's position in the context of its environment (ibid:256), while disjointed incrementalism results in a chronic suboptimization of organizational performance (Bryson 1988:13).

An alternative planning mode emphasizing strategic thinking - the strategic choice approach - was developed already in the 1960s (Friend and Jessop 1969). It is labelled 'the IOR School' by Faludi (1987) (Institute for Operational Research). Faludi and Mastop (1982:241) describe the approach as 'the second main stream of planning-methodological thinking in British urban and regional planning of the sixties and seventies', next to the systems approach. I include strategic choice in Table 2.2 because (1) the approach was further developed in the 1980s (Friend and Hickling 1987), (2) it seems to have a growing influence on West-European planning - not least thanks to the work of Faludi (1987), and (3) it has not been related to any particular planning paradigm in recent efforts to classify planning theories. The approach is essentially decision-centred. The purpose of planning should be to solve problems in the present rather than to draw pretty pictures of the future. Planning is seen as addressing the problem of making interrelated choices under conditions of uncertainty.

Friend and Hickling (1987:6) assume that practitioners 'arrive at commitments to action in an incremental or piecemeal way, however committed they might be in theory to the idea of taking a broader, more comprehensive view ...'. Consequently, they are in opposition to unbounded rationality in the sense of optimization. The IOR School sees this kind of rationality as opposed to its pragmatic approach which articulates the kinds of day to day dilemma that experienced decision-makers repeatedly face. The basic text on the strategic choice approach from 1969 was followed by a book (Friend, Power and Yewlett 1974) emphasizing the inter-corporate dimension of public planning. Faludi (1987:97-8) sounds more than a trifle disappointed when commenting that the text 'goes overboard with praising Lindblom's view of planning as mutual adjustment'.

The type of rationality presupposed in the strategic choice approach is spelled out by Friend (1983) and Yewlett (1985). The latter finds the normative basis of rationalism misplaced, given its practical and philosophical limitations. Yewlett regards strategic choice as designed to integrate rational analysis with a creative synthesis. He is sympathetic to March's (1971) 'technology of foolishness' as an antidote to overemphasis on rationality.

Paradigms related to communicative rationality

The introduction on dialogue in planning theory in Chapter 1 has already established that Friedmann's transactive planning is based on the dialogical ideal. His warning against turning dialogue into an instrumental relationship is essential for justifying the association between transactive planning and communicative rationality in Table 2.2.

In contrast to disjointed incrementalism, the dialogical incrementalism outlined in Chapter 1 is a nearly perfect planning response to Habermas's concept of communicative rationality. It denotes the planning mode emerging when communicative rationality and dialogue are fused with disjointedness and a sequence of small, tentative steps. The aim of the planners would be a genuine symmetry among all participants, permitting them to interchange role-taking completely.

Bounded communicative rationality is the outcome when mutual understanding is aimed for despite restrictions inhibiting dialogue. Communicative distortions erect boundaries between private and public language, making some social groups unable to articulate their deprivations and aspirations in public.[10] Distortions violate the claims for comprehensibility, sincerity, legitimacy, or truth. The misrepresentations may have an ad hoc character or be systematically caused by the way society is organized. Furthermore, one may think of some distortions as inevitable and others as socially unnecessary. Governmental propaganda and concealment, mass media censorship, and other violations of the freedom of expression are examples of socially unnecessary distortions. Tett and Wolfe (1991), Healey (1992) and Forester (1992) show how communication in planning can be discussed and evaluated.

The logic of advocacy planning takes for granted that the ability to make arguments influence political decisions is unevenly distributed among social groups. Advocacy planning aims at strengthening the negotiation power of weak groups, thereby creating a more symmetrical communicative situation (Davidoff 1965, Piven 1970, Heskin 1980). The paradigmatic essence of advocacy planning is its attempt to increase the power of deprived or suppressed groups by

(1) fighting apathy by demonstrating to the potential losers that they have a case, and that it might pay to tell their story;

(2) guiding their complaints and viewpoints through the right channels of communication; and

(3) formulating their arguments in a language acceptable and understandable to the public bureaucracy, often translating emotional utterances to the businesslike narrative style of experts.

In short, advocacy planning works by counteracting communicative distortions and assisting in building a convincing argument.

A central admission of John Forester's critical theory of planning is that communicative rationality is always imperfect. The following is the 'ethical framework for the everyday practice of planning analysts: to eliminate distortions, to foster open and authentic communication, ... to make true political discourse and dialogue possible' (Forester 1977:xxvi). This is also the paradigmatic core of planning as questioning and shaping attention. Forester (1989:46) affirms that there is a strong affiliation between his approach and advocacy planning: 'progressive planning practice represents a refinement of traditional advocacy planning, a refinement based on the practical recognition of systematic sources of misinformation'. This recognition will help citizens reveal attempts at 'misrepresenting cases, improperly invoking authority, making false promises, or distracting attention from key issues'. Forester's questioning satisfies Davidoff's demand that the advocacy planner point out the nature of the bias underlying information that is presented in plans set forth by the establishment,

48

and thereby perform a task similar to the legal technique of cross-examination. Shaping attention corresponds to Davidoff's claim that the advocacy planner should be an educator, informing other groups, including public agencies, of the conditions, problems, and outlook of the group he represents (Davidoff 1965:333).

In this section it is argued that some established and some recent planning theories can be arranged in groups, each with a clear connection to a comprehensive or a bounded type of rationality. Each of the four groups connected to instrumental or communicative rationality represents a planning paradigm. These paradigms are surveyed in the next section, which, moreover, finishes the explanation of the classification table by commenting on recalcitrant planning.

Reconstructing the basis of the SITAR classification

Since the appearance of the SITAR package of planning traditions in 1979, more than half a dozen classification schemes identifying competing or succeeding planning paradigms have been suggested.[11] None of them form an ordering principle by directly applying the rationality concepts sustaining the planning theories. I find this extraordinary because of the planners' persistent commitment to some kind of rationality, whether perfect or bounded. The reticence may indicate a dominance of instrumental thinking among planning theorists. Such dominance is demonstrated by the well-known title 'After rationality, what?' (Alexander 1984), where rationality is assumed to be of the instrumental type. No rational alternative to the instrumental way of thinking is mentioned. What planners can do, following the severe criticism of instrumental reason, is to modify it or start defending procedures and decisions that are *not* rational. Acknowledging communicative rationality opens for new answers to Alexander's question.

The Habermasian view of the rationality concept expressed in Table 2.2 provides a new foundation for a well-known systematization of the field of planning theory. The SITAR package of planning traditions (Hudson 1979) is still widely used for pedagogic purposes. The theoretical modes forming the acronym were selected by Barclay Hudson as representatives of five main traditions, because they offer different solutions to the problems of public interest, human dimension, feasibility, action potential, substantive theory, and self-reflection. However, Hudson admits that these criteria are rather subjective, 'a kind of Rorschach test of one's own cognitive style, social philosophy, and methodological predilections' (ibid.395). One cannot entirely escape the subjective. Still, I think the situation is improved when the planning theories are arranged by their relation to one basic concept, as in Table 2.2. What Hudson called 'the heuristic rubric of SITAR' may not be so heuristic after all.

I will now sum up how the recent planning theories briefly outlined in the preceding sections relate to the main traditions constituting the SITAR, and hence to the corresponding paradigms for planning. It has already been argued that strategic planning corresponds to the synoptic paradigm, and that the strategic choice approach is akin to incrementalism. Furthermore, I let the term 'transactive' cover all planning modes based on the assumption that dialogue will bridge the communicative gap between the planners and their clients. Dialogical incrementalism is then in concord with the transactive paradigm. As stated, Forester's critical and communicative approach has important traits in common with the advocacy paradigm. It is nevertheless acknowledged that Forester's anticipation of structural mobilization of bias takes his planning-as-social-critique some steps further in the direction of radical planning. In Table 2.2, then, the first four letters of the SITAR signify planning paradigms corresponding to the first four rationality types specified.

But what about the R in the acronym? In the rationality-based reinterpretation of the SITAR, it is expedient to let the R denote 'recalcitrant planning' instead of radical planning. Planning theories on the fifth line of Table 2.2 are recalcitrant because they resist the authority of the central instrumental/communicative dichotomy. Although applying instrumental and/or communicative reasoning, other and often overlapping types of rationality are brought to the fore, for instance political or ecological rationality.

To exemplify what belongs in the 'rest categories' on the bottom line of Table 2.2, I choose political rationality. The question is then if there are planning theories based on this type of rationality. My answer is affirmative, and such theories must address the problem of the political function of planning in society. An interest in this topic is found in several theories, e.g., advocacy planning, transactive planning, and in Popper-Faludian theory (Faludi 1986). I leave these aside here, however, and draw attention to two groups of theory treating the political function of planning as essential. Hence, the theories do not merely apply political rationality, they are based on it.

One can distinguish a left wing and a right wing current of the literature profoundly concerned with the function of planning in society. A large part of radical planning (Hudson 1979) belongs to the Marxist tradition. In Marxist urban and regional planning it is a crucial question whether it is possible to prevent planning in a capitalist society from solidifying the capitalist mode of production and reproduction.[12] Planning facilitates a smooth accumulation process by mediating the conflict between labour and capital and by regulating some of the secondary contradictions within the capitalist class (McDougall 1982). The experience as interpreted by the political left, is that it is hard to 'beat the system' and prevent planning from being politically rational as judged from the viewpoint of capitalism. Temporary success in alleviating the hardship of underprivileged groups tends to improve the adaptability and responsiveness of capitalism, and so put any deeper transformation farther off. Some Marxist scholars (Castells 1978, Scott 1980) have pointed out the apparent paradox between the inability of urban planning to reach its stated goals and its continuous widespread use. Part of the explanation may be that the political rationality of planning compensates for the lack of instrumental success.

The right wing current concerning the function of planning in society started off as a direct counterpart to the Marxist approach just described. In the interwar period and throughout the 1940s the right wing regarded planning as a threat to democracy and the market and as a road to socialism and serfdom (Hayek 1944). There is still a libertarian, minimal-planning line of thought that follows Hayek (Sorensen and Day 1981). According to this view, the political rationality of planning is not to replace the market, but to improve the decision-making system based on market transactions.

There is but a short step from the libertarian posture to the anti-planners (Jacobs 1965, Banham et al. 1969, Fishman 1980). Sennett (1970) is the anti-planner building his arguments most straightforwardly on political rationality. He hypothesizes that planning keeps the society in a state of prolonged adolescence. The function of planning is to create order. Simultaneously, planning decimates the number of conflicts and leads to a mediating professional bureaucracy. In these circumstances, the new regime preferred by Sennett cannot be realized. His aim is a disordered, unstable, and direct social life forcing people to deal with others different from themselves and to experience in their own lives the movement from conflict to agreement (ibid.160). The result is supposed to be freedom, diversity, and maturity.

Recalcitrant planning theory may be based on other than political rationality. For instance, Dryzek (1983) and Bartlett (1986) describe ecological rationality. It is 'the rationality of biogeochemical systems, their integrity, maintenance, reproduction, evolution' (ibid.234). Functional ecological rationality organizes actions consistent with an ecological ideal, e.g., the maintenance of a healthy life-enhancing interaction between man and the environment. Meier (1985) argues for a 'community ecology' paradigm for planning which is in accordance with ecological rationality. The focus of his planning theory is the set of reinforcing accommodations arising between the populations and functions of many different species maintaining themselves in close proximity. Masser et al. (1992) indicate that a shift to an environmental paradigm is about to take place in transport planning.

It is clear from the above examples that several of the recalcitrant planning theories are guided by what Max Weber denoted substantive rationality (Brubaker 1984). Each of the theories just mentioned espouses a particular set of values and political beliefs. The Marxist theories rely on class conflict to bring about the classless society, the right-wing theories are premised on the success of the market in maximizing social welfare, the libertarian theories are based on the value of unfettered individualism, the anti-planners believe in disorder and diversity, and ecological theories emphasize the value of the bio-environment.

The examples of what can be grouped behind the R in the reformulated conception of the SITAR do not exhaust the set of recalcitrant planning theories. This is a heterogeneous and open category including all planning theories giving prominence to other than instrumental and communicative rationality. There cannot exist a common paradigm for all recalcitrant planning. The more well-known and important planning theories that belong to the recalcitrant category, the more unfeasible Table 2.2 will be for surveying the field of planning theory. However, most recalcitrant theories still exist on the periphery of Western planning communities. Changes over the last few years have made this less so for the ecological theories and more so for the Marxist ones.

Conclusion

Several contemporary planning theorists exploit the possibilities of Habermas's theory of communicative action as a foundation for a critical theory of planning, e.g., Forester (1989) and Healey (1992b). There are also attempts to integrate his ideas in mainstream planning theory. The present chapter is part of this effort. The introduction of communicative rationality makes it easier to realize the intelligence of tending interpersonal relations throughout the planning process. The process is not designed just to ensure a satisfactory product. Planners deliberately introduce elements making the process valuable in itself. Dialogue serves democracy and personal growth as well as the search for acceptable solutions.

I offer a new answer to the old question 'why plan?' by drawing on Habermas's concept of communicative rationality. The composite rationale gives some advantages:

A) The distinction between integration, politics and production as the main aspects of planning makes the rationale correspond to the intentions behind most of the well-known theories of planning. A rationale involving both instrumental and noninstrumental rationality seems needed if we want a common rationale for the main traditions, ranging from synoptic to transactive planning theory. A rationale applicable to the diverse approaches provides planning with an image of homogeneity; it helps to present planning as one discipline.

B) The rationale bridges the gap between substantive and procedural planning. On the one hand, it makes clear that planning should give results of a certain quality, i.e., efficacy in meeting material needs. On the other hand, the rationale underlines that the qualities of the preparation process are equally significant.

C) The multi-rationality rationale embraces the peculiar modes of thinking of most academic professions occupied with planning problems, from the technical-economical to the psychological-sociological. The rationale might turn out to be an expedient tool for promoting co-operation between the disciplines, as it demonstrates that no single discipline masters all of the three main aspects of planning.

Incorporation of Habermas's concept of communicative rationality opens for a systematization of planning paradigms based on their associations with particular notions of rationality. Students are offered a new method for perceiving order in the field of planning theory and surveying it. In contrast to most other schemes classifying planning theories, only one basic ordering criterion is applied. The kind of rationality conspicuous in the doctrines and recommendations of a normative planning theory is considered to be the essential characteristic of the theory. Ordering the planning paradigms according to this metatheoretical criterion is believed to reduce the subjectivity of classification.

One aim of classification is to expose structure and detect lacunae that might give direction to future research. The SITAR package helps to make explicit the possibilities of choice between the alternative planning styles and modes of reasoning. It also brings to light possible combinations of theory traditions. According to the classification scheme this can imply choice between or combinations of different rationalities. Thus, the scheme draws attention to the intriguing problem of how this is achieved in practice (Sager 1993a). There is nothing to indicate that planning will stop being a multi-paradigm field. This state reflects the continuing eclecticism of planning as an academic discipline, and its necessary adjustment to contrasting forms of political practice.

Notes

1   In Thomas S. Kuhn's (1970) model of scientific progress, a paradigm represents the collectively accepted beliefs and procedures of a scientific community which structure the pursuit of normal puzzle-solving science.

Correspondingly, a planning paradigm 'frames' ordinary problem-solving behaviour within a particular planning tradition. I am only dealing with paradigms for how planning should be conducted. There may be other paradigms stating how planning should be *described*. For instance, the 'garbage can' model is a candidate for a paradigm of the last type only (Cohen, March and Olsen 1972, March and Olsen 1986). Descriptive theories do not necessarily assume that planning is rational. The concept of paradigm is discussed in Lakatos and Musgrave (1974) and Barnes (1982).

The concepts of 'paradigm' and particularly 'theory' have a more precise and restricted meaning in epistemology than in planning. For instance, what is called 'radical planning theory' would not qualify as a 'theory' in the epistemological sense. I stick to the usage of the terms common in the planning literature.

2 Benditt's (1973:300) example 'enough to eat' is a likely candidate for a public interest, since it is hard to insist in a public debate that others should starve because the debater in question would not benefit from the arrangements catering for them:

> (I)f a particular action or policy is in the public interest because it will provide enough to eat for anyone who meets its conditions, no one can claim that such a policy is not in the public interest on the ground that he himself, being rich, is unlikely to benefit from it. Its being in the public interest has nothing to do with whether everyone will actually get some of the results of it. It has to do with whether having enough to eat is an interest of everyone's and with whether the serving of this interest is social in nature.

3 Fadiman and Frager (1976) give a brief introduction to the work of Maslow and Rogers, and Boelen (1978) creates a vivid picture of the integrated and mature personality that is the desired outcome of personal growth.

4 Faludi (1984:Ch.3) adopts the term 'human growth' and gives it a prominent place as the rationale for planning theory. There is, however, a peculiar feature of his outline of the rationale. Faludi frequently cites and refers to Diesing in that short but central outline, and his 'human growth' includes the integrative aspect of this concept which is to Diesing the ideal of social rationality. But Faludi pays no attention to the kind of thinking and deciding which Diesing claims to be necessary for promoting human growth. He seems to disagree with Diesing's contention that a rationality different from the instrumental type is needed to obtain the integrative ideal. I have criticized Faludi's position elsewhere (Sager 1990a:Ch.2.3).

5   Schattschneider's (1975:69) statement appears in the following context:

> All legislative procedure is loaded with devices for controlling the flow of explosive materials into the governmental apparatus. All forms of political organization have a bias in favor of the exploitation of some kinds of conflict and the suppression of others because *organization is the mobilization of bias*. Some issues are organized into politics while others are organized out.

Hajer (1989:Ch.5) gives examples of this mechanism in city politics.

6   Planning which is primarily arranged to meet material needs, may cause diverging effects along the harmony/controversy scale. Planning will be conflictful if enduring needs are seen as kept up by systematic social inequalities. However, planning may be a harmonious activity if basic needs are conceptualized as caused by inadequate technology, fate, God's will, etc. Then planned action to increase economic welfare is not necessarily perceived as an attack on group interests.

Communicative rationality may be conducive to the levelling of illegitimate social inequalities, as it accepts no power except the compulsion of the best argument, and aims for a genuine symmetry among all participants. On the other hand, one may question the realism of getting anywhere near an ideal speech situation when the actors hold a conflict view of society.

7   Illegitimate social inequalities may concern the distribution of material goods and require product-orientation for their correction. The inequalities can also concern the distribution of opportunities and regards, and a process-orientation may be required to set them right. Citizen participation as direct democracy gives the local inhabitants the possibility to rectify the inequalities both ways. Nevertheless, when planning is seen as politics, the desired procedure is undistorted communication, which confirms the primacy of the process over the product.

8   Klosterman (1985:10) contends that even the correction-of-market-production rationale should not be used alone: 'the case for planning in a market society cannot be based solely on the theoretical limitations of markets ...'. He writes that (ibid.10):

> Government decisions concerning the provision of public goods, the control of externalities, and so on can be made in a number of ways: by professional planners, by elected or appointed public officials, by the proclamations of a divine ruler, or by pure happenstance involving no deliberate decision process at all. If planning is justified by the economic arguments for government alone, it is impossible to

differentiate between government planning and government non-planning - 'government' is reduced to an undifferentiated mass.

I am not convinced by Klosterman's argument. The market correction rationale for planning does not imply denial of alternative governmental ways for dealing with market failure.

A transaction cost rationale for planning was recently proposed by Alexander (1992). It offers a more parsimonious argument for planning than the current correction-of-market-production rationales and explains the emergence of co-ordinative planning in both the public and the private sectors.

9   A number of bounded forms of instrumental rationality have been identified. The 'selective rationality' described by Leibenstein (1976) is affiliated with Simon's thoughts on satisficing in that they both break with the ideal of the maximizing economic man. Leibenstein holds that our concern for the constraints set by the economic realities varies considerably. Since it takes effort to fight the constraints, we settle for a comfortable level of constraint concern. That means we are not doing our utmost to maximize economic utility.

Goodin (1982:Ch.3) has coined the term 'retrospective rationality'. His model foresees many occasions on which the individual concerned might mistake his future interests. Thus, interference may be justified to save people from 'their former selves'.

March (1978) distinguishes several types of bounded rationality. One of them is 'posterior rationality', emphasizing the discovery of intentions as an interpretation of action rather than as a prior position. Elster (1983, 1984) offers extensive studies in the subversion of rationality.

10 Several kinds of communicative distortions are described by Habermas (1970), Mueller (1973), and Forester (1989). Classification tables are offered in Forester (1989:34,53,150).

11 Sager (1993a) surveys the paradigms for planning proposed after the SITAR package. A contingency paradigm is explicitly proposed by Alexander (1988). Contingencies are identified by combining three dimensions: (1) the purpose or orientation of the theory or model (real vs ideal), (2) the decision domain (individual-deliberative vs social-interactive), and (3) the actor's orientation or purpose (accomplishment-oriented vs consensus/understanding-oriented). My classification scheme in Table 2.2 is based on a simplification of this. I deal only with public planning, which is taken to always involve several actors. Thus Alexander's dimension (2) is dropped. Furthermore, my aim is to classify normative theories of planning. Purely descriptive theories are ignored, and Alexander's dimension (1) is transformed to bounded vs

unbounded rationality. Alexander's dimension (3) is kept, but reformulated to instrumental vs communicative rationality. In public planning guided mainly by instrumental rationality, 'strategic action' dominates. When communicative rationality is the guiding principle, 'communicative action' dominates. These are the terms used by Habermas to characterize interactive action.

12 Surveys of Marxist planning theory are given by Cenzatti (1987) and Kraushaar (1988). The Marxist authors contending that planning in capitalist society has a system-supporting function do not always imply political rationality on the part of the planners. For example, Kravitz (1970) regards the planners as handmaidens to conservative politics, who are not aware or conscious of the political effect of their work.

Popper (1966b, 1986) has drawn the attention to a strain of irrationality involving the Marxist historicist position '- the theory that society will necessarily change but along a predetermined path that cannot change, through stages predetermined by inexorable necessity' (Popper 1986:17). Under historicism the ideal of planning as a tool for 'man perpetually shaping this world, including the guidance of his own development' (Faludi 1984:42) would be an illusion. As Popper says, historicism 'denies to human reason the power of bringing about a more reasonable world' (ibid.50). Planned change would lose its meaning: '(a)ll social engineering, no matter how much it prides itself on its realism and on its scientific character, is doomed to remain a Utopian dream' (ibid.47).

Part two   Obstacles to communicative rationality: power and conflict

Part two investigates the relationships between conceptualizations of power, conflict, and conflict management and the 'ideal types' of synoptic and incremental planning developed in Part one. The result is a consistent set of notions for the study of domination and controversy in planning.

It is not to be expected that theoretical ideals can be fully realized amidst the political turmoil and the social imperfections of the real world. Part two is an analysis of some important phenomena that the planners are up against when trying to adapt theoretical paradigms to practice. Biased power relations and pernicious conflicts set severe constraints on the strivings for dialogue. This is so although power and conflict may be constructive as well as repressive. Even planning itself has ambiguous effects on freedom since it is, inherently, partly controlling and partly an exploration of new opportunities.

The analysis helps to solve a problem present in most mainstream planning theory: as planning is a highly eclectic discipline, the theories of planning should be so precisely formulated, that it is possible to determine how well the borrowed notions fit in. However, planning theory has no tradition for such rigorous theory construction, and little effort has been made to bring planning theory, sociological conflict theory and the power theories of political science close enough together. This is the more deplorable, as a critical theory of planning must be conflict-oriented and explicitly account for the many forms of power relations in society.

The analysis of power relations and types of conflict and conflict management is also important in a contingency approach to planning. The political planning environment can hold widely different opinions on what it takes to legitimize a plan, which kinds of power relations are acceptable, how to deal with conflicts, and how to design collective choice processes. This, and the actual distribution of power and the current social controversies in the community, restrict the planner's freedom of action as a professional. These are among the contingencies determining how the planners respond and how plans are made: more or less incremental, communicative, flexible, and so on. In a critical theory of planning, however, the role of the planner cannot only be to react on terms set by others. Critical theory is designed to achieve changes in the society, and this requires a more active role that allows for initiatives as well as responses.

Working to ease the burden of power relations, to change them, and to settle conflicts fairly are great challenges to the planner. The aspects of planning as production, politics, and integration are all involved. This requires an ability to combine instrumental and communicative rationality.

3 Power in a dialogue/technique perspective

The negative connotations of the term 'power' do not seem to be strong in the planning literature. It is probably realized that some degree of power is required to implement plans. Perhaps it is also acknowledged that power may be used to emancipate as well as suppress. The literature on power and related notions is overwhelming, and different approaches proliferate (Clegg 1989). Much of the text is based on the simple definition of power as a causal relation between preferences and outcome. This facilitates the discussion of power in terms of technique and communication.

A brief survey of the three ensuing sections follows. A concept of instrumental power is first defined and distinguished from influence. Johan Galtung's idea of structural influence occasions some critical remarks on Faludi's human growth rationale of planning. The communicative concept of power set forth by Hannah Arendt is presented as a contrast both to instrumental power and structural influence. Then, four main types of instrumental power relations are discussed. They are force, manipulation, persuasion, and authority. Their effects on the possibility for dialogue are spelled out. I comment on two special power relations of significance to planning, namely paternalism and seduction. The last section connects Michel Foucault's ideas about power/knowledge with planning theory. It is briefly surveyed how mainstream theories treat the knowledge-power-action relationship.

Definitions of power and influence

The section presents a definition of power as the causal relation between preferences and outcome. The distinction between power and a systemic notion of influence is applied to relate the discussion to 'human growth' and to criticize the rationale for planning which Faludi founds on this concept. I deal mostly with conceptualizations of power as the quality of an actor. The conventional idea is that of an agent who is capable of realizing his or her own will even against the resistance of others. This is the Weberian notion, which is currently challenged by several models (Ball 1992). Yet it will be seen that the coercive aspect is not explicit or prominent in the definition shortly to be presented. The perspective of regarding power as a constructive characteristic of a collective or a system is not commonly adopted by social scientists. However, this idea is encountered in the writings of Arendt and Foucault.

There are virtually innumerable vantage points for an attack on the problem of power in planning. Power has been a troublesome notion in the social sciences for many years, and the conceptual contents of influence, power, and the various power relations display significant differences among authors. My classification of the terms is shown in Figure 3.1, which is an adjustment of Wrong's (1979:24) categorization scheme to fit Nagel's (1975) power concept.[1] Interpreted from the top, each line can be read as 'may be achieved through'.

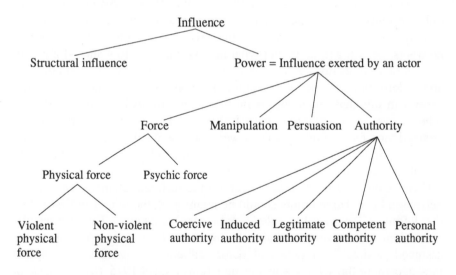

Figure 3.1 A hierarchy of concepts related to instrumental power

I use primarily the second and third levels of the figure. 'Power' and Johan Galtung's 'structural violence' belong to the influence level and are presented in the two subsections to follow. Treatment of the power relations on the third level is postponed until the next section.

A person may reach a higher preference level due to several causes. The event may come about by accident or by the will of other benevolent actors. In these cases his good fortune would not be credited his power. This is in accordance with Nagel's descriptive analysis of power, which rests on a relatively simple definition, only involving the variables 'preference' and 'outcome':

> A power relation, actual or potential, is an actual or potential causal relation between the preferences of an actor regarding an outcome and the outcome itself. (Nagel 1975:29)

Power, then, is the capacity to establish such causal relations.[2] When I refer to Nagel's definition of power, I combine this statement with the above quotation. Normally, the preferences of the controller must become known to the respondent. Communication is therefore at the core of power.

The definition leads us to regard as expressions of power some ways to reach results which are not customarily regarded as such (Parsons 1967). For instance, Elster (1978:49) would object that Nagel's definition requires only causality and not intentionality. It may not be sufficient that a person usually gets what he wants; powerfulness requires in addition that whatever he wants, he will get, no matter what he might happen to want. Along with several other objections which I will not discuss, this view suggests that the above definition may be too broad for some purposes. This objection is not serious in my analysis, as the point here is not to distinguish power from other ways an actor might gain influence. The necessary precision is attained not by delimiting the power concept itself, but by identifying specific kinds of interpersonal relationships which actors develop to establish a causal relation between preference and outcome.

There is no need to elaborate much on the different elements of Nagel's definition here. Three points should be mentioned, though. The first is that the definition incorporates 'rule by anticipated reactions'. This denotes the case when the respondent shapes his or her behaviour to conform to the assumed desires of a powerful actor without having received explicit message about the actor's wants or intentions (Nagel 1975:16). The case of anticipated reactions accounts for the term 'potential' in the definition.[3]

The second point concerns power as embedded in causal relations. Ball (1975:203) poses the question: 'If power relations are causal ones, and if cause is understood in mechanistic terms, then what, in political-scientific discourse, corresponds to the mechanist's principle of "no action at a distance?"'. There has to be some sort of 'connection' between the person exercising power and the one being influenced. Most writers on the subject agree that the human-behavioural substitute for actual physical contact or collision is communication. This cannot be taken literally as verbal communication, but must be interpreted as the interpersonal transmittance of signs or messages in general.

The third point is a clarification of how power can be increased in Nagel's model. For this purpose the term 'outcome' in the definition should be described more precisely. Nagel applies 'domain' and 'scope' to achieve this. 'The domain is the actor or set of actors influenced - an individual, group, collectivity, organization, nation, or whatever. The scope is the behavior, response, attitude, belief, or choice influenced' (Nagel 1975:14). Now, there are two ways in which an actor can increase his power. Firstly, upholding the preferences for a fixed outcome, he may strengthen the causal relation between these and the actual outcome. Secondly, developing a desire for an outcome having a wider domain or scope (but embracing the outcome formerly desired), he may succeed in making the existing causality work over the entire expanded outcome.

Stated goals or ends express the preferences of the actor wielding power. The part of this 'controller' may be played by the planner or the decision-maker. It does not matter much if we insert the goals instead of the preferences of the controller in the definition of power. We then see that power appears as a kind of generalized means to obtain ends. Power is necessary for transforming instrumental reasoning into efficacious action. Exerting power in interpersonal relationships implies treating men as means.

There is only a short step from Nagel's definition of power to prominent aspects of human growth. Faludi (1984:44) regards self-awareness as important, because 'an actor possessing consciousness is able to change himself in a deliberate manner, thereby to improve his chances of attaining his ends, and hence to grow'. Growth in this sense implies more power over some outcomes and most likely increasing indifference with regard to other outcomes.

Structural influence

The subsection introduces Johan Galtung's (1969) 'structural violence' as a kind of influence different from power. I prefer the term 'influence' instead of 'violence' for two reasons. It is closer to Wrong's (1979) terminology in Figure 3.1, where violence is seen as a kind of force. Besides, influence has wider connotations than violence, and is probably more readily associated with the inclination of a social system to create minor as well as major inequalities of life chances.[4] Fighting structural influence is tantamount to pursuing the planning-as-politics component of the compound rationale of planning.

Structural influence is not power in Nagel's sense because it is a characteristic of the system, and a system does not have preferences. When explaining structural influence with direct reference to Galtung below, I use his terminology. Galtung's (1969:168) point of departure is that 'violence is present when human beings are being influenced so that their actual somatic and mental realizations are below their potential realizations'. Violence is to him the cause of the difference between the potential and the actual realization. Concepts that depend on full information of potential states require perfect knowledge, and should thus be associated with synoptic planning theory.

Galtung would not call it violence when a person died from tuberculosis in the eighteenth century. But when a person dies from it today, with the medical technology now known and the resources now at hand, he would describe this as violence. Even if there is no single person or actor who commits the structural violence, 'individuals may be killed or mutilated, hit or hurt in both senses of these words, and manipulated by means of stick or carrot strategies' (ibid.170). The general formula behind structural violence is inequality. The violence is built into the structure and shows up as unequal power and consequently as unequal life chances. Galtung emphasizes process-oriented aspects of equality. In a critical comment on existing declarations of human rights, he concludes that 'it is the way in which decisions about distribution are arrived at and implemented that is basic' (ibid.188, Note 18). Thus, it is the power to decide over the distribution of resources which needs to be reallocated. Galtung sometimes refers to the condition of structural violence as social injustice.

There is a connection between Faludi's (1984) striving for 'human growth' and Galtung's ideal of 'minimal structural violence', because human growth can be regarded as the gradual closing of the gap between potential and actual somatic and mental realization. The two concepts can therefore be combined, and the combination covers the compound rationale of planning, broadly speaking. The emphasis of human growth is on the integration and production aspects, while structural violence accentuates the political dimension.

Galtung's exposition takes man-made injustice as the point of departure and retains an overtly egalitarian stand. This points at an unsatisfactory aspect of Faludi's rationale of planning. Faludi relates the task of planning - its logical basis and fundamental reason - only partly to structural characteristics of the society in which the planning takes place. His human growth rationale is wide enough to cover the abatement of structural obstacles to growth. But Faludi chooses to be unspecific regarding the substantive contents of this political part of the rationale, except for stating that he wants a society based on self-guidance.

Faludi wants to achieve 'a continuing enrichment of human life, and the widening of the range of goals which human beings are capable of pursuing' by the use of rational procedures of thought and action (ibid.35). Planning contributes by identifying the most efficient ways of attaining ends and by arranging for learning. When Faludi writes about fear and the desire of man to free himself, he refers to the fear and the limited choice caused by ignorance, not by a man-made and oppressive social system. Faludi elaborates his rationale by establishing close links between planning, rational action, and science, and by relaxing the bonds to political action and social emancipation.[5]

Faludi discusses human growth both as process and product within a system-theoretical setting without problematizing the constraining role of the system itself. He is fascinated by 'human growth as inextricably linked with the notion of man perpetually shaping his world' (ibid.42). While I share this fascination, I think that a helpful rationale of planning has to acknowledge that man is shaped by, as well as creating, the systems in which he acts (Giddens 1984).

Arendt's communicative concept of power

Hannah Arendt (1970:44) provides us with a communicative concept of power that is useful when discussing the pursuit of legitimacy. 'Power corresponds to the human ability not just to act but to act in concert. Power is never the property of an individual; it belongs to a group and remains in existence only so long as the group keeps together'. Arendt understands power as the ability to agree upon a common course of action in unconstrained communication. Power is a collective effect of speech in which reaching agreement is an end in itself for all those involved. The communicative concept of power is, thus, not instrumental but presupposes communicative rationality. '(P)ower, far from being the means to an end, is actually the very condition enabling a group of people to think and act in terms of the means-end category' (ibid.51). It serves to maintain the praxis from which it springs. That is, the advantages of being able to go unanimously in for a common course of action serve to strengthen undominated communication as the praxis for reaching collective decisions. This is a case of 'political rationality' in the terms of Diesing.

Politics in Arendt's sense is identified with the praxis of those who talk together in order to act in unison. She is interested in the production of power:

> Power is a good for which political groups struggle and with which a political leadership manages things; but in a certain way both find this

good already at hand; they don't produce it. This is the impotence of the powerful - they have to borrow their power from the producers of power. This is the credo of Hannah Arendt.   (Habermas 1977:21)

When the controller is a democratic collective, reaching decisions by dialogical exchange of views, the capacity to establish causal relations between preferences and outcome depends on the ability to agree upon a common course of action. First, the collective must be able to decide on the ends, meaning the preferences one should try to realize. Second, the causal relation will be stronger the more they agree on the means, i.e., on how to influence the outcome. Hence, for groups dedicated to dialogical practices Nagel's definition of power presupposes power in Arendt's sense. This is a confirmation, in terms of power, of Diesing's (1962:84) maxim that 'integration is a logical precondition for the successful completion of any social action'.

The basis of the communicative concept of power is 'the contract between free and equal parties with which they place themselves under mutual obligation' (Habermas 1977:23). This assumption of a contract has a function similar to the 'original position' in Rawls's (1972) theory of justice, which specifies the conditions under which individuals would behave as if they were equals, and under which they would therefore be able to communicatively agree on a fair procedure.

Habermas (1977:15) points out that 'Arendt traces back political power exclusively to praxis, to the speaking and acting together of individuals', and that this leaves her unable to grasp structural influence. The reason is that 'communicative power' and 'structural influence' are opposites on the power dimension: communicative power is a collective capacity that everybody is behind, while structural influence is a systemic capacity that nobody is behind; it is impersonal. Structural influence is built into political institutions: 'unperceived, it blocks those communications in which convictions effective for legitimation are formed and passed on' (ibid.21-2). Structural influence is incompatible with Habermasian dialogue.

Structural influence is damaging to a communicative production of power: this invisible kind of influence easily leads one to perceive social inequalities as something natural, not created by man himself. On this belief ideologies are formed, by which subjects deceive themselves about themselves and their situation (false consciousness). This kind of deception is especially dangerous because ideological illusions are outfitted with the authority of common convictions. Thus structural influence manifests itself in such forms that those trying to reach agreement in undominated communication remain unaware that they are all dominated by apparently 'natural', yet man-made, traits of the system.

Types of power relations

The purpose here is to describe four main types of social relations in which power is exerted (Wrong 1979). The section deals with the power relations force, manipulation, persuasion, and authority. They are methods for establishing causal relationships between preferences for certain outcomes and the outcomes themselves. A broad range of rewards and punishments can be combined with each kind of power relation, but I choose to omit sanctions from my discussion. Communicative aspects of the power relations are outlined, and some links to analytic technique are pointed out. The subsection on manipulation introduces a model of the planner as a seducer, which draws a line back to the personal growth paradox.

According to Nagel, the controller's housing of certain preferences causes a specific outcome. This implies that a power relationship cannot be purely dialogical. What causes a specific outcome from a dialogue, i.e., from undistorted communication, is the agreement resulting from mutual understanding. The strength of the arguments set forth is judged independently of the preferences held by the interlocutors. Hence, types of power relations may be communicative but not dialogical, and planning distorts communication to the extent that it makes use of the four power relations.

Force

I distinguish the actual use of force from the threat of employing it. The latter is an element in a social relation in which the threatener engages in communication with the respondent at the symbolic level. I return to threats under authority.

Force refers most commonly to 'the creation of physical obstacles restricting the freedom of another, the infliction of bodily pain or injury including the destruction of life itself, and the frustration of basic biological needs which must be satisfied if the capacity for voluntary choice and action is to remain unimpaired' (Wrong 1979:24).

A few comments on violent physical force will be helpful when discussing conflict management later on. The crucial point is the destructive effect of violence on communication. This is clearly spelled out by Cotta (1985), who states that violence generates a circuit in which the reciprocal recognition of the quality characterizing the other person is annulled, 'disfigured' by violence, so that the parties in the relationship can no longer recognize one another as human individuals.

(T)he possibility of personal communication may become lost, since it is achieved only when we have or find points in common, which

> constitute the criteria (the measure) of communication itself. ...
> (D)ialogue ... necessarily requires a common measure. And it is this
> very measure that is lost in violence, which, being unruliness, denies at
> the root the dialogical nature of existence, and so constitutes the most
> explicit and radical breakdown in communication. It cannot even be said
> to be a unilateral communication, since it does not communicate
> anything: it only imposes.   (Cotta 1985:65-6)

The violent man is prevented from dialogue and empathic coexistence,
keeping him enclosed within himself. He cannot be relied on to establish
a human relationship; he serves disintegration and hence acts contrary to
social rationality. Cotta's argument suggests that the communication
between the controller and the respondent may be restricted and to some
degree perverted also when other kinds of force than violence dominate
their relationship. I assume that this is the case, which is of significance for
the consequences of fight specified in the chapter on conflict.

I now leave the effects of force to examine when antagonistic behaviour
may occur. Perfect knowledge applied by rational actors would leave very
little disputed matter to be settled by conflictful behaviour. It would be
possible to calculate whose utility would increase or decrease. The use of
force under conditions of perfect knowledge would largely be due to a
rationality involving variables not included in the utility concept, which
may be honour and self-respect, for instance. Divergence from perfect
information and rationality creates some room for antagonistic behaviour.
Analytic techniques of option seeking, impact assessment, prediction, and
evaluation serve to narrow down the set of cases in which antagonistic
behaviour would seem a reasonable strategy. Techniques increase the
probability of convincing one of the actors that he misjudges the costs or
the benefits accruing from conflict. The higher degree of instrumental
rationality and initial amount of information, i.e., the closer to the ideal of
synoptic planning, the less scope left for uncertainty and the use of force
after the technical analysis.

Manipulation

In manipulation useful information is deliberately held back, which makes
this type of power relation a process of distorted communication. One
important kind of information concerns preferences. In the words of Wrong
(1979:28):

> When the power holder conceals his intent from the power subject - that
> is, the intended effect he wishes to produce, he is attempting to
> manipulate the latter ... Any deliberate and successful effort to influence

the response of another where the desired response has not been explicitly communicated to the other constitutes manipulation.

A special kind of manipulation involves the concealed mix-up of behaviour corresponding to different types of rationality. An association openly conceived by the one part as a subject-to-subject relationship may tacitly be regarded by the other as being subject-to-object, i.e., as an instrumental relationship. A means-end analysis of a close personal relationship is usually considered an abuse of technique. 'The deliberate giving of signals to another in order to elicit a desired response implies a degree of calculation, affective detachment and "playing on" another's feelings that is alien to norms of candour, emotional "warmth", and the mutual disclosure of motives which govern personal relations in primary groups' (ibid.29). This is to say that manipulation is normally at odds with the prevalence of social rationality in the same relationship.

Manipulators are not always cultivating instrumental behaviour, at least not in others. Planners tacitly organizing the process out of consideration for personal growth, at the expense of the lay participants' need for tangible improvements of the physical environment, may be unduly preoccupied with social rationality. They act instrumentally in a manipulative manner to promote social rationality.

Diesing considers political reasoning to be more fundamental than the other forms of rationality. 'This means that any suggested course of action must be evaluated first by its effects on the political structure' (Diesing 1962:228). Nothing is basically solved until the political problems (in this narrow sense) of an organization or society are solved. The reason is that without a well-functioning decision-making structure the system is unable to deal with its other problems in a continuing fashion. One should make the priority of the rationality considerations clear to the participants in the planning process in order to minimize manipulation. It is well known to planners that what is considered the best solution with reference to analytic technique does not always earn political blessing. They should not leave the lay participants with the impression that the paramount aim is to design the project so as to best serve the local users, knowing that the elected officials will give first priority to an alternative that is satisfactory on political considerations.

Wrong (1979:31) points out a similar kind of manipulation where 'the primary aim of power holders is always to establish and maintain their power for its own sake rather than to achieve a substantive goal, serve an ideal or fulfill a duty'.[6] Such behaviour is not, usually, what is expected from democratically elected decision-makers. They are more often supposed to represent the preferences of their constituency.

Hayek (1944) regards manipulation as inevitable in comprehensive planning. The planner resorts to 'common welfare', 'the public interest', and other obscure notions to manufacture the agreement needed. The controller does not state his intentions clearly. Knowing that there is not agreement on the concrete ends he is pursuing, he still pretends there is, and thereby manipulates. As people affected by a comprehensive plan do not have compatible interests, they cannot simply be persuaded into accepting the plan. Acceptance has to be produced by manipulation and propaganda, or else the minority must be forced to submit. The choice under comprehensive planning is one between manipulation and force, and thus planning is seen as the road to serfdom (Sager 1990a:Ch.3.5).[7]

I do not think that manipulation in the sense of holding back one's preferences is necessarily censurable. With reference to self-altering predictions, Chapter 5 will show that silence concerning the preferences of the planner will, in some circumstances, benefit most persons affected. In cases where the integrative gains are expected to be great, silence on the ideal of personal growth may also be warranted. Self- altering predictions exemplify how manipulation may be related to the use of analytic technique. Such a prediction may be published, not to inform the public of what is most likely going to happen, but to encourage them to change their behaviour so that, e.g., what was predicted will not occur after all.

Before leaving the manipulation theme I will follow Lilja (1988) in her comparison of the planner and the seducer, as portrayed by Kierkegaard (1971). His *The Diary of the Seducer* is an elaborate description of a manipulator. Lilja sees him as a symbol of the planner as practitioner of instrumental reason. Those of her arguments most closely related to my own subject matter are reproduced here. I add a few points to her analysis, and it will be seen that the seducer example has close parallels to the personal growth problem.

Kierkegaard's seducer is special in that he does not want to possess the woman. His idea of conquering her is a purely intellectual process. He arranges for the relationship to break before it demands any sexual involvement from him. Lilja points out that to him the seduction is simply an interesting planning process. He uses all his energies and cleverness to work out a detailed plan step by step. The woman is merely a means that offers him the opportunity for this fascinating intellectual game.

The interest of the seducer is aroused by what the process can do to the woman, not by what he might do with her once she is seduced. There is an analogy here to planning giving precedence to the personal growth component of the compound rationale. The deepest interest of the planner is then what the planning process may do to the other participants. The planner does not focus his interest on what they might be able to perform together when he has made them accept his proposal. The concrete project merely provides a necessary setting for the arrangement of a personal growth process. This kind of planning is process-oriented and procedural.

What does the seducer imagine that his conquering process will do to the woman? He wants to develop her aesthetically, to lead her to a world of endless reflection. His aim is to give her inner freedom, to rescue her femininity, to give her the opportunity to develop and be fulfilled, as pointed out by Lilja. The guidance towards endless reflection really is to direct the woman into the seducer's own way of being. This is not sufficient to legitimize the project of the seducer, just as consciousness-raising usually does not provide reason enough for planning. Hence, we find an analogy between the seducer's further arguments for his project and the legitimizing concepts of emancipation and personal growth. The seducer believes he is an expert in promoting such growth.

The strategic principle of the seducer, the law governing every move in his campaign, is to work the respondent into interesting situations. This implies that he has to design ambiguous situations, as infinite possibilities are precisely the interesting. If the respondent is able to predict his future steps, the relationship loses its meaning for Kierkegaard's seducer. Manipulation on the side of the controller (the planner or seducer) requires unpredictability for the respondent. This was strongly felt by his victim Cordelia, who complains that: 'No word of mine was without effect, and yet I cannot say that my word did not fail of its effect; for it was impossible for me to know what effect it would have' (Kierkegaard 1971:306).

Seduction implies the destruction of meaning, as advocated by Baudrillard (1985). Seduction, thus, is distorted communication and has no place in dialogue. If the respondent acquires the ability to predict, a logic and hence something meaningful has been found. Predictability means that the seducer has lost the game. There is a close connection between interesting situations, ambiguity, and aesthetical development. The respondent cannot be made reflective unless he or she is in doubt about what is going to happen. A confused person is easier to lead, also in directions not serving his or her interest. Manipulation ruins the respondent's possibility for fully realizing what is in his own best interest. It is required that the respondent faces choices, so that the controller can influence the decisions. The planner is often obliged to make the situation ambiguous by working out alternative plans. Furthermore, the planner is usually not in a position to make the situation unambiguous again, as the decision-making authority rests with the politicians or with higher bureaucrats.

Lilja (1988:2) states that 'the seducer is a manipulator in that he very consciously evokes her interest and certain expectations in her mind and dreams, that he never intends to fulfil'. Furthermore, the seducer conceals

71

his preferences. He has a clear picture of femininity and intends to change her accordingly. The woman does not know about his mental picture and she does not realize that she is being fashioned. Thus she is manipulated. Again one will see the analogy to the previous discussion of planning stressing the personal growth component of the compound rationale. The point is that the manipulative role of the seducer is necessarily inherent in planning when the personal growth part of the rationale dominates.[8]

It would have been comforting, at this stage, with a clear conclusion as to the acceptability of manipulation in planning. Unfortunately I cannot offer this. While, as a rule, I take manipulation to be a feature of planning that should be played down as far as possible, examples in the two following chapters indicate that there are cases in which it is best tolerated.

Persuasion

Persuasion is argumentation intended to make the respondent adopt the opinion of the controller. 'Where A presents arguments, appeals or exhortations to B, and B, after independently evaluating their content in light of his own values and goals, accepts A's communication as the basis of his own behaviour, A has successfully persuaded B' (Wrong 1979:32). Persuasion is a kind of 'indirect influence' in Nagel's terminology. This means there is a variable intervening between one actor's preference and the outcome, and this intervening variable is the preference of the respondent (Nagel 1975:101). Nimmo (1978) agrees with Wrong's notion, distinguishing persuasion from other communicative modes in that it is
- purposive, interested communication,
- dialectical and, in principle, reciprocal, and
- influential, i.e., making people act differently from the way they would have behaved in the absence of persuasive appeal (ibid.99-100).

Types of persuasion include propaganda, advertising, and rhetoric. These are all examined by Nimmo.

Under conditions of perfect knowledge, no actor can possibly influence the preferences or behaviour of another rational agent by persuasion. This is because the respondent already knows what serves him best, and because persuasion per se does not change this by imposing penalties or rewards. In the absence of uncertainty, it is futile for an actor to engage in this kind of communication. Admittedly, the above conclusion is purely theoretical. Even when the actors know all the facts about their environment, persuasion makes sense if there is some uncertainty with regard to one's own preferences. Rhetoric grows in importance as uncertainty affects some actors more than others (Downs 1957:82-4). It may now be rational for those who are most certain to try to influence those who are less so. The biased distribution of uncertainty is a consequence of the inevitably hierarchical structure of the communicative pattern exhibited by complex systems.

A biased distribution of income and wealth also contributes to the unevenly allocated uncertainty. The application of analytic technique to systematize and produce useful results from bits of information is usually not free. Hence, the ability to reduce uncertainty by technique tends to be positively correlated with the access to economic resources. Downs rightly holds that '(p)ersuadors are not interested per se in helping people who are uncertain become less so; they want certainty to produce a decision which aids their cause. Therefore they provide only those facts which are favorable to whatever group they are supporting' (ibid.83). Persuaders usually rely on experts who know what data are required to utilize a specific technique, and what kind of result is likely to emerge. Any technique can be, and is of course, used for persuasion, and more often so as the technification of planning and politics makes progress.

The communicative situation is very different for persuasion and manipulation. When the manipulative element is absent, the respondent always knows when somebody tries to persuade. He also knows who the persuader is, and he is, in principle, free to develop counter-arguments and answer back. Formally, as pointed out by Wrong, persuasion lacks the intrinsic asymmetry of other power relations. The difference between persuasion as a power relation and the mutual exchange of arguments in a dialogue is highlighted by Brown's (1963:25) definition of propaganda:

> The fundamental mechanism employed by all forms of propaganda is ... suggestion, which may be defined as the attempt to induce in others the acceptance of a specific belief without giving any self-evident or logical ground for its acceptance, whether this exists or not.

Emotional pressure, whether it takes the form of arousing positive or negative collective feelings, or simply that of presenting emotionally biased views, is not just something accidentally affixed to propaganda. It is fundamental to the whole process. Propaganda serves not only to change opinions. More importantly, it aims to intensify existing trends, to sharpen and focus them and, above all, lead men to action. It employs a totally different technique than rational and dispassionate argument. As Brown notes, 'the propagandist does not engage in genuine argument because his answers are determined in advance' (ibid.12).[9] The dialogue, on the other hand, is free from domination. The purpose is not to change the actions of the interlocutor to match one's own preferences and outcome. The purpose is mutual understanding in an attempt to arrive at a consensus on what are generalizable interests.

The dispassionate dialogue would seem to be a paradigm for public discussion in a democracy. However, Ellul (1973:121) makes a strong case for what he terms the dilemma of the modern state: 'Propaganda is needed in the exercise of power for the simple reason that the masses have come to participate in political affairs'. The dilemma is largely constituted by the following assertions:

1. The government cannot operate outside the pressure of the public opinion.
2. The public opinion is only imperfectly expressed in government based on majority vote.
3. Public opinion is so variable and fluctuating that a government cannot base a course of action on it.
4. Ergo, even in a democracy, a government that is honest, serious, benevolent, and respects the voter cannot follow public opinion, but it cannot escape it either. Thus, it 'must channel and shape that opinion if it wants to be realistic and not follow an ideological dream' (ibid.126).

When public involvement in planning is extensive, the dilemma can be brought to bear on this specific activity: propaganda is needed in planning because the local constituency has come to participate in the design of public projects. Hence, Ellul's dilemma leads to a reinforcement of Hayek's (1944) claim that planning necessarily produces extensive propaganda to manufacture agreement where in reality there is none.[10]

Authority

Authority is defined by Wrong as implying the untested acceptance of another's judgement, whereas persuasion results in the tested acceptance of another's judgement. Authority is exerted by issuing commands. It distorts communication and blocks the discourse, because the respondent is likely to abstain from counter-arguments.[11]

The above statements do not imply that authority is without foundation in reason and communication. Friedrich (1972:48) argues that '(w)hat makes a particular course of action authoritative ... is that convincing reasons may be offered in support of it'. These reasons may not be conclusively demonstrable for such reasoning to be authoritative. Indeed, only where they are not thus demonstrable is authority in the strict sense involved. Whenever logical proof cannot be offered - the usual situation in politics and planning - reasoning is apt to seek support in authority. Rhetoric is the technique of giving convincing reasons in politics. Thus, the basis for authority is established by a kind of communication. As the content of the communication is not questioned, one might say that certainty - instead of the uncertainty conducing persuasion - is reinstalled in the mind of the respondent. The source of the message guarantees the quality of its contents. The signature induces voluntary submission. '(I)t is not the content of a communication but its source, that is, the perceived status, resources or personal attributes of the communicator, which induces compliance' (Wrong 1979:35).

All the kinds of power relations are not open, neither to the seducer nor to the planner pursuing the Faludian human growth ideal. The seducer dissociates himself from the Don Juan type of behaviour, which he regards as rape. 'Most men enjoy a young girl as they do a glass of champagne in a single frothing moment. ... This momental enjoyment is ... a rape: it is like a stolen kiss, a thing that requires no art' (Kierkegaard 1971:337). Force is not attractive to the planner because personal growth becomes harder to achieve when the will of the participants is deliberately trampled on by the growth-agent. Persuasion, on the other hand, is admissible. Authority, too, is useful in small doses, but exaggerated authority might lead to immediate subjugation. This would eliminate the process of seduction, and no change would take place in the respondent. The parallel is that the ability of the planner to make the persons affected by the plan adopt his point of view, may be too high. When the lay people immediately admit that he is right, no process of citizen participation is meaningful. Everything that causes the process to be too short or redundant eliminates the possibility for personal growth. Hence, when the authority of the planner is too great, no personal growth will take place.

Threats belong under coercive authority in Figure 3.1. They announce actions to be implemented by the controller, and these measures are thus at his disposition. Warnings, on the other hand, refer to actions or incidents beyond the control of the threatener. Threats are clearly based on self-interest, and are often difficult to use openly in public planning controversy. Concealing threats as warnings is to replace an argument based on self-interest by another one based on the public interest. This results in strategies for disclaiming responsibility (Elster 1992). For instance, the town planner 'warns' the local residents' association that their continued struggle for hard surface roads in the neighbourhood might, if successful, induce the local road administration to demand humps and improved sight at crossroads - leading to expropriation of parts of the adjacent gardens. The planner conceals that he is in the position to influence the decision of the road administration, and thus manipulates.

The role of technique in making authority function is entirely different from that of making persuasion effective. The techniques are now valuable, not per se for the results they yield, but because they demonstrate a desired expertise. Technique may, for instance, lend the user the authority of scientific investigation, a case of competent authority in Figure 3.1. McAllister (1980:142) asserts that 'it is not uncommon for decision-makers and interested citizens, after having read a CBA evaluation, to find themselves in a position of either having to accept on faith the estimated monetary impacts or ignoring them'. When choosing the first, authority is established at the hands of the planners.

Planners gain authority by technical mastery, and by creating an image of themselves as objective and neutral, above the political conflicts of interest. Their aim is furthered by the idea of a clear-cut means-end scheme fixing preferences only to ends, while the planners claim responsibility for the means. After the intense social science critique of positivism during the last decades and the proliferation of policy studies showing the relativity and intermingling of means and ends, this myth of the neutral planner is discredited but far from dead. The technocratic pattern of thought prevails and provides planners with authority:

> Once the idea that we can empirically calculate and administratively design 'the right way' to accomplish our goals is accepted, there is little reason to engage in the exploration of other views. The 'rational' person is the one who agrees to submit to the properly derived technical and administrative knowledge of the experts. The authority of the expert, from this perspective, must take precedence over the democratic exchange of opinions. (Fischer 1990:43-4)

In Bråten's terms, the authority of the expert is based on 'model power', i.e., knowledge of causal relationships and analytic techniques. Dealing with citizen participation in local planning, we can usually assume that such processed knowledge is unevenly distributed. Now, imagine citizen participation procedures that give all parties equal access to information and provide for open communication between the planners and the local public. The theory of model power aims to show that the influence gap is not necessarily narrowed by this, when there was a severe bias in the initial situation. The ability of the model-weak party to acquire, discriminate, structure, and process the data has to be improved. This development is dependent on models. Without models of the phenomena to be influenced by participation, the information obtained by involvement in the planning process is of no use. Stein Bråten (1973:98) has given an instructive account of the theory of model power, and he concludes:

> If a model-strong actor and a model-weak actor are coupled in an open information exchange system, the former may be expected to gradually increase his control of the other actor. Offers of information are useful

only to the extent that there is model capacity for processing the information offered. Thus a successful transition in the name of democratization to a more open communication structure may freeze - or even increase - the influence gap. Independent development of system model resources among the less influentials is required.

When the planners have a model monopoly or are model-strong, while the local lay participants are model-weak, any information from the lay public can be processed and used by the planners. The local participants, on the other hand, can only utilize information from the planners to the extent that it fits the participants' simple and partial models. Even if these under-developed models gradually improve during the open exchange of infor-mation, the planners might strengthen their influence. The reason is that at any time, they have a higher capacity for data processing and model improvement at their disposal. The planners will be in full control if the local public, following a torrent of information from the planners, adopt the planners' images of reality and take over models formerly employed by them. This would equip the planners with power to even simulate the simulations carried out by the lay participants. At any time, then, the planners would have an adequate picture of the lay public's view of the situations emerging throughout the planning process (ibid.104-5).

The first step in a process to neutralize the mechanisms of the theory of model power would be to make the participants familiar with it. Then they may invalidate the theory in a particular planning process by
1) being aware of the planners' (and other experts') inclination to prefer consistent and unequivocal reasoning limited in perspective and area of validity to fit the prevailing analytic techniques, therefore generating only *some* models among several acceptable alternatives;
2) changing the borderline of the problem area so that no experts possess models which adequately cover it all;
3) consulting independent model sources; and
4) breaking off the communication temporarily, giving the model-weak party time to develop models on its own terms (ibid.126).

Advocacy planning aims directly at strengthening the negotiation power of model-weak groups, thereby creating a more symmetrical communicative situation. In my context a critical question concerning advocacy planning is whether it implies a device for indoctrinating lay people to the planners' way of looking at the world. Does the advocacy planner succeed in mixing processed knowledge with the personal knowledge of local under-privileged groups and come out with a powerful receipt for how to formulate arguments in negotiations with other planners and politicians? 'Do advocate planners strengthen the poor's fight against City Hall? Or does their influence divert the poor from the most effective forms of action?' (Piven 1970:32). Regardless of the answers, advocacy planning implies a concession to technocracy: it is based on the assumption that lay people cannot make it without the expert.

Wolff points out a dilemma in his discussion of the possibility of being a morally responsible individual, yet acknowledging a government. The state demands authority, i.e., the right to rule. On the other hand, the fundamental assumption of moral philosophy is that people are responsible for their actions. Responsible people arrive at moral decisions which they express to themselves in the form of imperatives. They are self-legislating and thus autonomous. The autonomous person is not subject to the will of another. Wolff (1970:18) formulates the paradox of authority this way:

> The defining mark of the state is authority, the right to rule. The primary obligation of man is autonomy, the refusal to be ruled. It would seem, then, that there can be no resolution of the conflict between the autonomy of the individual and the putative authority of the state.

Moral autonomy is a combination of freedom and responsibility. Autonomous man 'may do what another tells him, but not because he has been told to do it. He is therefore, in the political sense of the word, free' (ibid.14). In so far as it aims at instrumental rationality, planning is a branch of government activity that can embody a strong element of steering and control. The state and local government demand the right to prepare and implement plans. The dilemma of autonomy under authority can, accordingly, be transformed to one of freedom under planning. Friedrich Hayek's position can thus be recognized in Wolff's philosophical anarchism.

Autonomy is defined by Sennett (1981:86) as self-possession, a mastery of the self. He regards autonomy as a kind of authority which 'removes the necessity of dealing with other people openly and mutually'. The one who appears master of himself has a strength which intimidates others and creates an unbalance. Others are likely to show their need for him more than he shows his need for them. This puts the autonomous person in control and erodes the incentives for dialogue. Sennett's idea of autonomy as an aspect of ego's own authority may be contrasted with Wolff's conception of autonomy as the refusal to accept the authority of others. If we approve both points of view, we reach the conclusion that emancipation (from authority) creates new authority - a result which is a suitable prelude to the emancipation/freedom paradoxes of Chapter 5.

Force, manipulation, and authority do not necessarily involve communication, while persuasion does. Furthermore, force, manipulation, and persuasion can be seen as techniques for increasing the preference level of the controller by deliberately influencing another's behaviour. There are also techniques for obtaining authority and techniques for getting the most out of it, but authority itself is probably best regarded as a capacity or a resource.

Paternalism

In a much cited article, Dworkin (1971) understands paternalism as the interference with a person's liberty of action justified by reasons referring exclusively to the welfare, good, happiness, needs, interests or values of the person being coerced. Although others have suggested that the terms 'liberty of action' and 'coerced' are not always to the point (Gert and Culver 1976), Dworkin's definition catches the essential combination of power and benevolence. A person may think himself entitled to paternalistic interference, because he feels qualified to act on the respondent's behalf and even do so independently of the immediate consent of the respondent. Therapists, educators and experts of various professions - including planners - tend to acquire such ideas. This is one of the mechanisms making the power/knowledge theme of the next section of interest to planners.

I link paternalism to power by using the definition of Gert and Culver (1976:49-50), which is in line with the conceptualization above:

A is acting paternalistically toward S if and only if A's behavior (correctly) indicates that A *believes that*:

(1)   his action is for S's good
(2)   he is qualified to act on S's behalf
(3)   his action involves violating a moral rule (or doing that which will require him to do so) with regard to S
(4)   he is justified in acting on S's behalf independently of S's past, present, or immediately forthcoming (free, informed) consent
(5)   S believes (perhaps falsely) that he (S) generally knows what is for his own good.

Requirements (3) and (4) are crucial for classifying paternalism as a power relation. In point (3), Gert and Culver have in mind moral rules prohibiting deception, disabling, or deprivation of freedom or opportunity, for instance. Violating such moral rules means acting in a power relation; deception implies manipulation and disabling means force. Paternalism does not belong to one particular of the power relations force, manipulation, persuasion and authority; it is based on them and can be combined with any of them.[12]

The paternalistic controller feels better off himself, when his assistance makes the respondent reach a higher level of preference. To arrive at a new and preferred state, the respondent must - in the opinion of the controller - change his preference structure to be more like that of the controller. In this situation the controller has power according to Nagel's definition, if he establishes a causal relation between his and the respondent's preferences and is a successful paternalist. The controller trusts that posterior rationality will bring the preferences of the respondent in accordance with the controller's prediction of the respondent's preferences, thereby leaving the respondent with an approving view of the action and making him altogether better off.

Paternalism may be justified in some cases, but I do not discuss the exact criteria (see Hodson 1977 and Husak 1980). The problem is approached here by a planning example in which the paternalism is not legitimate in my view. Imagine a proposal for a monumental suspension bridge crossing a fjord. The project has a social benefit-cost ratio no higher than the required minimum, but the economic benefits to the local communities are beyond dispute. Although the social and ecological drawbacks are negligible, the village people on each side of the strait are opposed to the bridge for aesthetical reasons. It is a graceful and slender construction with elegantly curved ramps and impressive towers - all according to the planners. Nevertheless, its giant dimensions are out of proportion with everything else in the adjacent communities, including the landscape. The planners know from previous cases that audaciously designed landmarks like this often become tourist attractions in their own right. Local dissatisfaction usually vanishes quite fast when people experience the advantages of the bridge, hear approving comments from impressed foreigners, and get used to the new sight. The conclusion of the planners is that the project is marginal to the society at large, while it will do a lot of good to the local economy. They recommend the project for this reason and hence act paternalistically.

The general objection to paternalism is that it means treating persons as less than fully autonomous agents. Their choice is made *for* them, and to this extent they are treated as if they lacked the capacity to choose (Husak 1980:37). It should be a task for critical planning theory to identify cases of paternalism, so that it can be openly discussed if they are legitimate in a democracy. Carefulness is required, however, because the concept of 'false consciousness', playing a key role in critical social theory (Fay 1987, Leonard 1990), has paternalistic implications. By accepting the notion, one might easily reach the conclusion that the social critic is in the best position to identify the real interests of an oppressed group (West 1987).[13]

In the example above, the planners cannot claim ability to predict the future preferences of the local people more accurately than they are capable of themselves, and legitimately ignore their political opinion on that basis alone. The planners should instead try to communicate to the local public how practical their everyday life will be when the bridge replaces the ferry. They should attempt to make concrete the spreading economic impacts following from increased through traffic, and compare the bridge to other constructions generally accepted as attractions. The trade-off between local economic gains and the preference for the traditional scenery should be made explicit. As a general rule, the planners should not violate autonomy by recommending a good which is not recognized as such by the persons for whom the good is intended.

The power/knowledge dilemma and planning theory

This section links the ideas of one of the most influential postmodern scholars to the planning related discussion of power. Foucault's view on the power/knowledge complex provides a perspective in which the dialogical ideal of Habermas can be criticized. Furthermore, it shows clearly that the relationship between knowledge and power can be conceived of in a way very dissimilar from the prevailing view in planning theory. It is briefly argued here that the critical theory of planning founded on Habermas's thought is currently coming closer to the problematic of Foucault by incorporating a phenomenologic approach.

Several books spell out Michel Foucault's view on power, e.g., Dreyfus and Rabinow (1982), Foucault (1980), and Rouse (1987). The present brief exposition barely suffices for appreciating the significance of the power/knowledge dilemma for planning theory.

Foucault's view on power/knowledge

To Foucault, power is strategic games. It is decentralized and exists in a network of relationships. Power is strategically deployed without strategists (Hiley 1984:201). Such paradoxical statements show that it is dubious to classify Foucault's concept unambiguously as either influence or power in Figure 3.1. Like most authors, I shall be using the term power.

According to Rouse (ibid.13) 'the received view' of the relationship between scientific knowledge and power has three components:
(1)   Knowledge can be applied in order to achieve power.
(2)   Power is used to impede or distort the acquisition of knowledge.
(3)   Knowledge can liberate us from the repressive effects of power.
A fourth point is added here:
(4)   Power is used to acquire knowledge.

The formulation of the points indicates that power and knowledge are separable. This is a premise in Habermas's theory of communicative action, as it is argued that truth emerges from communication from which power relations are suspended. Hence, the same premise is made in planning theories based on the concept of the 'ideal speech situation', like dialogical incrementalism. The first point says that the preferences of the controller can be more effectively realized if one can accurately describe one's situation and the effects of one's instruments. This idea permeates synoptic planning. The second point is important in the critical theory of planning practice advocated by John Forester. Power is seen as introducing communicative distortions biasing the knowledge of the citizens. The planner should reveal true alternatives and correct false expectations created by actors influencing the planning process in this way to further their private interests. Power also impedes knowledge when subordinates are reluctant to come forth with information because they fear the negative response to their implicit criticism. Similarly, lay people may keep ideas to themselves in meetings with planners, intimidated by the authority of those talking with professional knowledge. In some settings, effects like these can be counteracted by structured group processes, e.g., the nominal group technique (Delbecq, Van de Ven and Gustafson 1975, Olsen 1982, Moore 1987). The third point stresses that knowledge can uncover the distortions power imposes and unmask the disguises that permit power to operate with reduced interference. The belief that knowledge linked with collective action in the form of planning can serve an emancipatory purpose, is reflected in the compound rationale for planning advocated in Chapter 2. The fourth point leads the thought to interrogation and forms of authority giving certain individuals the right to know. Furthermore, a corollary to power is in many cases income, which can be used to buy information. In some countries the government has access to long-term and short-term macroeconomic models in its planning and budgeting, while the opposition may be denied such access. The rationale of advocacy planning is to counteract social unfairness following from the fourth point.

It is outlined below how Foucault's thinking on the interaction between power and knowledge differs from the received view. Especially in his early work, Foucault is interested in the spectacular modern growth and ascent in influence and prestige of the human sciences (Gordon 1980). What made such science possible, according to Foucault, is not an advance of rationality into the domain of human behaviour, but the emergence of new forms of coercion and disciplinary techniques for the control of bodies. In turn, the human sciences produce conceptual tools contributing to the success of such control. 'Biopower' is Foucault's term for this interdependence of power and knowledge. He studies the technologies elaborated in human science for the governance of people. Public planning may be seen as such a technology, although not explicitly examined by Foucault. Both planning and (other) fields of human science are linked to the philosophical conception of man as being simultaneously the subject and object of knowledge.

The power and knowledge of the human sciences are used in a normalization process. Foucault investigates how this knowledge comes to use in mental health care, the penal system, and in the control of sexuality. Knowledge is used in defining the normal and in the treatment of deviation. McCarthy (1992:129) points out that 'Foucault's account of the interrelation between social institutions geared to normalization and the growth of knowledge suited to that purpose parallels Habermas' account of the interconnection between the administrative colonization of the lifeworld and the rise of objectifying social science'. The ideology of public planning rests on the same quest for normality as that of the other institutions: it is regarded as necessary that individuals act in accordance with the public order and the common interest. Only now it is their behaviour within the economic system that is in focus, i.e., their use of land and other economic resources. Judging from his treatment of the human sciences, it is in the spirit of Foucault to be sceptical to the idea that planning has a liberating function. In planning as in other spheres of life, biopower succeeds through normalization. It maximizes utility at the same time that it maximizes docility. Planning belongs among the human science technologies arranging for the success of biopower and thus cannot emancipate us from its effects. Hiley (1984:193) continues:

> Biopower, that is, functions to achieve the Enlightenment dream - a society in which everything is regulated, calculable, rationalized, and efficient. It individualizes, and makes individuals into 'cases', both as objects of study and targets of power. Individuals are examined, described, measured, compared, classified and judged ... It makes us subject and subjugated. The emergence of the sciences of man which has man as its subject is one and the same as the emergence of biopower which has man as its target.

Hence, power cannot be separated from knowledge, truth, and rationality. One cannot speak a truth to power that would itself be free of power relations. This is the core of the power/knowledge dilemma.

Foucault's conception of the power/knowledge relationship dissolves any transcendent position which can be constituted outside of discursive practices. That is, truth is an outcome of communicative practice, which in turn is always influenced by power - except for Habermas's utopian ideal speech situation. Lindblom (1990:46-7) argues that even in dialogue one never goes beyond analysis of how best to adapt an outcome to prior continuing impositions. 'One cannot even conceive of a solution or outcome reached wholly by examining its merits. For all participants in problem solving live in a network of existing impositions and coercions, born as they are into an economy, polity, and culture that they never chose.' Their solutions to social problems, even when emerging from dialogue, are never independent of the pre-existing power relations that have made their imprint on the social context in which the dialogue takes place. In his view, the outcome is no more the result of dialogical arguments than of the impositions.

At base, the concern is with strategies of discursive power. This is an intriguing field of research, because no discourse in Foucault's sense is only repressive or unambiguously emancipatory (Tett and Wolfe 1991). Discourse is where power and rationality are intertwined.

This exposition comments on the ensuing three aspects of Foucault's conception of power, which are all opposed to the received view (Hiley 1984:200-1):

A. Power and knowledge are co-constituting. Knowledge cannot exist except through relations of power. Power structures a domain of knowledge at the same time that inquiry isolates areas as objects of knowledge, making them targets for the deployment of strategies of power. Biopower is wielded not through ideological distortion but through surveillance, coercion and disciplinary techniques for the management of bodies.

B. Power cannot be reduced to repression; it does not only exclude, censor, mask, and conceal. This follows from facet A. The composition of power/knowledge is productive. It produces domains of objects and 'regimes of truth' and makes possible our actions and social relations. Thus:

C. Power, as part of the power/knowledge composition, is local and omnipresent. It is dynamic and functions permanently rather than something occasionally exercised by individuals or by law. Biopower circulates throughout the social body continuously.

I have already commented on point A, pointing out the doubt cast on the possibility of truth beyond power relations. The argument is extended here to comment on ideology and planning theory. Foucault draws attention away from power in the sense of setting agendas and affecting or forming the felt needs of people (Bachrach and Baratz 1963, Lukes 1974). This is power preventing our problems and desires from even being formulated - and then masking that fact. Attention is thus directed away from ideological forms of power that can be counteracted by knowledge, and towards biopower that cannot be fought by the same means. In the biopower perspective there is no room for the emancipation inherent in the planning-as-integration part of the compound planning rationale.

The very ideas of false consciousness and of the critique of ideology imply the possibility of nonideological thinking or of *true* consciousness. Ideology is the result of distortion sustaining asymmetrical relations of power. Its hardly visible mobilization of meaning serves to make the public accept economic and social inequalities as something natural, even though man-made. Only if such distortions were seen through and the repression dispelled, could truth be established. 'The concept of ideology, Foucault thinks, thus implies the traditional view that knowledge must be disinterested, that truth can be ascertained only in the absence of distorting power relations' (Hoy 1986:131).

Critical theory in the Marxist and the Frankfurt School tradition has emphasized the critique of ideology as an emancipating analysis. It is no wonder then that critique of ideology has also entered planning theory, e.g., with Forester's approach to planning as questioning and shaping attention. According to Foucault, a social state free from what Forester (1989:34) denotes 'socially unnecessary distortions' can never come into existence. Neither can a state without misrepresentation caused by power shaping felt needs (ibid.38) or a truth uninfluenced by the political-economic structure (ibid.150). Because ideology bounds rationality (ibid.53), unbounded rationality is utopian. Forester's book has a practical as well as a theoretical aim. He wants to advise planners on what to do in practice, while Foucault offers no guide to action. I consider the recommendations of Forester valid despite Foucault's critique of the notion of ideology, which strikes some of Forester's theoretical categories. What is needed in the wake of Foucault's power/knowledge dilemma, is a caveat that the planners, even if they succeed in disclosing some ways in which an asymmetrical class or power structure rationalizes itself, still convey views reflecting power relations.

Point B, objecting to unwarranted reductionism, is sustained both by Hannah Arendt and Foucault - as well as some current feminist literature (Baker Miller 1992, Wartenberg 1988). The ideas of Foucault and Habermas on this theoretical aspect are juxtaposed by Hoy (1986). Foucault states that 'relations of power are not something bad in themselves, from which one must free one's self' (Foucault 1987:18). To him the problem is not one of trying to dissolve the power relations in the utopia of a perfectly transparent communication. The problem is to give one's self the right rules of law, the right techniques of management, and also the right ethics and practice of self. They should all be arranged so that the ensemble of rules and procedures producing power relations can function with a minimum of domination (ibid.18). The important implication of acknowledging the constructive facet of power is that Habermasian 'dialogue' is not an ideal to Foucault. It is not only utopian but also potentially harmful to aim for the 'ideal speech situation' when knowledge and power are co-constituting and knowledge and hence power have positive functions. It follows that dialogical incrementalism would be a meaningless 'ideal type' within the conceptual universe of Foucault.

The critique of Habermasian dialogue can be pushed to extremes by an analogy to Jeremy Bentham's Panopticon. Foucault is using the Panopticon as a paradigm for a surveillance structure. It is originally a prison designed to let the inmates keep nothing hidden or personal. Everything they do can be observed by the controller. Dialogue in Habermas's sense can be seen as a 'panoptic discourse' in the public sphere. There is a regime of 'pan-transparency' pervading the public domain. In contrast to the original Panopticon, however, the openness is two-way in all directions. The interlocutors are simultaneously inmates and wardens. The surveillance is shifted from bodily movement to speech. The conversation shall only be motivated by the aim for mutual understanding and agreement. All utterances motivated by personal goals and interests are invalid. The implementation of the dialogue model implies a 'Pancommunicon', in which the process of normalization, disciplining and mutual surveillance is extended to the limit.

Point C should not be taken as an assertion that there is no liberty. On the contrary, Foucault (ibid.12) states that 'if there are relations of power throughout every social field it is because there is freedom everywhere'. This does not mean that the situation is satisfactory. It implies only that the controllers of the social fields have not eliminated all forms of resistance on the part of the respondents. When all the possibilities for opposing the controller are gone, there is no longer a power relationship according to Foucault. Maintaining power implies preserving the experience of choice. Although power can be repressive, it also challenges and confirms freedom. 'At the very heart of the power relationship, and constantly provoking it, are the recalcitrance of the will and the intransigence of freedom' (Foucault 1982:221-2).

The ambiguous relationship between freedom and power - power that can also be used for emancipation - is illustrated in the emancipation/freedom paradoxes of Chapter 5. When contemplating the role of planning in sorting out the tangles of power and freedom, some Foucaultian scepticism is warranted. He thinks that 'it can never be inherent in the structure of things to guarantee the exercise of freedom' (Foucault 1987:245). Institutions always serve a system, and even an initially emancipatory social system turns into its own opposite and becomes repressive, just because it is a *system* and as such totalizing. Thus, liberty is a practice that institutions cannot assure. Incorporating 'emancipation' in the rationale of planning, as in Chapter 2, can do nothing to change this.

The knowledge-power-action relationship in planning theories

The knowledge/power relationship, in the complex form analysed by Foucault, is scarcely treated in planning theory; Boyer (1983), Flyvbjerg (1991), and Roweis (1988) are exceptions. What *is* discussed, is simplified relationships of knowledge-action or knowledge-power-action (Forester 1989:29-33). The concept of power referred to in these discussions is far more closely affiliated with Nagel's definition than with biopower. I now give some examples of how prominent theoreticians of planning write on the knowledge-power-action relationship. Following that, it is surveyed how well-known planning theories connect to the power/knowledge complex.

Chadwick's (1971) explanation of what planning is - in a systems view - involves both information and power. Knowledge and information, true or not, create an 'Image'. The Image is knowledge of the world, and a person's behaviour depends upon the Image. A plan must be added to explain and control the order in which a sequence of operations is to be performed. The reciprocal influence between knowledge and action is explicit: 'Plans depend on the content of the Image for motivation and information, whilst the Image is modified by the activities engendered by the plan' (ibid.23).

Lindblom is acutely aware that planning is determined by power relations. Policy is drawn forward 'in the light of what recent policy steps have shown to be probably realizable' (Braybrooke and Lindblom 1963:71). Choosing goals for their attractiveness without thought of their feasibility is far from the spirit of disjointed incrementalism. Power is not seen as monolithic but as distributed among numerous actors. Disjointed incrementalism is a strategy for using one's own limited knowledge and power to achieve what little can be achieved in a political hubbub where the planner is continually up against the power of a multiple of partial interests.

Lindblom and Cohen (1979:Ch.7) hold that professional social inquiry often positively obstructs social problem-solving. That is, planners may organize knowledge in a way hampering action, which is an unusual suggestion in planning theory. They list several reasons for this anomaly:
- Waste. Professional social inquiry requires resources but fails to deliver results.
- Noise in the system. The solution to many problems has to be sought in communicative interaction and by applying personal rather than professional knowledge. Professional social inquirers distract problem-solving by pretending to make a contribution to the solution.

- Hyper-rationalism. Variants of systems analysis are proposed, recommending the pattern of problem formulation, option seeking, forecasting and impact analysis, comparison and evaluation of alternatives, even when practical judgement will do. The comprehensiveness and formal completeness of the analysis hamper the process of mutual adjustment and social learning tending to the political aspects of complex social problem-solving.

The last point in particular is elaborated by Lindblom (1990:270-4).

Friedmann and Hudson (1974:2) find that 'a useful way to look at planning is to consider it as an activity centrally concerned with the linkage between knowledge and organized action'. The task of the planners is societal guidance by organizing society in learning groups. Planning links scientific and technical knowledge to processes of societal guidance. The guidance implies a central involvement of the state, a top-down management of public affairs. The notion of 'societal guidance' is adopted from Etzioni (1968), who wants to counteract alienation by social mobilization and the formation of a group consensus around important social tasks. The greater this consensus, the less explicit, repugnant, and alienating would be the forms of control needed.

To Friedmann (1987), the knowledge-action theme is central. The planners' conception of truth is validated by becoming the basis for the mastery of the social system, the social world. In Friedmann's view, science has become almost entirely a form of manipulative knowledge. Planning is a scientific endeavour, 'and in that tradition, the specific agent of mastery and control is, first, last, and always, the state' (ibid.413). Friedmann's own concept of action is not exclusively teleological, however. Goal achievement is not an essential part of it. Thus, moving from knowledge to action does not necessarily imply control. He thinks that the ideas from the Enlightenment are about to give way, opening for new theories transforming the nature of the basic relation of knowledge to action. He advocates planning as an emancipatory and radical practice in the tradition of social mobilization. Planners should use their power to assist people in organizing resistance to forces that have subjugated their lives to an alien logic and worked to ensure their passive compliance through the bureaucratic powers of the state. They should assist in the recovery of an active political community facilitating collective action in the self-production of life and livelihood (Friedmann 1989:11).

Faludi (1984) focuses on the rational features of planning. It is seen primarily as instrumental rationality, and as such it requires knowledge. Faludi regards planning 'as analogous to another learning vehicle: *scientific method* meaning a set of procedural requirements which propositions must meet in order to pass as scientifically valid' (ibid.51). This theme is followed up by Faludi (1986) in a study of Popperian thought in planning theory. Faludi's strongly decision-centred view of planning is notable in the present context. Decision is inserted as a crucial link between knowledge and action. In this respect Faludi can be seen as the heir of Davidoff and Reiner (1962) and their choice theory of planning. In both contributions it is claimed that the right course of action is always a matter of choice, never of facts. There has to be some kind of organization or institution so that choices can be made; i.e., somebody must have the power to make decisions. Furthermore, power is needed for the effectuation of decisions and plans. Implementation is an important theme both to Faludi (1987) and Davidoff and Reiner. The latter perceive the planning process as value formation, means identification, and effectuation.

Power is not really treated as a problem in the planning theories of Faludi and Friedmann. It is primarily seen as an implementing tool, a vehicle for moving from knowledge to action. This is the typical way power enters the central knowledge-action relation of mainstream planning theory. Surely, power can also hamper implementation, but this does not make it a *theoretical* problem complicating the relationship between knowledge and action.

The various planning theories imply different simplifications of the general knowledge↔power↔action complex (k-p-a). In synoptic planning the goals are given, there is no conflict, and power and action are not separately treated. The general k-p-a relation collapses into knowledge→action. Disjointed incrementalism is designed as a learning by doing process. Although conflict is acknowledged as adding to the uncertainty of planning, power is not addressed as a problem. The k-p-a relation is simplified to knowledge↔action. Transactive planning theory does not pay much attention to power, although this planning mode would require substantial social change to be implemented. The basic structural problem of the existing guidance system (of the US) is believed to be its rising level of ignorance. 'Mutual learning' and a 'learning society' are therefore central concepts. The two-way relationship between knowledge and action is accomplished theoretically by separating types of knowledge. 'Personal knowledge' is acquired from practice, and knowledge↔action here signifies interchange of the 'processed knowledge' of experts and the personal knowledge of local inhabitants.

Advocacy planning is based on the assumption that the knowledge of planners can empower local groups that are in danger of being run over by the society at large or by powerful local interests. The general k-p-a relation breaks down to knowledge→power. Advocacy planning has been more of a protection against repressive action than a plea for substantive change. The action-orientation is more conspicuous in radical planning and in

Forester's critical planning theory. The shaping of attention is employed as a bridge from analysis to implementation (Forester 1989:157). Planners need knowledge to pose critical questions and power to frame attention. These resources must be combined to plan and act 'in the face of power' to the benefit of openness and fairness in decision-making. By applying Habermas's critical theory of communicative action, Forester also shows how power distorts communication and thus impairs knowledge. The conceptual pair attention-shaping/questioning confirms the relevance to planning theory of Foucault's power/knowledge dilemma. Questioning provides knowledge. More knowledge increases the planner's ability to direct attention and thus to exert power. Enlarged power augments the interrogative pressure and expands the capacity to compel answers. Higher propensity to respond improves the knowledge of the planner. The general k-p-a relation takes the form knowledge↔power→action in the approach to planning as questioning and shaping attention.

The explicit appeal to phenomenology in the recent work of Forester (1990b, 1992) and other planning theoreticians (Dryzek 1982, de Neufville 1987, Healey 1992a) gives increased consideration to the way planning knowledge is derived from practice and action by reading meaning into fragments of experience from everyday life. These contributions also shed light on the way power relations form and are reproduced by the interpretations and the meaning-making required to formulate the planning problem and visualizing a realistic compromise. In planning theory then, the approach based on the critical theory of communicative action seems to be the one most fully addressing the various interactions of the general knowledge-power-action relationship. Planning theory has not yet taken into account the numerous ways power bounds and constructs knowledge. However, phenomenology paired with Habermasian critical theory is a promising approach for taking into account Foucault's insights on the power/knowledge dilemma.

Notes

1   Wrong (1979) sees power as intended influence, which he contrasts with unintended influence on the second line of his version of Figure 3.1. I have replaced unintended influence with structural influence, which is a capacity of a system. Structural influence is not intended, as a system does not have intentions. Power, as I use the term, has to be exerted by an actor (possibly consisting of more than one person) and is intended or unintended.

2   Nagel's concept of power does not contradict the intuitively reasonable idea that if two individuals can bring about the same desired result at different expenses, the one who is able to produce the result at the least cost is the more powerful. The resources saved can be used for other purposes and thus help to reach a higher preference level.

   A critique of Nagel's concept could possibly be developed from the claim that preference and outcome are not fully independent 'things' (Clegg 1989:43-4).

3   Planning may be practised as anticipated reaction. A special case is the historicist planner who anticipates the direction of the future lawlike development of society and adjusts to it. His vision may be the inevitable victory of the market forces or the dialectic path towards the final revolution following self-destructive monopolistic capitalism. In any case, historicism places the planner in the role of a respondent reacting to social forces that are sure to have their way in the end.

4   Stone's (1980:980) concept 'systemic power' is affiliated with structural influence: 'that dimension of power in which durable features of the socioeconomic system ... confer advantages and disadvantages on groups ... in ways predisposing public officials to favor some interests at the expense of others ...'. Stone offers an interesting discussion of the relationships between systemic power, anticipated reaction, and nondecision-making.

5   In a parenthesis Faludi (1984:42) mentions that inequitable distribution of resources may be a barrier to human growth. He offers the following receipt to overcome this political hinderance: 'to remove some of the barriers to human growth means to change ourselves. But only by being aware of our own habits, our ways of looking at this world, including how they affect our actions, may we deliberately guide our own development towards the removal of barriers to human growth'. Here is certainly no conflict of interests, illegitimate power or violence. However, Faludi does not entirely cut the bonds between human growth and politics. The following seems to be his most balanced statement, making room for both scientific and political action:

> I am proposing to regard human growth as an ideal in the sense of man firstly transforming his physical environment and utilizing its resources; and secondly shaping human institutions, thus including the social environment into the orbit of his control. Because growth in the latter sense also means self-guidance, this concept incorporates a view of man as gaining mastery over himself by power of his faculty of reason.
> (Faludi 1984:45)

6   One may wonder how a government ruling according to this principle can carry out its functions, as any attempt at legitimation must be based on fraud. Downs (1957) deduces his theory of democracy from the assumption that parties formulate policies in order to win elections, rather than win elections in order to implement formulated policies. He constructs a defense of this, founded on the belief that 'social functions are usually the by-products, and private ambitions the ends, of human action' (ibid.29).

7   In local planning the tighter networks and the shared values and beliefs of a community will often reduce the need for force and manipulation. Taylor (1982:140) states the point clearly:

> (C)ommunity makes possible the effective use of social controls which are an alternative to the concentrated force of the state. These controls, the use of which is widely dispersed among the community's members, may be thought of as more egalitarian than those associated with the state, less liable to be used for purposes not widely approved; but they are controls nevertheless: because of them people are deterred from doing things they otherwise would do.

The schism into a majority and a minority can be concealed both in a large society and in a small community by avoiding decisions where the discord would be clearly demonstrated. The dilemma to which Hayek directs our attention therefore makes nondecisions important.

8   Seduction as pure manipulation is a too lopsided point of view according to Baudrillard (1985). This is especially revealed in his chapter on 'the ironic strategy of the seducer', in which he comments on Kierkegaard. Cordelia is to be seduced (and 'rescued' or 'destroyed' as one sees it) because she is the one who by nature is equipped with the ability to seduce. Kierkegaard's seducer can say, without hypocrisy, that he does not hit upon anything by himself, but learns everything from Cordelia. The calculated seduction is a mirror of the natural one. The manipulator steals her own seduction and turns it against her. The reciprocity is not necessarily acknowledged, however, and it is not communicated. In this lies a difference from persuasion.

9   Brown (1963:13) states that: 'Inasmuch as he is for the creation of certain attitudes, the propagandist is necessarily against others; and the extirpation of what he regards as false beliefs and doctrines is as much his concern as the propagation of the 'right' ones.' This is Brown's starting point for treating censorship as a form of propaganda. I choose to exclude censorship from my discussion of persuasion, although it is a phenomenon closely connected to public communication. Censorship serves to evince that propaganda is not only intended to lead men to

action, but also to make them conform. Ellul (1973:70-9) makes the division between agitation propaganda and integration propaganda one of his main distinctions.

10 Popper (1986) echoes Hayek on this point. He thinks it very unlikely that free discussion of the holistic plan and its consequences will be tolerated. Every large-scale plan causes considerable inconvenience to many people, and there will always be a tendency to complain and to oppose the plan.

> To many of these complaints the Utopian engineer will have to turn a deaf ear if he wishes to get anywhere at all; in fact, it will be part of his business to suppress unreasonable objections. But with them he must invariably suppress reasonable criticism too ... Unable to ascertain what is in the minds of so many individuals, he must try to simplify his problems by eliminating individual differences; he must try to control and stereotype interests and beliefs by education and propaganda. (Popper 1986:89-90)

11 Hannah Arendt does not regard authority as a kind of power. Nevertheless, she draws the line between authority and concepts like force and persuasion in much the same way as Wrong:

> (A)uthority precludes the use of external means of coercion; where force is used, authority itself has failed. Authority, on the other hand, is incompatible with persuasion, which presupposes equality and works through a process of argumentation. Where arguments are used, authority is left in abeyance. (Arendt 1961:93)

12 Sennett (1981) treats paternalism as (ibid.2) a kind of authority. It is seen as authority exercised for the good of others. This is an exercise of power which - besides manipulation - is typical for the thought of Kierkegaard's seducer. What he does, is done for the alleged good of Cordelia. He is convinced that he knows what is best for her, wanting to rescue her femininity, develop her aesthetically, etc. However, he is not recognized by her as such a strong authority, so he has to manipulate in order to act out his paternalist disposition.

The 'transformative' conception of power advocated by some feminist writers is related to paternalism (Wartenberg 1988). Most women experience power through their role as nurturers. Here, power is centred on helping the person over whom it is exercised instead of making him or her subservient.

13 The fear of paternalism is seen in Held's (1987) interpretation of the central point in Schumpeter's critique of the 'public interest' concept:

If one assumes the existence of a common good and asserts that it is a product of rationality, then it is a short step to dismissing all dissension as sectarian and irrational. Opponents who are merely 'sectarian and irrational' can be legitimately marginalized or ignored; they might even be restrained 'for their own good' if they are persistent in their protest. The notion of the common good is an unacceptable element of democratic theory.   (Held 1987:172)

The public interest is not the only legitimizing notion that commands consensus and at the same time is claimed to be a product of rationality. This is also the case for Habermas's rationally communicated consensus. The point is that an ideal, a goal, a situation, etc., may be set forth as (1) the only outcome which it is rational to pursue, and as (2) the only outcome that is acceptable to society; and the majority's devoted belief in the combination of these statements endangers the freedom of dissenters.

4 Communicative manifestations of power relations in controversial planning: a case study

The purpose of the chapter is to exemplify how the power relations of force, manipulation, persuasion, and authority become manifest in planning practice. The case study concerns the planning and implementation of a toll ring around a Norwegian city. It is suggested that the development of toll technology sheds light on the power/knowledge dilemma.

The toll ring case

There are toll rings around the three biggest cities of Norway, namely Oslo, Bergen, and Trondheim (Lewis 1993). A map is shown in Figure 8.1. Motorists were already heavily taxed in Norway, paying twice the amount spent on road investment and maintenance. Consequently, the car drivers cannot be expected to see the need for extra fees to finance main roads in the biggest cities, which is the main purpose of the toll rings. The populations of the cities are 650,000 for Oslo, 190,000 for Bergen, and 140,000 for Trondheim. Especially in the smallest city, congestion has been modest by any international standard. Nevertheless, even here a system of cordon tolls was introduced in October 1991. The only precursor abroad is Singapore, and observers have seriously doubted that similar systems would stand a chance in western-type democracies. A narrative of the planning and implementation of the Trondheim toll ring is the story of how one can make the unlikely happen.

This is no account of the planning process, however. I concentrate on the expression of power in the written arguments of public debate, although other instances of force are mentioned as well. Data are collected from a comprehensive study of the newspaper articles on the Trondheim toll ring from its conception in 1985 to the end of 1992. The written information

material from the County Roads Office and from opponents to the toll ring were also examined.

It is necessary to present the case briefly, so the reader can appreciate the arguments shortly to be commented on. The Trondheim toll ring is described by Tretvik (1992), and I draw on his exposition below. The original political agreement was to raise private sector money, to be matched by extra government funds, to fulfil urban road building programmes in much shorter time than otherwise possible. The private/ public investment split is 60/40 percent. The Trondheim scheme is unique in that it was electronic from the start, with ten out of the twelve toll plazas being unmanned and automatic. More than 90% of the cars have an electronic tag and use the no stop lanes during the morning peak hours. Thus, traffic is not delayed by queues at the toll plazas. Only inbound traffic is charged, and the payment period is Mondays through Fridays from 06:00 to 17:00. Drivers are charged for each crossing, even if they have pre-purchased toll credits. However, subscribers to the Q-Free tag pay only for the first 75 entries per month and only for one entry per hour. Another unique detail in Trondheim is that tolls during the morning peak are higher than later in the day, indicating that the idea behind the payment scheme is not entirely fiscal. The design influences the car drivers' choice of mode and departure time.

The revenues produced by the tolls feed a development plan denoted the 'Trondheim Package'. It focuses on a system of new and improved main roads outside the city centre and the residential areas. Bus lanes, facilities for pedestrians and cyclists as well as various environmental improvements are included. The contents of the investment package and the design of the scheme have changed somewhat in line with stagnating traffic, increasing environmental awareness, and technological development. The intention is to spend about NOK 2 milliard (about £200 million) spread over fifteen years.

Some drivers pay more than others as a consequence of their home and work place locations, not necessarily as a result of how much they benefit from using the road network or their marginal contribution to congestion. About 40% of the city population live inside the toll ring. A single ring is basically a fairly crude revenue generating mechanism. It can, however, be regarded as the first step towards more comprehensive road pricing.

In the sections to follow, it is shown how the validity claims to dialogue were challenged. Power relations are exemplified, and particular attention is given to strategies of persuasion. I comment on the types of argument used often and rarely. It is of particular interest here if the differences seem affected by the distribution of power in the society. Some comments on the entire communicative process are offered on the basis of the press debate, and the toll ring is seen in the power/knowledge perspective of Michel Foucault.

Examples of force, manipulation, and authority

Communicative validity claims

For the public debate to unfold in a dialogical manner, validity claims concerning truth, sincerity, legitimacy, and comprehensibility have to be met. These claims are all disputed in this case, as opponents to the toll ring maintain that:

Contesting truth:	The toll ring is not needed. There is little annoying congestion in Trondheim. Other than road investment ought to be given first priority.
Contesting sincerity:	The real purpose is to relieve the pressure on the local and central public purse, so that a smaller share of the ordinary tax revenues is needed for roads.
Contesting legitimacy:	There are enough fees and taxes on cars already. Classified roads are the responsibility of the State, and should be built without local financial contribution.
Contesting comprehen-sibility:	When traffic decline gives a possibility for cancelling the toll ring, its proponents shift to a new line of arguments and go sturdily ahead with it.

The validity claims of the opposition were challenged only later on. When the toll ring had been in operation for ten months, the City Council decided to postpone further road investment in the Trondheim Package for at least two years. The projects for public transport, pedestrians, and the environment progressed as planned. At the same meeting, the City Council said 'no thanks' to NOK 160 million (about £16 million) from the State meant to improve the E6 towards the city centre. The postponement decisions met with harsh reaction:

Contesting truth:	The roads are still needed, even if traffic has not increased. The Trondheim Package is largely meant to accommodate for the traffic level reached already in the late 1980s.
Contesting sincerity:	The purpose of the postponement is not really to co-ordinate with other transport planning or wait for new traffic increase, but to erode the basis of support for the toll ring and hence to cancel the Trondheim Package.

Contesting legitimacy:	The revenue paid by the car drivers should be used for road construction, as was the original idea, and not for any transport purpose whatever, like a tax.
Contesting comprehensibility:	The realities in Trondheim have not changed sufficiently in one year to warrant both the installation of the world's first automatic toll ring and the interrupted construction of the projects it was meant to finance.

The validity claims set demands on the planning process (Flyvbjerg 1991: Vol. 2, p. 381):

(1)　Generality: Affected parties should not be excluded from the communication process;

(2)　Autonomy: Representatives for all interests should have equal possibilities for raising and criticizing validity claims;

(3)　Ideal role taking: The participants should be able and willing to show empathy towards the validity claims of others;

(4)　Power neutralization: Power relations among the participants should be neutralized in order to prevent power effects on the formation of consensus.

(5)　Transparency: The participants should neither conceal their goals and intentions nor act strategically to fulfil them.

The two sets of statements above form the foundation of a large part of the arguments for and against the toll ring. It goes for these statements as for those to be reproduced further on, that I do not assess their reasonableness. I now turn to the exemplification of the power relations and start with force.

Force

The toll ring is itself a manifestation of force. This is so whether the toll stations can be circumvented or not. Car drivers are forced to pay or change their behaviour by making detours, changing destination or transport mode, or making the trip during a non-payment period. This force hits arbitrarily, and is probably hardest felt by people living on one side of the city and working on the other, passing the toll ring both ways. Only about one third of the car drivers in Trondheim pay regularly several times a week.

As a counteraction, some motorists are induced to apply physical force, like driving on cycle tracks or across lawns and fields to avoid payment. There were a few incidents of physical violence during the introduction period. Motorists sabotaged the equipment at some toll plazas. Later, some advanced electronic components were stolen. It is hard to say whether this was sabotage or industrial espionage. Force includes deliberately delaying other traffic, as when insisting to pay only with small coins. Such sabotage of the system is only possible at the two manned toll stations, and has effect only when cars are queuing for manual payment.

Force in written communication usually takes the form of slander, insult, defamation, or harassment. Accusations of theft, lies, stupidity, and weakness of character appear time and again in the newspapers:

- 'It is high time our local politicians start to acquire viewpoints having durability beyond the next public opinion poll.'
- 'Arbeider-Avisa (a local newspaper) holds that the proponents of continued road construction have neglected eco-political elements in the discussion on the main road system in Trondheim. Everyone following the debate knows that this is a lie.'
- Comment to the postponement decision: 'This is theft of people's money and a game that may be costly for Trondheim. The most stupid is nevertheless saying no thanks to 160 million *kroner* from the state for use on E6 east. I cannot remember having experienced foolishness matching this.'

The two first examples show that force in the planning process is not necessarily something dramatic. Politicians in western-type democracies are expected to put up with this kind of criticism.

Manipulation

The trend in Norway towards allowing ever more road projects to be partly financed by the car users, gives rise to suspicion of manipulation on a national scale. The tolls are meant to realize strongly desired new roads *in addition* to those included in a normal road budget. With user fees, however, roads are built even if the ordinary state grants should decline. Then the tight budgets might tempt politicians to tacitly reallocate state funds from road building to other pressing tasks. The car drivers will suffer increased expenses in this case, but receive fewer extra roads than they were led to expect. Such a manipulation implies a concealed tax increase for this group.

The fear of being manipulated in this way seems to reside in a fair share of the adult population in Trondheim. In an opinion poll half a year before the opening, 25% believed that one of the reasons why the politicians want the toll ring, is to introduce yet another tax to get hold of people's money. This suspicion colours some of the sharply adverse reactions to the postponement decision:

Stop the recovery of tolls! The politicians in this city are about to abandon their own decisions. They want to cancel further road construction even before the first half of the Trondheim Package is implemented. If the City Council decide against the planned road projects, the motorists of this city must, from that day, be exempted from the obligation to pay road tolls. When one party fails to fulfil the contract, the other party is excused from his duties. The politicians cannot collect money for goods they do not deliver.

Political goals sometimes stand in so blatant contrast to political action, that people doubt if the politicians really intend to pursue the stated end. The Trondheim City Council proclaimed the goal of considerable reduction in car traffic, which, if fulfilled, would lead to economic disaster for the toll projects approved by the same Council - and for which the Municipality of Trondheim had assumed a heavy liability. When the politicians vote in favour of projects based on the premise that their own goals are not fulfilled, people are alerted to goal setting as a manipulative strategy. Even among the politicians a warning was called out: 'We must avoid messing up things so that we need to push more cars out on the roads in order to collect a revenue big enough to cover all the expenses.'

If one believes that the politicians take their own goal seriously, there is still reason to suspect manipulation. It would be tempting to use the toll ring as a means for ensuring permanent traffic reduction, which would contradict its announced function as a temporary financing device. The point is made in a reader's letter from 1991, when the toll ring had been at the planning stage for six years:

At last the politicians speak straight from the shoulder: the intention behind the toll ring is to reduce car driving. The goal is even quantified to 30% decrease within the year 2000. This confirms what I have been afraid of all the time, namely that the toll ring will become permanent.

Authority

The law and the budgetary procedures are important in forming the relations of authority between politicians and populace. Two examples will show that these institutions are also significantly affecting the toll ring debate. Firstly, the Norwegian Road Law says that user charges cannot be collected for the purpose of regulating traffic. The Public Roads Administration has to present the favourable environmental effects of the toll ring as by-products of the financing device. Secondly, there will always be claims that money be used for other purposes: 'It is a paradox that hundreds of million *kroner* are spent on roads in Trondheim, when the city cannot afford to take care of its eldest and weakest citizens in a worthy manner.' Due to widespread respect for the democratic budgetary process, it is unnecessary for the Public Roads Administration to answer this kind of objection.

Competent authority in the toll ring case is based on practical engineering skills and analytic technique. Claims to technically advanced and smart solutions abound: 'First in the world with a full scale electronic collection system and a network of unmanned stations.' 'The world's most advanced toll ring system.' 'The system has attracted international attention, and the people behind it have been around the world presenting it.' The technical success is not disputed. The implicit message is that those behind the system are really smart, so the idea of a toll ring cannot be that bad. Logical inconsistency of this sort is a typical result of authority shifting the attention of the receiver from the content to the sender.

The common man opposing the toll ring may try to exploit his authority as a voter. He can threaten to withdraw his vote from the political parties in favour of the ring. A number of such 'democratic threats' were published in the local newspapers. However, to be effective the voters need to co-ordinate their efforts. The Action Committee against the toll ring collected 19,000 signatures in twelve days by placing lists at the petrol stations. The signatures were presented to the Mayor and referred to in some newspaper articles. The authority of dissatisfied voters can be strengthened if it is demonstrated in opinion polls that they are an impressive number. Half a year before opening the ring, 68% of those asked in a poll answered that the Trondheim Package ought to be postponed or cancelled.

Opponents to the toll ring can try to raise doubt about the competent authority of the experts in the road administration. Some newspaper articles objected to a cost-benefit analysis of one major project calculating that savings to society amount to NOK 2.1 milliard (about £210 million). This approximates the total investment in the entire Trondheim Package, and much of it is made up by the value of time savings. One critical newspaper response to the planners was that:

> The Public Roads Administration and the Municipality of Trondheim present nonsense and build castles in the air when maintaining that the benefits from the Ring Road are large enough to pay for the entire Trondheim Package. Such calculations of the so called utility to the society are often carried out to justify extensive road construction. Real and fictive numbers are deliberately mixed in order to make the net benefit appear as large as possible. Before the Transportation Plan is decided on, the political parties should note how easily the road

authorities turn to mirages to ensure that political decisions on unrealistic plans go their way.

The indistinct border separating warning and threat based on authority is demonstrated by the response of the Chief County Roads Officer to the City Council's postponement decision:

> I have never experienced a more uncertain situation. What will the majority of the City Council decide four years from now? Are we then supposed to resume road construction? I feel like balancing on floating log. We will obviously be careful undertaking projects in Trondheim when we do not know if we will be disregarded. It is very difficult to work under these conditions. We have a big construction organization in Trondheim, and we are well equipped to build effectively. However, if we cannot build in Trondheim, we have to reduce the organization and transfer resources to other tasks.

This may have been intended as a warning, but with the high unemployment in Trondheim and the road authorities' disappointment with the postponement decision, the statement was conceived as a threat by several local politicians.

Persuasion strategies

Many of the arguments for and against the toll ring and the Trondheim Package could also be used in a Habermasian dialogue. They are strictly to the point, do not exaggerate, take the ball and not the man, do not play on ideological connotations, etc. Here, however, the task is to list some arguments that do not fit into a dialogue. For various reasons they distort communication and turn argumentation into a power strategy. In general, this occurs when arguments say too little or too much; concealing or linking sober information with propaganda, respectively. The strategies below serve the purpose of instrumental success rather than mutual understanding.

Strategy 1: Emphasize attractive parts of the project that are peripheral, and remain silent about the central and controversial part of the project. 'Never before has Trondheim experienced such enormous efforts to improve the environment, the safety, and the public transport.' The Trondheim Package and thus the toll ring are proclaimed the saviour of the environment, while keeping quiet about how the projects considerably facilitate driving and consequently stimulate the use of private cars.

Strategy 2: Paternalism, i.e., create the impression that your policy will benefit everybody - whatever they say: 'The toll ring is an arrangement to the benefit of everyone travelling in Trondheim.' Paternalism is not perfect when the controller is only *pretending* to act for the good of the other. Still, the core of the strategy is easily recognized in the following two citations from local papers:

> Give the revenue from the toll ring to the public transport company. The politicians aim to expand the supply of public transport by using surplus money from the motorists. Let us give precedence to public transport and extend the tramway immediately. The more people go by bus and tram, the more pleasant it will be to remain a car driver. Hence, our policy must also be in the interest of the car users. I do not understand that anybody can be opposed to setting the priorities like this.

> The road supporters forget that the motorists will be better off with investments in cycle tracks and public transport. It will be more attractive for them to leave the car at home, as an increasing part of them want.

It is nothing wrong in pointing out that the policy you prefer will have some desirable effects even for your adversary. When I engage in a paternalistic strategy, however, I take these benefits to be decisive, and conclude that my opponent will be better off if my policy is implemented, although he is unable to see it himself.

Strategy 3: Advocate the product because of the process. 'This road construction scheme benefits our society because it is based on a comprehensive administrative treatment and broad political considerations.' This line of reasoning is not common in the debate.

Strategy 4: Indicate that the opposite party is not trustworthy, for example by asserting that if offered a finger, he grabs the entire hand. One possibility is to question if future toll charges will be allocated only to investment: 'The next time we risk being up against demands for user financed road maintenance.' Two additional quotes from a paper catch more common sentiments:

> When first decided on a few years ago, the Trondheim Package was calculated to cost 800 million *kroner*. The next year the price was doubled to 1,600 million. Nobody in the City Council gave the alarm. Now the price is 2,500 million *kroner* - 2.5 milliard. How high must the bill grow before the majority of the City Council are willing to think?

> The toll stations will probably be there permanently, as milch cows easily resorted to when seeking funds for ever new road plans.

Strategy 5: Tactical use of passion (Bailey 1983). The chairman of Trondheim Chamber of Trade declared in an interview: 'We are furious and convinced that the toll ring means the deathblow for commercial enterprises in the centre of Trondheim. The proposed toll ring scares the pants off us. It is unbelievable and depressing. Proposing a toll ring is to play with the biggest working place in Trondheim, which is commercial business.'

Strategy 6: Draw a caricature of the policy you oppose. 'The risk is that Trondheim will be transformed into a giant road junction. The dimension of the Trondheim Package is better suited for a metropolis like Los Angeles.'

Strategy 7: Ignore differences in degree. Argue as if a negative effect always cancels out the positive, and vice versa. Hence, do not concede to a single one of your opponent's arguments. In the question of traffic increase caused by new road projects, this strategy was used by both camps, as shown by the following two citations:

> The production of traffic is independent of the standard of the road network. The production depends on factors like car ownership, income, number of inhabitants, land use, etc. The quality of the road network only affects the choice of route and destination.

> Cars need roads, so when roads are built, car sales are zooming. The more and better roads, the more cars. When the Chief County Roads Officer and others want to build roads in order to improve the environment, they forget that better supply generates increased demand. What you gain on the roundabouts you lose on the swings. And in the meantime milliards are spent.

Strategy 8: Tactical advocacy. There is always a group not receiving its share of the benefits; find it and use it: 'Road tolls should not be paid until the projects are built. Think about all the students forced to pay for roads that will never be of any use to them.'

Strategy 9: Associate the policy you dislike with a political metaphor sounding distinctly disgusting to all involved. Pretend that turning down the policy means rejecting an evil or stupid political system. The Norwegian Automobile Federation accused the politicians dealing with transportation in Trondheim of spreading a 'big-brother-sees-you' mentality. When the collection of tolls started, it was referred to as the 'closing' instead of the 'opening' of the toll ring, and the federation depicted the ring as a new Berlin wall. A reader's letter takes this strategy to the extreme:

> I pass in the manual file and pay ten *kroner*. Why? Because protection of privacy is a human right in Norway. The Q-Free tag gives a registration that others may use against you. Do you have any guarantee

against sale of this register? Can you be sure that the authorities do not register you in other places as well? Stay alert, motorist! Tomorrow is unknown.

Strategy 10: Maintain that your opponents base their reasoning on models that do not fit with the conditions here and now. Trondheim Chamber of Trade want special subscription rates, and they protest against higher rates during rush hours. 'Those going in for such increased rush hour prices are people comparing the situation in Trondheim to that in Singapore and London.'

Strategy 11: Deduce from one particular judgement you disagree with, that your opponent has lost the capacity to think clearly. He has not got good enough vision to walk, he has lost touch with reality, etc. Two newspaper articles comment that:

> Car traffic is decreasing, not increasing. It is equal to losing one's head when claiming that Trondheim is in desperate need of the planned roads and for the life and movement that go with large scale road construction.

> The planned main arterial road through Trondheim carries the unmistakable sign of megalomania.

Strategy 12: Convey an image of crisis. Create the impression that conditions are rapidly deteriorating, so that immediate and radical action seems appropriate. I quote from two contributions to a paper:

> Let us solve the problem now, not fifty years from now. Congestion and pollution. Busses trudging slowly ahead. One exhausted biker. Children spurting over the pedestrian crossing. The traffic problems concern all of us. And we will soon witness a collapse of the traffic in Trondheim, if we do not make a valiant effort now.

> The roads will soon be overloaded. Imagine a litre measure. When you pour water into it, your problems start only when it overflows. Then you reach out for the two-litre measure. In Trondheim this costs 1.4 milliard *kroner*.

The list of persuasion strategies could be made much longer. Most of the strategies mentioned seem to be quite common, and most of the examples are commonplace and undramatic. Approaching dialogue does not usually require heroic effort from the planner. Neither does it imply that participants in public debate are denied the right to argue as displayed in the examples. The important thing for the planner is to see through the rhetoric. Is there a core that would make a valid point even in dialogue? What effect can the rhetoric be expected to have on the other interest groups? How can the planner bring the valid core to the fore when the parties meet?

The communication process

When assessing a public debate, e.g., judging if the number of statements and utterances from each side is reasonable considering the size of the contending groups, the possible effects of the 'spiral of silence' (Noelle-Neumann 1974) should be taken into account. Her hypothesis is summed up by Sanders, Kaid and Nimmo (1985:xvi):

> People are reluctant to become social isolates. If they form an opinion on an issue, they pay close attention to the climate of opinion, assessing that their individual opinions are either the views of a majority or of a minority. If of the majority, and if sensing that the majority is stable or growing stronger, individuals willingly express their views in public. If they are in the minority, they remain silent. There are two qualifications, namely, 1) people sensing themselves members of a majority that is declining in numbers may be reluctant to speak out, and 2) those sensing themselves members of an ever-growing minority that may eventually become dominant are more willing to express their views. A key feature of the view, however, is that so long as people evaluate themselves in the minority and, hence, remain silent, this adds to a general sense of their views being minority views. Silence reinforces a perception of minority status, thus bringing on more silence - that is, the spiral of silence. The paradox is that were people to speak out they might actually find themselves adherents of an unvoiced majority.

The effect of such a possible spiral on the toll ring debate is not known. It may be small, as the majority and the minority seem to be of similar sizes, and both pro and con opinions are 'in good currency'. There is not an insurmountable borderline between the yes and no groups. As demonstrated by the actual development of the case, it is quite possible for a political party to change its opinion, leading to new coalitions on both sides.

Earlier in the chapter I listed five demands on the planning process set by the validity claims. In this section the written and public communication process concerning the toll ring up to 1992 is considered mainly in the perspective of generality, autonomy, and power neutralization. The two other demands, on the degree of ideal role taking and transparency, are not easily judged from the written material. When it comes to transparency, it is clear that the main parties in the toll ring debate act strategically. The goals of the interest groups are reasonably clear. The political parties have to take incompatible interests into account, however, and this sometimes blurs their real ends (as exemplified in the subsection on manipulation).

The major and minor local newspapers support the Conservative Party and the Labour Party, respectively. Both parties voted in favour of the toll ring. It is noteworthy, therefore, that when counting the number of times pro and con arguments appeared in the papers, I found approximately twice as many cases of con arguments (135 cases). The amount of pro and con mentioning of the toll ring is more balanced when correcting for cases of approving mention not sustained by arguments. Anyway, it can be ascertained that the columns of the newspapers were open to the opponents of the ring, and that they used this opportunity to state their case. Both the press debate and the hearings ensured the generality of the process.

The County Roads Office has produced quite extensive information material on the toll ring and the Trondheim Package, partly in a joint effort with the Municipality of Trondheim. Four information newspapers have been distributed to all households in the city. As expected, the information material promotes mainly the viewpoints of the road authorities. Pro arguments appear at least four times as often as con arguments. Accusations of propaganda have nevertheless been rare. The following exception serves as a reminder that communication does not only consist of words: 'It is totally meaningless to present a new four-lane motorway in Elgeseter Street (the heavily trafficked approach from the south) as an "environmental street". In the drawing there are lots of trees, a bus, and some prams. But there are virtually no cars. It is unbelievable!'

Despite its propaganda function, the information material has probably broadened the debate. It propagated pro arguments receiving little mention in the papers, as for example:
- The toll ring generates money to be invested in traffic safety, public transport, and environmental improvement.
- The road projects are profitable and give employment.
- The Trondheim Package is improved, and the alternatives to it are clearly inferior.

Only one con argument is regularly set forth by the road authorities. From the initial phases of the toll ring process, they have pointed out that one ring is an unjust and arbitrary payment device. The strategy of persuasion seems to be to yield on the one point which it is in the interest of the road authorities themselves to correct. The intention of the County Roads Office has all along been to develop the toll system in the direction of road pricing. Then more motorists would have to pay, which means increased funds for road investment.

When the writings in the newspapers and from the County Roads Office are seen as a whole, the conclusion is that the papers have contributed significantly to the neutralization of the power relation between the resourceful road and car interests and other groups affected by the toll ring.

In order to consider the autonomy of participating groups, I take as my point of departure the four pro and con arguments most frequently used in the written public debate (between one and two dozens of articles each).

Frequent pro arguments:
(1)   Funds are built for investment in traffic safety, public transport, and environmental improvement.
(2)   The toll ring regulates the traffic.
(3)   State funding of classified roads is insufficient.
(4)   The ring pays for an improved network of main roads.

Frequent con arguments:
(A)   The toll ring harms trade in the city centre.
(B)   As a payment device, the ring strikes unjustly and arbitrarily.
(C)   Motorists pay enough already; classified roads are the responsibility of the State.
(D)   The toll ring is not well designed.

The preferences of three important interest groups are taken into account by the pro arguments. Argument (1) reflects the interests of those in favour of expanded supply of public transport, (1) and (2) serve the environmental movement, and (3) and (4) accord with the interests of the motorists and the road authorities. The interests of the users are expressed also in the con arguments (B) and (C). In addition, the interests of two other groups are voiced. Argument (A) takes care of business interests, and (D) serves, for a large part, the interest of inhabitants of nearby dwelling areas. They were afraid that the toll ring would induce motorists to drive through residential districts to avoid payment.

The con argument claiming that society invest in other sectors at the expense of transport, is used almost as frequent as the above arguments. That is, interests outside transport have also made their voice heard in the debate. It is my impression that guardians of personal freedom have played a modest role in the toll ring debate compared to the experience from Hong Kong and Singapore. This side of the toll ring has been questioned in less than half a dozen articles, while for instance the harm-to-business argument was found in nearly two dozen cases. This notwithstanding, the most frequently used arguments indicate that the main groups affected by the toll ring have been able to articulate their interest and participate in the public debate.

There is a conspicuous difference in character between the pro and the con arguments. The listed pro arguments do not refer to concrete improve-

ments of personal economic or other welfare components. The three most frequently used con arguments, on the other hand, point directly to economic loss easily associated with individuals. This difference may disappear with growing city size. It is remarkable that the following arguments are almost absent from the public debate in Trondheim:
- Efficient flow of traffic is important to trade and industry.
- Congestion is time-consuming and frustrating for the motorists.
These pro arguments have the same economic and individual orientation as the con arguments listed above. And the two pro arguments are likely to be frequently used in bigger and more congested cities than Trondheim. To the extent that the important pro arguments appeal to common interests and the con arguments appeal explicitly to economic group interests, the implementation of the toll ring seems to depend on considerable communicative power in the city (in the sense of Hannah Arendt). It requires ability to act in concert and to reach a sufficient degree of agreement upon a common course of action in relatively unconstrained communication.

The communication process in Trondheim was influenced by the economic cycles. When the debate started in the middle of the 80s, there was a general upswing in business conditions, causing an eight percent annual traffic increase. As shown above under the persuasion strategy conveying an image of crisis (Strategy 12), the strong traffic increase was reflected in the pro argumentation. However, the cycle turned downward in 1988, followed by a slight decrease in traffic over the next few years. This led to a marked change in the argumentation in favour of the ring. Investing to prevent a congestion crisis did not any longer seem as a good idea. Instead it was maintained that the Trondheim Package was largely meant to accommodate for the traffic already on the roads in the late 80s. The postponement decision of the City Council strongly indicates that the majority of the representatives did not accept this argumentative twist. Nevertheless, the Director General of Public Roads insisted, when commenting on the postponement decision in a speech, that 'the projects now turned down were primarily needed because of their contribution to safety and environmental protection'. There is a manipulative element here, consisting of an attempt to conceal that the logical basis for upholding the toll ring to finance new road projects is weakened. One pretends that safety and environmental considerations were the only core arguments from the start, and that accessibility never had anything to do with the rationale behind the investments.

It is of course tempting for the opponents to the toll ring to exploit the stagnation of traffic in their argumentation: 'For the first time since the car was introduced on Norwegian roads, the traffic has in fact declined. The right thing to do then, is to pause for thought until 1995'. However, the con-party should be careful not to get trapped in a similar way as the pro-party. Traffic might increase again, and with con arguments too dependent on traffic stagnation, manipulation would be hard to resist.

Toll technology in a power/knowledge perspective

The private car has long been associated with freedom in the sense of an almost unrestricted possibility to go when and where one pleases. In many cities this freedom is threatened by the sheer number of people eager to enjoy it. In the three biggest Norwegian cities this has given rise to a paradoxical situation, in that the car owners' freedom is kept up by technology with a very high potential for control. The further the knowledge of payment devices is developed to meet demands for environmental protection, efficient allocation of road space, and just distribution of payment, the higher is the possibility for detailed steering and individual control. This follows from the increasing number of electronic registration points on the road network and the possibility to match the collected data with registers containing personal information.

I sketch the development of road toll technology briefly as a background for considering the increase of potential control. The initial payment technique was manual cash transfer. Payment machines have been in use for many years, some of them with throw-in of coins while passing at low speed. Cash payment has in many cases been replaced by seasonal cards and other passes. Electronic onboard units are introduced in ever more tolling systems. Passive electronic tags are used in Trondheim. Transponders and smart-cards will probably be the next step. The use of the smart-card can be restricted to the toll road system, or it can be valid also for ferries, parking, and public transport. Technically, an ordinary credit card may be employed. This will considerably increase the potential for tracing the owner's movements and activities.

The initial plaza infrastructure was manned stations with bars. In Trondheim most toll stations are unmanned and equipped with payment machines and traffic signals showing if the passing was paid for. There is a development towards simpler and less visible antenna stations. Potential controlling arrangements are more likely to be implemented the less they are felt as direct regulation. Space-consuming and conspicuous control posts with bars going up and down, guards, obligation to stop, and cash payment would scarcely stand a chance of being implemented as a part of a road pricing system. Unmanned antenna stations emitting discreet light signals may have a higher possibility of acceptance. If not as a fully fledged road pricing system, then maybe as a double cordon, possibly supplemented by a few radial sectors.

The inconvenience to the drivers when passing has diminished considerably. Manual cash payment implies stopping and often queuing and searching for coins. With electronic payment only slightly reduced speed may be required - if there is any inconvenience at all. The electronic technology is cheaper to operate, less space-consuming, and handles differentiated prices without problem. Because the number of registration points can easily be increased, a higher percentage of the motorists will pay. Thus, future systems can be more just and can readily be designed for traffic regulation as well as financing. It can be concluded that both users and road authorities have a motive for endorsing the new electronic technology.

At least two distinctions are important when assessing the control aspect of the toll road systems. The first distinction is the control visible to the motorist at the toll plaza vs the control procedures carried out by the back system. There has been an unambiguous trend towards less overt control at the plazas. The fully manned stations implied continuous surveillance by the human eye, and no back system was required. It is now common to use video cameras to register irregular passings. In Trondheim the number plates on the pictures are checked manually. The number file is matched with the National Vehicle Register. Name and address of the car owner are transferred to the toll road company, and an invoice is sent. The owner's data are deleted when payment is received. Data on the motorists passing in a regular way are deleted the following day when payment is drawn from their accounts.

The second distinction is the degree of anonymity when the rules are observed vs the potential for surveillance if they are not. The motorist may in principle be anonymous in the Trondheim system. He can open an account with the toll road company without revealing his identity. As long as there is money on the account, the company is satisfied. The motorist can remain anonymous with the future smart-card technology. An amount of money is stored in the card. When passing a toll gate, the payment is transferred but not the identity of the card owner. The toll road company will not know who paid that particular sum of money or who passed the toll gate at that particular time. There are several ways to break the rules, though:
- Photographing both regular and irregular passings.
- Failing to delete the data.
- Extracting personal identity numbers from the National Vehicle Register and matching the information with other registers.

- Using the information for other purposes than identifying non-paying motorists; e.g., checking that a taxpayer really uses his car to and from work, like he states in his income tax form.

The potential for misuse rises with the number of registration points, the percentage of the passings being photographed, the number of registers available, and the amount of information in each register. The relative weights put on the possibility for anonymity and the potential for misuse depend on how the constituency trust their authorities and politicians.

When one knows where and when people are going, one has the information to control much of their lives. Developing ever more refined payment technology, the risk is that we simultaneously take steps towards the caricature of the Enlightenment dream: a society in which everything is regulated, calculable, rationalized, and efficient.

Knowledge ensuring efficient behaviour can arrange for effective control, and consequently a fear of surveillance has been expressed in the toll ring debate (Strategy 9). There have already been cases setting the authorities' will to abstain from surveillance on a test. The prosecution authorities wanted to use a picture taken by a photo box as evidence in a theft trial, since the stolen goods were visible on the roof rack. They were not allowed to in this case, but what if the photo had destroyed the alibi of the main suspect in a murder case? It may be symptomatic for the future trend, that it is already mentioned approvingly in the toll ring debate that antenna stations can be used for speed control and facilitate the calculation and preparation of fines. By the way, there are also private 'authorities' in search of control. In a few cases, the toll road company has received inquiries from husbands wanting a list of passing times for the car used by their wives. There might also be employers wanting to check where company cars have been driven. In accordance with existing rules, the toll road company does not comply with such requests.

This section should not be read as an indictment against the toll ring. The power/knowledge dilemma of Foucault is a real dilemma just because technological and social knowledge are needed even if control is a corollary, and because control itself may have constructive social functions. The point is that to strike a balance, we must know how our instrumental knowledge produces control, and how that control can in turn be kept in check. To accomplish this last task, there must be a public sphere accessible to recalcitrant groups (Habermas 1989, Calhoun 1992). In this public space, critical social theory and dialogical debate will find conditions of viability.

5 Dilemmas of power in planning

The three sections of this chapter deal with problems of applying concepts of power in theories of planning, and problems of exerting power in planning. It is a basic idea behind most concepts of power that exercising it means influencing the decisions of the respondents. Conceptualizations of power can, consequently, often be connected with decision theories, and this, in turn, links them more easily to planning theories. The first section treats a number of ideas and concepts of power in order to examine if they are compatible with synoptic and incremental planning theory, respectively. The second section continues the examination of power as causation of outcome by preference. The relationship of power to technique and communication is clarified. Self-altering forecasts are studied as an example of communication affecting the power of technique. It is analysed how the posterior formation of preferences delimits power. Furthermore, it is shown that some tacit ideals of planning cannot be fulfilled by exerting power. Section three questions if there are limitations on what can be achieved by working to establish strong causal relations between preferences for certain outcomes and the outcomes themselves. The insight offered is that ideals may be beyond reach no matter how powerful planners and their employers are, because there are goals that might not be compatible with the act of planning. The problem is discussed by studying some general and puzzling difficulties encountered when trying to transform the process of liberation into a state of freedom. I also investigate some extra conundrums faced when planning is to play a significant part in this transformation. Thus, both the second and the third section illustrate limitations to the use of power in planning.

Matching notions of power to modes of planning

The section treats a number of ideas and concepts of power in order to examine if they are compatible with synoptic and incremental planning theory, respectively. It is demonstrated for some well known notions of power that they should not be uncritically inserted into either planning theory. Neither do the power relations fit equally well with both synoptic and incremental planning. Perfect information leaves little room for manipulation and persuasion.

Theories of planning are, broadly speaking, theories of how decisions concerning the community or the society at large are prepared or should be prepared. The most common approach to power has been to regard it as primarily revealed in decision situations. It has been a basic idea behind most concepts of power that exercising it means influencing the decisions of the respondent (however, Bachrach and Baratz 1962 introduced another approach). Conceptualizations of power can, consequently, often be linked to decision theories, and this, in turn, links them more easily to planning theories. It should be underlined here that the literature on social power is truly immense. The definitions and the features of power concepts mentioned in this section are selected from a far larger number of potentially relevant notions.

The lower aspirations and the satisficing under incrementalism and the maximizing behaviour in the synoptic mode make the planning types differ from the point of view of power. The lack of information forces the controller to adopt strategies leading to lower levels of preferences than he would have been able to reach under perfect knowledge. Incremental planning has both the ability and obligation to yield to outside pressure. This is an implication of the search for agreement. Synoptic planning comprises no procedures justifying submission to the pressure from powerful interests once the 'best' solution to the problem has been calculated. Yielding would be a result of either computation error or new information changing the input to the analysis. The first violates the assumption of unlimited calculative capacity, and the second is unlikely with perfect information.

Concepts of power consistent with synoptic planning theory

I list some characteristics of synoptic theory below, which are featured in particular concepts and theories of power. Most of the properties are derived from the perfect information assumption and are not compatible with incremental planning theory. The list is followed by some examples. The characteristics are:

a) Instrumentally rational actors

b) Preconceived operational ends
c) Knowledge of all the possible options
d) Complete knowledge of consequences
e) Complete knowledge of the actors
f) Decisions as events of great importance
g) Unaltered preferences over the entire planning period.

Property a): The mathematical theory of games is the typical example (Rapoport 1966, Ordeshook 1986). The outcome of the game, the consequences of power and conflict, is (usually) determined already at the outset. The actors are nearly always assumed to possess all relevant information. Therefore, they can make decisions concerning every move throughout the course of the game without limitations.

Property b): In his brief account, West Churchman (1961:323) introduces power as 'the measure of his ability to attain anyone of a set of his desired goals'. In general, definitions embodying the notion of achieving goals formulated in advance are not in accordance with incremental planning. There, ends develop as one moves along.

Property c): Two serious objections to the definition above should be mentioned. First, the reference to personal ends does not permit inter-individual comparisons. Second, a person having a high level of aspiration will be less powerful than a more modest person. Therefore, Churchman suggests another definition, releasing power from individual goals. 'This abstraction can be accomplished by defining an individual's power in terms of his potential choices. In this sense, X is more powerful than Y if X can exhibit all the behavior that Y can, and more besides' (ibid.324). What is crucial to my argument is the use of the term 'potential choice'. To apply the definition one should know all the options, all the actions open to the actors. This can only be assumed in a synoptic model.

Property d): Karlsson (1962) defined power formally in terms of utilities, focusing on the extent to which the controller is able to affect the outcome accruing to the respondent. The controller holds more power the larger the difference is between the maximum and the minimum reward which will be earned by the respondent depending on how the controller decides to act. Karlsson's proposal is only compatible with a synoptic model, because calculation of maximum and minimum rewards requires perfect information. Moreover, I suggest that the maximum reward is of little interest as a reference-point in an incremental model. It is unlikely that an incrementalist respondent will realize the maximum-state in any case, regardless of the controller's attempts to influence him.

Property e): This applies to a definition proposed by Bierstedt (1974:231): 'Power is the ability to employ force, not its actual employment, the ability to apply sanctions, not their actual application'. The amount of power, according to this definition, cannot be determined by observation of actions, but requires perfect knowledge of the actors forming the relationship.

Property f): Lasswell and Kaplan (1950:75) hold that 'power is participation in the making of decisions: G has power over H with respect to the values K if G participates in the making of decisions affecting the K-policies of H'. This approach is in harmony with the synoptic mode, in which projects are large and the single decisions may be of great importance. The definition would appear less fertile the more markedly incremental the planning process. Each decision is then less significant. Planning approaches a smoothly running process lacking the characteristic of decisions as milestones.

Property g): Shapley and Shubik (1954:787) proposed a definition of power which presupposes that the preferences of the actors are known: 'Our definition of the power of an individual member depends on the chance he has of being critical to the success of a winning coalition'. For the necessary calculations to be carried out, instrumentally rational actors must be assumed. The authors apply a game theoretic and synoptic approach. In an incremental process where stable goals may not exist, where preferences change, and coalitions are formed and dissolved accordingly, such an approach would be difficult to use.

I now leave the definitions of power to investigate if the power relations are congruous with the synoptic assumptions. The actual use of force is compatible with both planning modes. Threats of force, however, have little place in the synoptic model as long as perfect knowledge is presupposed. It is of no use saying that 'if you do that, I'll do this', when the other part is already aware of it.

Manipulation is not reconcilable with synoptic planning theory when perfect knowledge is assumed. Manipulation implies that the respondents do not know the intention of the controller. Some forms also require that the respondents do not know what is in their best interest, but this is no necessary condition for manipulation.

Persuasion can be ignored in a perfect synoptic model for largely the same reason as manipulation. When an actor has full information and clearly formulated preferences, he can calculate which actions are the best. Persuasion could only be conceived of before this calculation is completed. However, the calculative capacity under synoptic planning is assumed to be so high that attempts at persuasion would not be rational.

When certainty prevails and information gathering is free, there is no reason to conform to the untested judgement of others. Nobody can judge your interests better than yourself, so why bow to the source of the message? Authority, if it is to be a phenomenon recognized at all, would have to be based on qualities other than impressive knowledge and judgement. For example, the quality of having good intentions may be universally recognized as superior to the ability of producing desired results.

It goes almost without saying that in the modified forms of synoptic planning found in practice, all the four types of power relations are logically applicable and frequently observed.

Approaches to power compatible with incrementalism

In general, models of power based on imperfect knowledge should be combined with incremental rather than synoptic planning. Such models may presuppose, for instance, that the respondents wrongly ascribe some sort of special competence to the controller, or they obey because they do not know what is in their best interest. The following paragraphs focus on posterior reasoning and adjustment of preferences.

Posterior reasoning introduces an ambiguity into the concept of power (Nagel 1975:108-10). It reverses the causal relation; not only does outcome follow from preferences, but preferences are formed by experience. The result is a permanent lag in preference formation, making preferences an unreliable aid in decision-making. One may constantly hold a negative view of past acts, even if each of them was carried out in perfect harmony with the preferences prevailing at the moment of choice. With the volatility of preferences, it becomes reasonable for the actor to be careful and not expose himself to heavy 'costs' - of exercising power, for instance - in order to realize promising projects. In principle, the actor does not know if the use of force, manipulation, etc. brings him closer to the goals that will be embraced after implementation of the project. The actor's ex ante positive assessment of the attempt to influence may dwindle in the act of exercising power. This is because unforeseen resistance may be mobilized, motivation for co-operation on other projects may drop off, and the project causing it all may in retrospect be judged to have looked better than it tasted.

It is more interesting, however, that power in Nagel's sense is turned into a less important concept under posterior reasoning, although it is still logically applicable. A controller may achieve high positive correlation between his ex ante preferences and the outcome of action, but it may not help much to be powerful in this sense. A high percentage of cases displaying a favourable ex post assessment of the outcome of actions just carried out will inform us that the actor is satisfied or lucky, but it does not tell us much about power. It is hard to conceive of any meaningful causal relation directed from preferences to action in this case.

Posterior reasoning is not compatible with synoptic planning, so the above analysis only affects the application of power concepts in incrementalism. The mechanisms guiding ex post formation of preferences may make a person positive to his previous actions in order to relieve cognitive dissonance. Hence, acknowledgement of posterior reasoning does not imply less powerful actors.

Posterior reasoning may also affect plans that are implemented in conformity with the communicative concept of power. One cannot trust that a plan will have lasting support even if an ex ante dialogical consensus is achieved. What is agreed to be generalizable interests may not be identical in the before and after situations.

The nondecision-approach of Bachrach and Baratz (1963:632) grows in importance as the planning becomes more incremental:[1]

> Many investigators have also misleadingly assumed that power and its correlatives are activated and can be observed only in decision-making situations. They have overlooked the equally, if not more important area of what might be called 'nondecision-making', i.e., the practice of limiting the scope of actual decision-making to 'safe' issues by manipulating the dominant community values, myths, and political institutions and procedures.

The nondecision-making strategy involves the organizing in and out of issues (Schattschneider 1975:69). This may be convenient in disjointed incremental planning in search for agreement and taking the line of least resistance. Nondecision-making implies a distorted communication process (Clegg 1989:77).

Incremental planning may be part of a nondecision-making strategy. Antagonism among local groups can be exploited so that only incremental changes are possible, and even these may be designed to cancel each other out. The power strategy may lead to a circle of incremental steps. Devoting one's energy to such tasks as creating or reinforcing social and political values, may pay off in an incremental planning process. In synoptic planning, on the other hand, preferences and values are considered as given or determined once and for all in the initial phase of the process.

The practice of limiting the scope of decision-making to 'safe' issues is equivalent to the limitation of analysis to a few somewhat familiar policy alternatives, a practice defended by incrementalists. Synoptic planners, on the contrary, are obliged to pursue whatever line of action seems best suited to achieve the predetermined ends. The incrementalists' practice is a version of the 'rule of anticipated reaction'. The planner A may seem powerful, but 'though B regularly accedes to A's preferred courses of action, A in fact lacks power over B because A just as regularly tailors his demands upon B to dimensions he thinks B will accept' (ibid.635).

Learning may cause adjustments of values and ends as part of a conscious or subconscious psychological 'cost reduction'. This is a process reducing the pains incurred in meeting the demands of a powerful other. When an unbalance favouring A has arisen in the power relationship, the balance can be restored in several ways (Emerson 1970:49):

1. If B reduces motivational investment in goals mediated by A.
2. If B cultivates alternative sources for gratification of those goals.
3. If A increases motivational investment in goals mediated by B.
4. If A is denied alternative sources for achieving those goals.

Some of these strategies for alleviating the pressure caused by the power of another are based on the idea of posterior reasoning and changeable preferences.

Incremental planning theory is compatible with force, manipulation, and persuasion. With regard to persuasion Lindblom (1979:524) writes that:

> In partisan mutual adjustment and all politics, participants make heavy use of persuasion to influence each other; hence they are constantly engaged in analysis designed to find grounds on which their political adversaries or indifferent participants might be converted to allies or acquiescents.

Thus, even if analysis is simple and one does not apply evaluation technique in a rule-like fashion when making choices, analytic technique is by no means absent in disjointed incrementalism.

As isolated cases, threats - even empty ones - may be rational when information is defective. In general, however, authority is devastating to any rational planning conducted under the circumstances of imperfect knowledge. The reason is that 'authoritarianism must discourage criticism', as pointed out by Popper (1966a:159). The controller will then lack the information necessary to discover whether his measures achieve the desired aim. Thus, authority prevents Popper's 'piecemeal engineering', and the planning methodology that Faludi (1986) builds on it, from operating as a rational research strategy. For the same reason it also destroys the rationality of disjointed incrementalism.

Several conceptualizations of power lack outstanding features that tie them to a specific theory of planning. My aim in this section, however, has been to demonstrate that a number of definitions and ideas of power rest on distinctly synoptic conditions, while others are based on unmistakably incremental ones. Planners are part of power relations, weakening some and creating others. A theory of planning in society has to accommodate the concept of power. One can only hope for consistency in this endeavour when the contents of the concepts borrowed from, e.g., sociology and political science are carefully considered and not arbitrarily injected into just any planning theory.

Power as causation of outcome by preference: the communicate/calculate perspective

The section inquires what can be inferred from Nagel's definition of power about technique and communication in planning. Examples of self-altering forecasts are used to demonstrate that the power of planners is not always increased by communicating their preferences more effectively. Self-altering forecasts are also demonstrated to cause a synoptic paradox of prediction. Furthermore, there are limitations to the power of planning regarded as coercive technique and control. I address the relationship between power and communication by clarifying how manipulation, in the sense of delibe-rately holding back information on intention, may be required to realize the purpose of the planning effort. One aim is to point out some obstacles facing dialogical planning.

The relationship of power to technique and communication

Technique and Nagel's concept of power are both defined within instrumen-tal rationality. However, they are far from being identical concepts. Power may be experienced without the use of techniques, as in the case of anti-cipated reactions. Neither is the use of techniques or technology a guarantee for the satisfaction of preferences, i.e., of power. Other actors might possess more effective techniques. Nevertheless, the point of employing analytic techniques in planning is to help us transform theoretical and predictive knowledge into control and guidance. More effective techniques augment the likelihood of enlarged power. Improved technique makes the same resources yield more outcome; or the same outcome may occupy more modest resources. These may be reinvested to strengthen the causal relation between preferences and outcome in other areas of interest, thus increasing the overall power of the controller. Power in the sense of Nagel is a more general instrumental competence than technique.

Power is also a more general competence than technology, which consists of a set of techniques tied together by a model of the system one wants to control, predict or understand. Nevertheless, technology conceptualized as knowledge of how to influence and control the world suggests a close con-nection between power and technology. Power implies knowledge of how to make the respondents comply or to act as if they complied, at least when anticipated reactions are not involved. This points to knowledge of theories of how communication works as a process for gaining influence: attitude formation, dissonance theory, decision theory, social judgement theory, stimulus-response theory, theory of social choice, and so on. In short, technology as applied theory, as analytic techniques, is an important tool for power conceptualized as knowledge. Even if not entirely theoretically adequate, in practical planning there is much to the slogan that 'power is effective use of technology'.

I now turn to the relationship between communication and power. When Nagel's definition is employed, a power relation does not logically imply communication between the controller and the respondent. When the reactions of the controller are anticipated, he can remain passive while his preferences become known to the respondent by any number of mechanisms. The mediation can include all of the procedures by which one mind may affect another. This involves not only writing and speech, but in fact all human behaviour (Nagel 1975:33).

If we want to make communication a prerequisite for a power relation, 'preferences' should be substituted by, e.g., 'pronounced preferences' in Nagel's definition. Even then, the definition would not require that the pronouncement is actually perceived by the respondent. It is a basic theme in communication theory that the message does not always reach the receiver, and often not in the form intended (Schramm 1971). Power is frequently restricted by the capacity of the information-carrying channels between the controller and the respondent.

Etzioni (1968:333) underlines the functional interplay of coercion and communication. They 'are the two main implementing factors which "transmit" the signals of the controlling centers to the performing units and carry their "feedbacks". Organizational networks and consensus-formation structures are, above all, institutionalized power and communication pathways'. A government can, accordingly, be seen as a communication network or a web of nerves, as it is by Deutsch (1966).

Both being quite general 'means' to affect behaviour, coercion and communication can, to some degree, be substituted for each other:

> If the message is less clear but more enforced or less enforced but more clear, similar results may be obtained. But such substitutions are limited in scope; when faced with resistance, the clearest communication will be useless unless it is backed with sufficient power, and a large application of power will yield little action if the control centers receive vague or conflicting information about what the performing units are doing and how the environment is changing.[2]   (Etzioni 1968:336)

The substitution case rests on the assumption that compliance will be more complete as the preferences of the controller grow clearer. There are important exceptions to this, as will be demonstrated shortly in discussions of self-altering predictions and indicative planning, and the promotion of personal growth through planning.

Self-altering forecasts: communication affecting the power of technique

By 'the power of technique' in the heading I mean the capacity of technique - e.g., forecasting - to establish or reinforce the causal relation between preferences and outcome. The self-altering forecast (self-denying or self-fulfilling) is a common phenomenon in social science. Simon (1954) and Grunberg and Modigliani (1954) proved that there is always a self-fulfilling prophecy. They claimed to have established 'the falsity of the proposition that the agents' reaction to public prediction necessarily falsifies all such prediction and that therefore social scientists may never hope to predict both publicly and correctly' (ibid.478). If behaviour varies continuously with forecasts and the future realization is a continuous function of behaviour, there exists a forecast that causes itself to become true (Arrow 1987:210).

Imagine now that the controller is the Planning Commission in the Directorate of Telecommunications. It has predicted that within, say, five years, more than 70% of the Norwegian population can be reached by cable-TV. This published forecast convinces the national and local producers of cable-TV programmes that it is worthwhile expanding and improving their supply. It will also be more attractive to buy the Norwegian distribution rights to programmes produced abroad. The public will display increased willingness to pay as a response to the improved supply. Political pressure to develop the cable-network will grow.

The dissemination of the forecast-information will make the prediction self-fulfilling. The prediction itself has become a part of the interacting set of social conditions that determines future social states. Henshel (1978:99) defines a self-altering prediction as one generating 'a sequence of events in reaction to prediction of a future state such that the reaction alters what would otherwise have occurred'. Wachs (1982:563) has noticed that forecasts in policy-making are fascinating exactly because self-altering predictions represent an inherent and generic dilemma of circularity:

> The future is made by people, and is not beyond our control. But to
> choose wisely from among alternative actions we seek information about
> conditions which will form the context of those actions. We want to

know what the future will be like so that we can act, yet actions will determine what the future will be, and may negate the forecast.

We now look at two different planning situations in the above cable-TV example. In the first, the preferences of the Planning Commission coincide with the announced prediction. In the other case the Commission advocates a far lower rate of development than the prediction implies.

In the first situation the published prediction increases the likelihood that the plan will be implemented. The analytic technique of forecasting strengthens the power of the controller in this case. The effect depends on the prediction being communicated and trusted. It is not necessary that the Planning Commission states its preferences. The self-fulfilling effect would be obtained even if the respondents did not know that the prediction was also the plan of the controller. That is, there are relevant cases to planning in which the controller can increase his power without making his preferences known and without trusting the rule of anticipated reaction. However, in the example, the self-fulfilling effect is probably fortified when the controller makes his preferences known. Such a pronouncement will presumably consolidate the credibility of the forecast among the firms offering programmes on cable-TV. In this case, stating the preferences increases the power. We thus have a case of positive correlation between power and communication.

In the second situation the plan deviates substantially from the prediction. The preferences of the Planning Commission are then best served by not publishing the forecast. Its power is reduced by making the prediction known. However, the Commission may cushion this effect by also publishing its preferences, if the respondents are confident that the controller will have his way to some degree. This exemplifies the general mechanism that predictions are less self-altering the less they are trusted.

Admittedly, it is not self-evident that the probability of realization of the Commission's preferences will increase when they are publicly stated. Clearly stated preferences may stimulate the political opposition. Knowing that the public planners are negative to a quick development might make people want it all the stronger. They might intensify their political work to make the Directorate of Telecommunications change its policy, e.g., to give political acceptance of private developers. In a case like this, the power of the controller decreases the more information is disseminated both on the prediction and the plan. It is a general point here that information on preferences can impair the power when the message encourages conflict or sharpens competing interests.

Self-altering predictions may be self-defeating as well as self-fulfilling. The next example is self-defeating. A Town Planning Unit releases a prediction to the effect that the district is going to be a typical over-populated area. Housing prices will zoom, there will be traffic jams, and the provision of service-facilities will generally lag behind the population development. Announcement of the forecast might counteract the predicted trend. The preferences of the Planning Unit are to maintain a balanced development of population and service. The Unit plans to achieve this goal by controlling commercial and industrial activity. Planning permission may be withheld, untraditional (private) financing of roads and other service-facilities will be encouraged, and there will be co-operation with neighbouring towns to obtain dispersion of enterprises. Proclamation of the plan might well offset the positive effect of publishing the original forecast. In this case, increased communication makes it more doubtful if the future development of population and service will conform with the preferences. Communication thus reduces the power of the Planning Unit.

It is a somewhat paradoxical feature of situations like this that a low degree of confidence may increase the power of the Planning Unit. In the example the power is augmented by trust in the forecast and by low confidence in the plan. The authority of the Planning Unit, both as a technical-analytic oracle and as a political agency, will thus affect its overall power. The controller may be aware of the effects of communication, while nevertheless having obligations to release information on both the prediction and the plan. The reactions of the respondents can then be influenced to some extent by formulating the messages so as to affect the relative credibility of the prediction and the plan.

The examples show that the actions of the respondents depend on their expectations and information. Taking advantage of the connections between power and communication, this provides the foundation of what is known as 'indicative' planning. In indicative planning the government influences the development more by co-ordination and by providing information than by direct decisions and commands (Johansen 1977:7). The main tool is an exchange of plans and information about the future between the controller and the respondents.

From a democratic point of view, the fact that power and communication are not always positively correlated is important. The controller might feel tempted to withhold information, restrict communication, and manipulate the respondents. Oscar Morgenstern studied self-altering predictions already in 1928 and recommended that forecasts of trade cycle developments should not be published. Leif Johansen pointed out (in the mid 1970s) that Norwegian national budgets up till then avoided publishing figures concerning expected rates of inflation. One feared that such forecasts might in themselves contribute to enhancing the rate of price increase (ibid:133-4).[3]

The question of manipulation in the sense of holding back information is in some cases a difficult one. There is occasionally a trade-off between the amount of information and the economic welfare for nearly everybody. The publication and wide media coverage of an increase in nominal wages for some groups have been criticized for this reason. Knowledge of successful wage-negotiation for one group creates higher expectations in other groups. The effect may spread and cause an overall wage increase that significantly exacerbates price levels. The result may be shrinking market shares abroad, an untenable trade-deficit, devaluation which raises the prices of imported goods, and a restrictive economic policy that makes nearly everybody worse off in the long run. Thus, manipulation might be in the public interest.

In indicative planning, where realization of the preferences of the controlling authority is very susceptible to the reactions of the respondents to the information communicated, the temptation to manipulate the amount and timing of information may be irresistible. One has a choice between an indirect and 'soft' form of planning based on co-ordination and information, or a direct form based on restrictions and commands. These types might well imply a trade-off between manipulation and demotivating, detailed regulation. Which will be considered the most legitimate cannot be generally stated. It is not only a question of preferences for different kinds of power relations as such, as the economic output may be quite dissimilar in the two cases.

As pointed out by Gill (1986), prediction may be paradoxical, and the concept of self-altering forecast is the basis of a synoptic paradox of prediction. A paradox is a logical progression that circles back to contradict one of its premises. In this case, the critical assumption is that a synoptic planning process exists.

When specifying synoptic planning I postulated that calculations are peremptory to achieve full knowledge of how to act in the future. Most computations concerning the future are predictions, and some of them are of the self-altering type. Assume now that there is immediate and perfect information of past and present, so once a result is calculated, it must also be regarded as published. The correctness of forecasts can only be guaranteed if the various actors' reactions to the calculated results are taken into account. The assumptions of synoptic planning imply that estimates are always right. Before calculating, then, the planner has to know how people are going to respond to the forecasts. But such information cannot be available unless the calculated results themselves are known in advance. In that case, however, the computations would be superfluous. Without the calculations the synoptic process is emptied of most of its contents. The conclusion is that the phenomenon of self-altering prediction undermines the logical foundation of synoptic planning with perfect information.

The controller may be tempted to employ impermissible means to influence the planning process and the plan itself. However, it is essential that the controller does not use threats, force, manipulation, violence, etc. so as to make the respondents feel oppressed, powerless, and of no value. Implanting a self-image of impotence into the minds of the respondents is contradictory to personal growth. In other words, power over the process and product of planning may be bought at too high costs, i.e., at the expense of the ultimate goal.

The ensuing paragraph on Hegel's dialectic of 'lordship and bondage' will make the point clear (Bernstein 1971, Sennett 1981:127-30). The stage of a fully developed and free self-consciousness that is recognized and reflected in another self-consciousness is taken to be the highest level of the spirit of man. The aim of the master is to realize himself and gain recognition by dominating the bondsman or slave.

> It would seem that the master does achieve his project of affirming himself and negating any limitations, by making the slave subservient and dependent upon him. But ironically ... the more the master succeeds, the more he fails. 'Just where the master has effectively achieved lordship, he really finds that something has come about quite different from an independent consciousness. It is not an independent, but rather a dependent consciousness that he has achieved' ... In his desperate attempt to become an independent self-consciousness, a true master, he has actually enslaved himself, made himself dependent on the slave for his own existence qua master. It is by virtue of the slave, who was initially taken to be unessential, that the master has achieved lordship.
>
> (Bernstein 1971:26-7, who quotes Hegel)

The master's use of force to gain power has its limitation. If the master literally destroys his slave, he does not succeed in his project. He then eliminates the possibility of gaining the recognition that he demands to assert himself as a fully developed, free self-consciousness. As seen in Chapter 3, the planner's use of authority to gain power over the plan design exhibits similar limitations when there is disagreement between the controller and the respondents. Just as the planner has gained control of the plan, he may discover that the foundation of the rationale of planning is eroded. The dilemma is that the means securing the power of the planner, in one important respect may leave him or her powerless. The ultimate goal of personal growth will not be achieved when exaggerated authority prematurely interrupts the process, and he may not be able to legitimize further planning.

In the case of both the master and the planner one may conclude that personal growth cannot be compassed solely by instrumental reason, which is the rationality sphere of Weberian power. The two cases reveal an antagonism between instrumental and social rationality. Excessive use of force to gain power (instrumental control) annihilates the slave and impoverishes and humiliates the lay participants in planning. In both examples the processes of integration and personal growth are interrupted, i.e., social rationality is retarded.

We have already seen that personal growth is a tacit ideal. I will stress the partial impotence of planning by calling attention to another state desired by planners, yet abrogated by planning itself. In later years strong preferences have been voiced for 'townscapes' that give an unplanned impression. Attractive examples are probably found in all countries, from the medieval Italian city centres (De Wolfe 1963) to the white-painted, wooden-built coastal towns of southern Norway (Lorange 1986). The impression given is disorderly but cosy, narrow but sheltered, unmodern but charming, inefficient with regard to mobility, yet functional concerning the development of community.

Despite scattered calls for non-planning (Banham et al. 1969, Jacobs 1965, Sennett 1970), there is little to indicate willingness to abandon the advantages of the prediction, co-ordination, functionality, and control of the established planning routines. So the dilemma is: how to plan to leave an unplanned impression? How to provide vernacular architecture with a 'self-grown' look while retaining the technical functionality of well-planned places? The dilemma is real because the planned orderliness and systematization required by technical efficiency is exactly what destroys the self-grown impression. Planning for spontaneity is paradoxical; it requires an explanation of spontaneity, thus pretending that spontaneity depends on preparation - producing a parallel to Elster's creativity dilemma: 'Any attempt to explain technical change sooner or later comes up against the paradox of turning creativity into a dependent variable' (Elster 1982:9).

I am not competent to analyse the aesthetics of the kind of places described, but it strikes me that the title *Nonplan: an experiment in freedom* (Banham et al. 1969) may provide a clue. Is there a kind of aesthetics of freedom? Is it partly the associations to self-management which make the self-grown townscapes appeal to us. Are we fascinated by the myriads of small imprints of actions made independently yet amounting to visual and social harmony? Our imagination may be stimulated by the innumerable physical details of the properties reflecting the individual interests and peculiarities of their occupiers.

A third example will strengthen the impression that we can perhaps be too sophisticated as planners, solving the technical and calculating side of the planning task a little too well. It might be possible to establish a basis for decision-making which is so comprehensive that it is harmful. Deliberation of expected consequences from actions is at the core of rational planning. Hence, the impact analysis is central in the synoptic planning scheme. When attention is directed towards conflict, the political consequences are of special interest. However, a survey of the risks of various kinds of conflict and a survey of other likely political effects due to the plan are seldom made (but see Wenk 1979). Luft (1976) and Robertson (1978), for instance, have therefore voiced the need for special 'political impact analysis':

> (T)he emphasis is on how each group will react to the proposal as it is being implemented. It will become apparent that transfer payments ... may be of paramount importance ... In particular, concern over the distribution of benefits and costs moves beyond questions of equity to whether certain groups that feel shortchanged will attempt to block the proposal. ... In fact, what is necessary is a 'feasibility analysis' that examines the project's economic, political, and organizational feasibility.
>
> (Luft 1976:437-8)

It is not decisive here whether the prediction of political impacts is accurate or not. What counts is that a certain option is chosen because it is believed to get the most favourable political reception. Then we might again be faced with a situation involving the 'essential by-product' argument. The dilemma is that by publishing the information that the recommended planning alternative was chosen because of its favourable political effects, one can reduce the chances for its implementation and at the same time compromise the political decision system. People usually want (e.g.) a road because it provides higher accessibility, fewer accidents or other concrete advantages. They expect the politicians - their representatives - to understand and accept these reasons, and so they might dislike hearing that the plan was accepted because it was politically the most opportune.

Politically favoured results are essential by-products of implementing plans that solve the practical problems of the constituency, as they define them (efficacious plans). Hence, political impact assessment can lead to decisions which are politically delicate if the real basis for them is leaked. On the other hand, hiding the real decision criteria is a kind of manipulation, and could eventually undermine the legitimacy of planning. The conclusion is that if the planners experience the reactions of the politicians to be unpredictable, closer co-operation between the two groups should be established. Instead of fortifying the technocratic impression of planning by submitting yet another area to technical analysis, one should communicate and in that way attempt to make the need for the new analytic technique vanish.

We have seen that the conceptualization of power varies considerably depending on the kind of rationality we apply when thinking about it. Different rationalities are used for different tasks. It is maybe not entirely perplexing, then, that different facets of power come to the fore under emancipation and under freedom. The next section explores some paradoxes connected to the problematic transition from emancipation to freedom.

Limits of instrumental power:
on the power to convert emancipation into freedom

The section questions if there are limitations on what can be achieved by working to establish strong causal relations between preferences for certain outcomes and the outcomes themselves. The control and steering aspect of planning relates it directly to instrumental power. Consequently, planning is not the kind of activity to succeed in realizing freedom. The insight offered in this section is that important ideals would be beyond reach of the planners even if they were powerful enough to be above every external claim. The problem is discussed first by studying some general and puzzling difficulties encountered when trying to transform the process of liberation into a state of freedom (as noncoercion). After that, I investigate some extra conundrums faced when planning is to play a significant part in the transformation.[4]

Is there something to which one can attach preferences, which still cannot be realized by a causal relation between these preferences and the 'something'? Freedom may be a case in point. Assume that there is substantial disagreement among the citizens on the aspects of civil liberties which need improvement. Then an over-dominating causal connection between an actor's preferences for a particular aspect of freedom and the incidence of this aspect of freedom in society may force freedom on a majority of the population. However, it is a contradiction in terms that freedom can be forced on the citizens in a dictatorial manner.

Planning presupposes preferences. If one is planning for freedom, and there is a very strong causal relation between the plan and realization of the preferred degree of freedom, it would mean that the preferences of those formally passing the plan are causing the freedom. In the case of disagreement, freedom would then be enforced. That is, the problem of using power to strive for freedom is closely linked to the problem of planning for freedom. Planning, even when it is an emancipatory tool, implies control and steering. So, planning may add to the general problem of transforming emancipation into freedom.

Emancipation is part of the legitimation of planning, yet there is Hayek's dilemma of lost freedom under planning. It is not primarily the combination of planning and emancipation that creates the knotty issues, but the conversion of emancipation into freedom by means of planning. The chapters to follow suggest two approaches to planning that aim at minimizing the negative effects of the freedom-under-planning dilemma. Planning as conflict management deals with the disputes bound to arise when groups have their freedom constrained by public plans. Flexible planning balances the control aspect against the possibilities for choice, adjustment, and correction necessary to preserve a degree of freedom.

Emancipation/freedom paradoxes

This subsection deals with paradoxes springing up whenever liberation is to be transformed into freedom. They are general in that they arise whether or not planning is a crucial feature of the liberation and transformation process. Generally speaking, the paradoxes relate to planning by problematizing the means-end scheme. They illuminate some important unintended consequences of instrumental power in planning. There is an analogy between a number of the paradoxes and the planning dilemma constituted by the ideal of personal growth giving rise to manipulation.

First I will call to mind that the essence of structural influence is systemic inequalities of power causing unequal life chances among members of the society. An illegitimately biased distribution of instrumental power interferes with further production of power in the communicative sense. To realize the freedom necessary to create communicative power, structural influence has to be surmounted. That is, one has to pass through a phase of liberation, defeating those taking advantage of the prevailing inequalities, to lay the foundation for dialogical power.

This points to an old dilemma in political science, already discussed by Machiavelli in renaissance Italy. Freedom requires liberation, but why would the liberator - strong enough to overthrow the old regime - be interested in reducing his power and create a society in which people are not politically suppressed? Freedom is impossible without liberation, but liberation calls for strong power in a Weberian sense (Ehnmark 1986:194-203, Machiavelli 1984).[5]

Ellul's distinction between agitation propaganda and integration propaganda sheds considerable light on the problem of letting liberation be succeeded by freedom. The difficulties spring from the contrast between leading men from mere resentment to rebellion, and persuading them to adjust themselves to desired patterns of obedience:

> When a revolutionary movement is launched, it operates with agitation propaganda; but once the revolutionary party has taken power, it must begin immediately to operate with integration propaganda ... That is the way to balance its power and stabilize the situation. But the transition from one type of propaganda to the other is extremely delicate and difficult. After one has, over the years, excited the masses, flung them into adventures, fed their hopes and their hatreds, opened the gates of action to them, and assured them that all their actions were justified, it is difficult to make them reenter the ranks, to integrate them into the normal framework of politics and economics. (Ellul 1973:76)

Paulo Freire (1972) acknowledges the Machiavellian dilemma. He wants freedom for the oppressed peasants of Latin America, yet he writes about them: 'Their ideal is to be men; but for them, to be a "man" is to be an oppressor. This is their model of humanity' (ibid.22). Freire develops a strategy for evading the paradox. What is needed is a pedagogy of the oppressed teaching them that being a free person implies to break out of the oppressor/oppressed duality. Initially, 'their perception of themselves as opposites of the oppressor does not yet signify involvement in a struggle to overcome the contradiction; the one pole aspires not to liberation, but to identification with its opposite pole' (ibid.22). If this situation is allowed to continue, political liberation is bound to create new oppression.[6]

The lines are easily drawn back to the concept of 'model power'. The oppressed need a new model of humanity. This model cannot be worked out by the oppressors; it has to be developed in a dialogue between the oppressed and a third party. It would be a contradiction in terms if the oppressors not only defended but actually implemented a liberating education. A new model, in which the oppressed are their own example in the struggle for liberation, can only be accepted and internalized in dialogue. And a dialogue cannot - per definition - take place between oppressor and oppressed.[7]

The planners may be guided by an advocacy paradigm. When they and those being planned for do not acknowledge common interests, planning as emancipation is not possible without the use of coercion. The planners may be convinced that the diverging opinions are caused by some kind of false consciousness on the part of the local constituency. Benton (1981, 1982) points out that this catches radical and democratic critics among the planners in a 'paradox of emancipation':

(I)f they are to remain true to their political values they may implement no changes without the consent of those who are affected by them, and if they seek to implement no such changes, then they acquiesce in the persistence of a social system radically at odds with their political values. (Benton 1982:15)

The paradox rests on the assumption that it is possible for the planners to know the interests of those planned for better than those affected know their own interests. This opening for paternalism is often created by conditions of ideological domination. To prevent the paradox arising because of false consciousness, those planned for have to be alerted to the prevailing conditions of structural influence before policies to smooth out inequalities are introduced. An analysis of ideology is important in this connection. If mutual understanding is not achieved, the planner's option is to establish what he regards as illegitimate power relations himself, or grudgingly submit to structural influence.

Benton's paradox repeats the ancient and essential knowledge which is also part of Machiavelli's paradox: the liberator must be willing to and strong enough to take control. Both paradoxes come into existence in situations requiring this simultaneously with a real democratic commitment on the part of the liberator. Despite the obvious similarities the paradoxes differ. The paradox of emancipation arises because of the liberator's real commitment to democratic ideals. Machiavelli's paradox springs up because certain situations notoriously give reason to doubt that the liberator will adhere to his democratic ideals: power corrupts.

The 'spirit' of the paradoxes differs; they reveal suspicion in different directions. Benton seems to say: If the liberator is really democratic, how, then, should he be able to seize power? Machiavelli seems to say: If the liberator is successful in seizing power, why, then, should he remain democratic? In the case of Benton there is a discrepancy between the preferences of the liberator and the public ex ante, and this causes the paradox of emancipation. In the case of Machiavelli the paradox accentuates as a fact that a discord will emerge between the preferences of the liberator and the public ex post.

The paradox of emancipation poses the question if one can possibly be forced to be free. This is what seems to happen if the planner in Benton's paradox decides to implement changes without the initial assent of those affected - and succeeds. Success requires that he is right in his judgement that those opposed suffer from false consciousness. And this has to be gradually realized by the opponents with the result that the planned changes are eventually appreciated. Then the respondents become free as a result of being forced.

The possibility that men might be forced to be free was discussed by Jean-Jaques Rousseau (1968) as part of his work on participative democracy.[8] He seeks a theory to rectify the most disturbing observation, the puzzle that 'man was born free, and he is everywhere in chains' (ibid.49). Participation is a requisite for freedom in Rousseau's sense. The obstacle to freedom is not necessarily false consciousness, but passivity and unwillingness to participate. Being forced to be free means being forced to participate. Involvement in collective affairs is necessary because only 'obedience to a law one prescribes to oneself is freedom' (ibid.65).

In relation to Benton's paradox, a related conundrum involving a kind of persuasion merits mention. It is the paradox of indoctrination founded on the assumption that what one is basically trying to pass on to students cannot be rationally taught. This is held to be the case with 'world-pictures' disseminated through general education.[9] Given this fundamental lack of rationality, Macmillan (1983:270) offers the following statement of the situation:

> The problem of indoctrination is this: in a modern society, the desired goal of education is that each student develop a set of beliefs that are rationally grounded and open to change when challenged by better-grounded beliefs. In order to develop such students, however, it would seem that they must acquire a belief in rational methods of knowing which must itself be beyond challenge, i.e., must be held in a manner inconsistent with its own content. Thus, students must be indoctrinated in order not to be indoctrinated: a pedagogical dilemma or paradox.

One will notice some common traits between the paradoxes of Benton and Macmillan. In Benton's case those affected by plans are not 'rational' because they are subdued to false consciousness. In Macmillan's case the students are persuaded to refrain from using their full rational and critical capacity simply because a world-picture cannot be rationally taught. In both cases the liberator-teacher is committed to democratic ideals, and he is tempted to pursue these ideals by an 'undemocratic' procedure. If the temptation is yielded to, he would in one case force people to be free and in the other indoctrinate students to resist indoctrination.

Problems of planning the transformation into freedom

Freedom is problematic under planning because planning has the dual character of being both control and creation of opportunities. A telling example is drawn from James Buchanan (1975:94), who points out that even Robinson Crusoe accepted the necessity of planning and used an alarm clock to impose constraints on his own choice behaviour:

As the alarm bell arouses him from his nap, Crusoe faces one paradox of 'being governed'. He finds himself frustrated by an external constraint on his choice set, and he feels 'less free' at that moment than he might have felt in the wholly voluntary act of rising from his bed. This sense of frustration may be repeated each and every morning, but Crusoe may continue to set the governing clock each evening. The rational rule-maker makes the trade-off between liberty and planned efficiency and includes an enforcement instrument in the contract.

It is common to all the conundrums of this subsection that they are formulated in terms particularly suited to highlight the problems of planning the transformation into freedom. One will find both the non-coercion aspect and the opportunities-for-choice aspect of freedom apposite to the discussion.

For instance, Macmillan's paradox of indoctrination which closed the last subsection, has some special relevance for local participatory planning. Such planning is often committed to democracy, and it has an educative purpose. It is to serve the acquisition of skills for participation in general political life. Besides, it is to give the individual a positive experience of his or her own competence, and of what can be achieved by acting collectively with neighbours or workmates. The participant is to gain personal growth through this experience. As already argued, this intention has to be played down, and so the pedagogy of the process cannot be completely rational. The basic ideal of planning - its rationale - is an analogy to a 'world-picture'. The lack of rationality involved is a parallel to that requisite for the paradox of indoctrination to arise. In both cases the 'world-picture' cannot be grounded in a way accepted as rational by the students or lay participants.[10]

There is also another connection between indoctrination and the problem of freedom under planning. Indoctrination is an effective means to make people conform, and conformity is a threat to freedom. On the other hand, planning conceived as control requires prediction; and the ability to predict is greatly improved by conformity. Change and variety in individual behaviour complicate prediction because the utility of past experience is deflated. Consequently, there will be an intrinsic tendency among planners to encourage conformity and thus persuade in an indoctrinating manner. This, in turn, makes planning a threat to freedom, reinforcing the basis of Hayek's fears. (Part of this argument was developed by Wilkins and Gitchoff 1969:126.)

Following Heiner's (1983) argument, the planner can induce conformable behaviour by manipulation as well. The game of the planner would then be to increase the complexity and uncertainty of the situations in which the individuals will have to act. As Heiner states, 'predictable behaviour will evolve only to the extent that uncertainty prevents agents from successfully maximizing' (ibid.561). Uncertainty makes individuals fall back on easily recognizable patterns, and conformity will result without direct indoctrination. Planning theory does itself offer a telling example. Under high uncertainty, planners fall back on the simple rule of incrementalism, keeping close to the existing situation. Prediction of planned action is then not likely to miss by much.

Combining the views of Kierkegaard (1971) and Baudrillard (1985) on seduction, another tension between planning and emancipation comes to the surface. Baudrillard holds that in the seduction, it is the manifest, the discourse on its most 'superficial' level, which turns against the underlying order to nullify it and replace it by the charm and the trap of the apparent. The seduction is what deprives the discourse of its meaning and leads it away from truth (ibid.59). This makes seduction the antithesis to the emancipating analyses described in Chapter 2, viz., analysis of psyche, conflict, and ideology. These analyses have one thing in common: a search beneath the observable surface to trace hidden motives, forces, structures, etc., which can ascribe meaning to human behaviour.

Inspired by Lilja (1988) I have given an account of the planner as an analogy to Kierkegaard's manipulative seducer. On the other hand, planning is legitimized by emancipation aiming at personal growth and the abolishment of structural influence. But how can the descriptions of planning as seduction and as emancipation be unified when seduction is contrary to emancipatory analysis? Have I fabricated an image of planning that is biased in some important respect? Or is it possible in practice to combine manipulation with emancipation? This puzzle is recognizably affiliated to the forced-to-be-free problem.

One way to settle the matter is exploiting Baudrillard's thoughts on the reciprocity of seduction (see Note 8 of Chapter 3). Ambiguity is introduced concerning the controller/respondent roles. The planner is answerable before the politicians, who are in turn given their mandate by the constituency seduced by the planner. In a way planning may be imagined as a seduction sanctioned by the seduced. The planner is the medium used by the collective of citizens to lessen the harm done by their individual pursuit of self-interest. The planner is himself seduced to believe that *he* holds the power to integration, redistribution, and production independently of those for whom he is planning. He is seduced when he considers his own projects and plans as the independent variables setting the social system in motion.

In the tradition of humanist planners, planning itself has been characterized in terms that make us recognize the Machiavellian dilemma. One can argue that planned effort and thus planning is an indispensable tool for liberation. But planning turns simultaneously into part of the new apparatus of power necessary to reform and reorganize the old one.[11] How can planning, always containing an element of control and steering, be combined with freedom? This is the problem Friedmann catches in his contradiction between 'social planning' and 'radical practice', which we can think of as planning and dialogue, respectively. The starting point of Friedmann is not Machiavelli's emphasis on liberation from oppressive political power. It is, rather, planning as a collective struggle to form our own world, emancipation in the sense of man creating himself:

> A grandiose vision: humankind collectively in charge of its own destiny! Through an exertion of sheer will we shall construct a fitting home for ourselves! The image is of pioneers who plant their fields and raise their cities where there was once a cosmic wilderness. And so we reappropriate from Heaven what properly belongs to us. Becoming human is a human act. (Friedmann 1979:19)

What is so disturbing to Friedmann, are all the restrictive measures we must adopt to preserve the feeling (the illusion?) that we are really in charge of our own destiny. In the process we risk that the emancipating project of becoming human is reduced to nought. Friedmann's version of the Machiavellian paradox is that 'in the measure that we try to control for uncertainty, pyramiding control upon control, we also destroy both the will and the ability to engage in social construction' (ibid.19). The discipline needed during the long march in pursuit of the vision transforms the marchers into robots to whom the vision has no meaning. In short, planning as control destroys freedom as self-creation.

Friedmann launches his attack on social planning through a critique of forecasting and 'model fetishism'. That is, he views planning primarily as technique, as technical analysis based on the means-end dichotomy within a system pretending to be closed. When everything in the system is connected to everything else in a vast, seamless web of cause and effect, nothing can be controlled unless everything is controlled. The core of radical practice, on the other hand, is dialogue. Friedmann focuses on the technique (as planning) fostering order, and dialogue creating turbulence. His admittance of the need for a unity of social planning and radical practice is an expression of the necessity to combine technique and communication.

Friedmann sheds light on the terms of freedom under social planning by referring to Lenin's analysis of the withering away of the state in the post-revolutionary higher phase of communist society, and concludes that:

Freedom in a totalized society is a learned, conditioned freedom. Our teachers are the armed workers of the state, whose punishment is terrible and swift. From them we learn how to obey the rules of the new order. When we have learned these rules, the state as a coercive power melts away. Freedom in a totalized society becomes the habit of obedience. (Friedmann 1979:36)

Friedmann sees social planning as a totalizing endeavour. Pushing the point to the extreme, he associates Lenin's armed workers with bureaucratic planners within large-scale and impersonal structures where they design a society of hierarchy, domination, and control. To the degree that social planners are successful in their project of controlling always more variables which could possibly interfere with the implementation of their plans, freedom is lost. 'Our freedom is part of the uncertainty that renders social planning indeterminate' (ibid.39):[12]

What in the perspective of social planners appears as the fatal flaw in their art - their inability to control turbulence, to render human responses more predictable - presents itself as the condition of my freedom. Where the social system becomes indeterminate, in the interstices of the planned system, I exercise an independent choice; I am autonomous. (Friedmann 1979:38)

Individuals should hold an inner conviction that they create and control their own life and are fully responsible for their actions. Planning aims to expand freedom by providing public goods and thereby widening the range of choices open to the subjects. In spite of this, enough activities must be left unplanned. This is so because the feeling of liberty can only be obtained by the experience of doing things hit upon by oneself, not figured out by others. The suspicion that the choice was foreseen by others and planned by a collective would ruin the feeling of freedom.

The self-destructive capacity of omnipotence, Hegel's vivid description of the lord destroying himself as a master the moment he destroys the slave, is also recognized in Friedmann's paradox. Just as the planners seem to have succeeded completely, when control is gained over the last variable that could possibly interfere with the implementation of the plan, and all uncertainty is removed, all freedom is gone. Planning has completely demolished its own rationale of emancipation and personal growth. The dialectic of uncertainty and control, nourishing the planning endeavour, has disappeared, and planning as a meaningful project for improving the human condition is dead.

Society could be blessed with completely well-intentioned planners possessing perfect information and all necessary power, yet the result might be dreadful. 'Of course!' one might respond; for how can planners hope to fare better than the Almighty himself: God is all good, all knowing, and all powerful, yet evil exists.

Notes

1   The aspect of power showing itself as the ability to make decisions, have one's way in negotiations, and win conflicts, is often termed 'the first face of power'. The nondecision approach was then, consequently, taken to reveal the second face of power. Lukes (1974) introduced the third face of power, pointing out that the controller may exercise power through affecting or forming the felt needs of the respondent. The controller may also influence the way the respondent perceives inequalities and injustice. The third face of power consists of mechanisms making possible 'structural influence'.
    The approach of Lukes does not introduce new ideas easily referred to either synoptic or incremental planning theory. However, it focuses on the way political communication is formed and given substance. Gaventa (1980:15-6) writes that:

> This may include the study of social myths, language, and symbols, and how they are shaped or manipulated in power processes. It may involve the study of communication of information - both of what is communicated and how it is done. It may involve a focus upon the means by which social legitimations are developed around the dominant, and instilled as beliefs or roles in the dominated. It may involve, in short, locating the power processes behind the social construction of meanings and patterns that serve to get B to act and believe in a manner in which B otherwise might not, to A's benefit and B's detriment.

Bråten's (1973) ideas on 'model power' and communication catch an important aspect of the third face of power.
2   In this citation 'power' is best read as 'coercion' to make the passage meaningful in my exposition. As long as we stick to Nagel's definition, power and communication cannot be substitutes for one another. But coercion and communication can be substitutes in the production of power.
3   Other striking examples are found in Wachs (1982). One tells how a mayor refused to publish a forecast predicting a dramatic and continuing shift in racial composition in his town. A second example tells how Robert Moses deliberately presented underestimated costs to politicians

and officials of New York to get his projects started. This kind of manipulation is discussed further in Wachs (1990).

4   It may be difficult to move from emancipation to felt freedom even apart from the paradoxes raised by power. Psychological adaption-level theory has found that '(e)ven as we contemplate our satisfaction with a given accomplishment, the satisfaction fades, to be replaced finally by a new indifference and a new level of striving' (Brickman and Campbell 1971:287). Habituation will produce a decline in the subjective pleasurableness of the input. Applied to my problem, emancipation may go on 'forever' without generating a lasting feeling of freedom. Adaption-level theory points to a planning dilemma because 'no planning for the good society (a task for optimists) can be successful unless it is done by people who thoroughly understand the relativistic and elusive character of subjective pleasure (an understanding of pessimism)' (ibid.289).

5   The problem is probably spelled out most clearly in the part of Book One, where Machiavelli writes about 'the transition from servitude to freedom':

> While with regard to modifying institutions all at once when everybody realizes that they are no good, I would point out that, though it is easy to recognize their futility, it is not easy to correct it; for, to do this, normal methods will not suffice now that normal methods are bad. Hence it is necessary to resort to extraordinary methods, such as the use of force and an appeal to arms, and, before doing anything, to become a prince in the state, so that one can dispose it as one thinks fit. But to reconstitute political life in a state presupposes a good man, whereas to have recourse to violence in order to make oneself prince in a republic supposes a bad man. Hence very rarely will there be found a good man ready to use bad methods in order to make himself prince, though with a good end in view, nor yet a bad man who, having become a prince, is ready to do the right thing and to whose mind it will occur to use well that authority which he has acquired by bad means.
>
> (Machiavelli 1984:Section 1.18)

6   Krippendorff (1991:189) formulates the dilemma of Freire more in the abstract. The paradox is that those who explicitly criticize the power of the powerful, implicitly accept power as a way to understand the world. They thereby constitute the very reality they seek to overcome. This is evidence of an entrapment in power that includes social critics as well. The ultimate problem is a pathological reality construction. Reality is neither external to its observers nor inside someone's head. It resides in social practice, and discursive practice in particular. The question is how

such practice can be changed. What is needed is an emancipatory theory of communication, according to Krippendorff.

If Friedrich Nietzsche is right, the projects of Freire and Krippendorff can never succeed. Nietzsche's position is that power is always oppressive. One's freedom comes at another's expense, because to be free is to conquer another. Universal liberation is absurd. One cannot be for or against liberation in general. The question under consideration is always whether to support group A increasing its power at the expense of group B (Read 1989).

7 Frantz Fanon (1967) has set forth ideas affiliated to those of Freire. O'Neill (1985) has connected the work of both authors to the critical theory of the Frankfurt school. He concludes that: 'There is a considerable complementarity between the practical aims of Fanon and Freire and the analytic and emancipatory enterprise of critical social theory' (ibid.72).

8 In Chapter 7 of The Social Contract on 'the sovereign', i.e., on the collective legislative body composed of as many members as there are voters in the assembly, the following passage is included:

> Hence, in order that the social pact shall not be an empty formula, it is tacitly implied in that commitment - which alone can give force to all others - that whoever refuses to obey the general will shall be constrained to do so by the whole body, which means nothing other than that he shall be forced to be free; for this is the condition which, by giving each citizen to the nation, secures him against all personal dependence, it is the condition which shapes both the design and the working of the political machine, and which alone bestows justice on civil contracts - without it, such contracts would be absurd, tyrannical and liable to the grossest abuse.
>
> (Rousseau 1968:64)

It might be of interest that the idea of forcing somebody to be free can be given an interpretation linking it to social choice theory. Runciman and Sen (1965) call upon the well-known 'prisoner's dilemma' to illustrate the point. There is a dilemma because each of the two prisoners will be rewarded if he, and he alone, confesses; but he does not know whether his mate will confess too. If they both confess, the sentence will be hard, and if they both keep silent the sum of their sentences will be at a minimum.

> They would both be ready to appoint an agent who would see to it that neither of them confessed. In the absence of sanction (or, we might even say, of a Sovereign), each prisoner may be driven by

rational self-seeking to break the contract which is to the common advantage of both. This gives an immediate and plausible sense to Rousseau's notion of the members of a society being 'forced to be free', ...   (Runciman and Sen 1965:556)

9 The term 'world-pictures' refers to Wittgenstein's 'Weltbilder'. Habermas's concept of the 'life-world' is derived from the same source, and consequently it would seem that a conceptualization of a lifeworld, too, cannot be appropriated by the means of rational reasoning alone (Habermas 1984:337). The necessarily irrational acceptance of the world-pictures seems to be an analogy to the basic axioms or assumptions of science, which must be accepted without proof before scientific results can be derived.

10 Affiliated with Macmillan's paradox is the close connection between education and propaganda pointed out by Ellul. Both indoctrination and propaganda can be considered types of persuasion. Ellul (1973:109) argues that the uncultured man cannot be reached by propaganda. 'Primary education makes it possible to enter the realm of propaganda, in which people then receive their intellectual and cultural environment'.

A similar paradox is mentioned by Elster to be proper to Rosa Luxemburg. The manipulative idea is that the working class can advance only by fighting for goals that the leaders have deliberately chosen because they are just out of reach:

> It is clearly impossible to say to the workers that they shall revolt in order to be defeated and by defeat acquire the class consciousness required for a mature revolutionary class, for workers ready to accept this argument would already be in possession of that consciousness. The alternatives for the leaders are either to abdicate from leadership for the benefit of less experienced members who can make their own mistakes, or to present victory as a real possibility for the rank and file although they know that defeat is certain.
>
> (Elster 1978:59)

Hence, according to this theory, the workers must be manipulated in order to be emancipated.

11 Nietzsche formulated this problem for liberal institutions. He could see no worse and no more thorough injurers of freedom than such institutions. Yet he states that they really promote freedom in a powerful way while they are still being fought for (Read 1989:73).

12 The concerns of Friedmann closely resemble those of Popper in his defence of the open society against its enemies, among them interventionist planning:

(I)f we do not strengthen our democratic institutions while giving more power to the state by interventionist 'planning', then we may lose our freedom. And if freedom is lost, everything is lost, including 'planning'. For why should plans for the welfare of the people be carried out if the people have no power to enforce them? Only freedom can make security secure. We thus see that there is not only a paradox of freedom but also a paradox of state planning. If we plan too much, if we give too much power to the state, the freedom will be lost, and that will be the end of planning.

(Popper 1966b:130)

6 Conflict management and integration

Planning serving a critical function in society should explore the power relations implied by various types of conflict resolution. Conflict management as an emancipatory process means elimination of or withdrawal from the most intolerable power relations, or at least a limitation of the domain and scope of such relations.

What I want to do here is to (1) argue that the levels of ambition for conflict management lead to different types of planning, (2) bring conflict theory and planning theory closer together; i.e., to connect conflict and conflict management with power relations and synoptic and incremental planning, and (3) describe a couple of communicative strategies for dealing with conflict in planning. First, however, I need to situate the conflict theme in my general discourse and introduce some notions to characterize conflicts.

Preliminary view of conflict and planning

Conflict exists as a potentiality in all interpersonal relationships, and the interactions taking place in a planning process are no exception. Communicative rationality is the main mode of thinking serving to integrate conflicting parties. It prescribes the attitude of treating other human beings as ends rather than means. When this behavioural mode permeates a society, it promotes a kind of freedom constituted by the absence of instrumental power relations; that is, a non-coercive concept of freedom. The quest for integration and reciprocal understanding is then the primary principle guiding human conduct. This is incompatible with the calculating attitude of always opting for the best outcome in an instrumental sense, and thus contradictory to the interpretation of social relationships as competitions that should be won.

When everybody can act, independently of a collective plan, to improve their own lot, this can strengthen the feeling of freedom even if the actors are not better off materially. In this unco-ordinated struggle, often manifest in competition for resources, conflict is frequently observed:

> We recognize that conflict is an essential component of a free society. Everyone has the right to compete for advantages. In a democracy, conflict produces new standards, new institutions and new patterns of relationships. Conflict may be necessary in the pursuit of justice.
>
> (Cormick 1985:3)

Hence, when everybody pursues his own interest on an individual basis, conflict is inescapable. So when freedom is seen as the opportunity of ordinary men and women to compete in the everyday arenas where they are usually active - for job possibilities, good bargains, decent housing, etc., conflict is an implication of freedom.

Conflict imposes uncertainty on future collective preferences and is a main source of ambiguity in planning. Friedmann's dilemma in the last chapter was that freedom is lost to the degree that planners are successfully controlling always more variables which could possibly interfere with the implementation of their plan. The analogy in conflict terms would be: to the degree that planners are successful in their project of managing and dissolving always more conflicts rendering planning indeterminate, freedom is lost. As peace comes about and freedom from domination is gained, another kind of freedom disappears. John Friedmann insists that freedom depends on uncertainty: only in the interstices of the planned system is independent choice exercised. The sacrifice demanded by peace includes the choice to compete. Everything is now foreseeable, so co-ordination is perfect, and there are no more interstices in the planned system making room for choice and competition.

With peace, planning is neither adequately depicted as a process of negotiation, mediation, and citizen participation, nor as a process of questioning and shaping attention. The incremental mode of seeking agreement through stepwise, disjointed analysis is impertinent. Once conflicts are gone and with them much of the uncertainty, the algorithmic, maximizing procedures of synoptic planning again enter the stage. Analytic techniques move to the forefront and communication withdraws to the peripheral task of monitoring to make sure the well integrated community endures. Under unanimity the four modes of planning discourse - advocacy, criticism, explanation, and deliberative judgement - do not seem crucial.

It is not uncommon to come across statements from planners with approximately the following contents: 'Compromise and conflict resolution are the everyday experience of the planner. What else are we doing but working out and advancing proposals, taking account of competing interests so that something may be done in practice which furthers the public interest'. Batty (1974), for one, advocates the notion of planning as conflict management, asserting that any model of the planning process that involves the notion of choice among alternatives must be based on the resolution of conflict. In the 1980s this view of planning finally attracted wider interest and sparked off several studies on mediation and negotiation in planning (e.g., Minnery 1985, Moore 1986, Sullivan 1984, Amy 1987, Watts 1987). The public planner, as a representative of (e.g.) the state or the county, is not impartial. Even so, he or she is still the one responsible for attending to the preferences of interests not otherwise represented, and the one to ensure that no special interest outwits the others. The planner is still the first person to turn to when dispute emerges between other parties in the planning process. Thus, negotiating and mediating skills are, indeed, required from many planners.

In the planning literature conflict is usually mentioned in a way making it obvious that it is regarded as a negative phenomenon: 'planners treat the scars of conflict, even their own, as a brand of shame rather than a badge of honor' (Hoch and Cibulskis 1987:99). Conflict makes it difficult to implement 'rational' decisions; it causes delays, extra work, and inefficiency. 'Unrealistic' alternatives and 'insignificant' consequences have to be assessed, and persons who 'very likely' will come up with nothing of interest have to be informed and listened to. It should be noted at the outset that I view conflict - whether within a society, a group or an individual - as not necessarily destructive. Controversy is not always detrimental to decision-making and not always contrary to long-range integration. At the interpersonal levels of society and group, this differentiated view is advocated by Coser (1956) and Fisher (1980), respectively.

Controversy is most likely to be productive when characterized by (1) the communication of relevant information, (2) acceptance of differences in perception, (3) efforts to identify common goals, and (4) the definition of the dispute as a problem to be jointly shared and resolved. Unproductive interaction follows from poor communication, the overt hiding of facts and data, perceptions of 'bad' and 'good' people, suspiciousness, hostility, willingness to exploit another's needs, imposed resolutions, and outcomes that are of the win-lose type. The likely result is additional anxiety, pain, and loss of resources (Cormick 1985, Fisher and Brown 1988).

My treatment of conflict and conflict management will be quite abstract and general, and the concepts applied are not limited to dyadic conflict.

However, I do not deal with alliances and coalitions. One may imagine that the parties have entered into this kind of co-operation before my discussion starts. Moreover, no attention will be paid to conflicts among the planners. When the planner intervenes in a dispute between other actors or engages in a controversy with another actor, the internal conflicts of the planning agency are considered to be already sorted out. An actor in a conflict is an individual or an organized collection of individuals (groups, firms, organizations, etc.) that has preferences concerning the outcome of the conflict and acts to affect the outcome. A rational actor will succeed to some degree in some circumstances, and thus he possesses some power. The interest of an actor in a certain conflict is equal to the difference in consequences to him or her following from the possible outcomes. Coombs and Avrunin (1988) provide a recent text-book overview of the field.

Dichotomies for characterizing conflicts

The main task here is to present a list of conflict features that is helpful when examining how conflicts differ with regard to communicative characteristics, presuppositions of power relations, and compatibility with planning theories. Two definitions of conflict are presented below, and I refer to one of them in particular only when it helps the discussion:

> Social conflict ... will provisionally be taken to mean a struggle over values and claims to scarce status, power and resources in which the aims of the opponents are to neutralize, injure or eliminate their rivals.
> (Coser 1956:8)

> Conflict may be defined as a situation of competition in which the parties are aware of the incompatibility of potential future positions and in which each party wishes to occupy a position that is incompatible with the wishes of the other. (Boulding 1962:5)

These two definitions suffice to demonstrate a profound indeterminateness in the conceptualization of conflict. Some, like Coser, require that conflict implies hostile actions. Others, like Boulding, attach the conflict term to certain background conditions, such as 'contradictions', 'opposition of interests', or 'emotional hostility'.[1] As Turner (1982:178) says: 'When the preconditions of conflict are lumped together with the actual emission of conflict acts, then theories are likely to be vague'. However, this need not concern us here. Both perspectives will be useful when conflict is related to planning, power, etc. I refer to conflict defined in the Coser and Boulding manners as behaviour-defined and condition-defined, respectively.

Some condition-based definitions of 'conflict' give a very broad meaning to the concept. Potential and latent conflict imply that there may be conflict without personal conflict behaviour, and even when the parties are unaware of their contradictory interests. In my terminology, 'conflict' includes several phenomena that are not usually considered destructive, such as debate and competition. There is neither reason nor possibility to eliminate conflict so broadly defined. It may nevertheless be useful to monitor even 'benign' conflict situations and prevent them from developing into harmful fights.

Throughout the ensuing paragraphs the following statement by Howard Raiffa (1982:11) should be kept in mind:

> Early in my research I had the grandiose idea of devising a taxonomy of disputes, in which the listing would be reasonably exhaustive and in which overlaps among categories would be rare. This was possible, I found, only after developing a host of abstract constructs - and even then the taxonomy was not very useful.

I have heeded the warning given by Raiffa, and the list of dichotomies in Table 6.1 is no attempt at a complete and non-overlapping classification of conflict types. The features are selected mainly because of their relevance to the technique/communication perspective on planning. Some explanations will now be given to the table.

When the conflict is latent, the foundation of the conflict is still present. The parties may be indifferent to this fact, however, or they may have some sort of 'false consciousness', believing that the underlying causes of the controversy are dissolved. Latent conflicts are most likely to be of the system-dependent type. It is not always recognized by the underprivileged that they are poor because mechanisms of the social system produce systematic inequalities. Communication, e.g., with third party observers, may change the status of the conflict from latent to perceived. This is the aim of agitators. Note that latent conflict is not compatible with all condition-based definitions, for instance Boulding's definition above.

Competing interests incite action. Manifest conflict consists of three elements; these are incompatible interests, power relation, and personal conflict behaviour. Potential conflict only requires contradictory interests, but power relations of authority are often present. Force, manipulation, and persuasion are not compatible with potential conflict as they imply action. Note that power does not presuppose manifest conflict, 'because preferences can determine outcomes without overt struggle when reactions are correctly anticipated, when power resources are well known, when one actor totally dominates another, when information or incentives are cleverly manipulated' (Nagel 1975:154).

Table 6.1
Features used to categorize conflicts

Yes	Are the following features present?	No
Perceived	Are the actors conscious of the conflict?	Latent
Manifest	Does personal conflict behaviour take place?	Potential
Real	Is the conflict correctly conceived by the actors?	Displaced
System-dependent	Is the conflict generated by structural influence?	System-independent
Zero-sum	Will some actors win what the others lose?	Variable-sum
Co-operative	Can information be exchanged and coalitions built among the actors?	Nonco-operative
Means-oriented	Are additional data and appropriate analytic techniques sufficient, in principle, to bring the conflict to an end?	Goal-oriented
Formal	Do the actors recognize each other as legitimate parties in the conflict?	Informal
Institutionalized	Is there a well-established procedure for terminating the conflict accepted by all actors?	Ad hoc

'Competition' is a kind of perceived potential conflict. The competitors know that they cannot all achieve their goal, yet they take no action towards each other (Fink 1968:444). In sports like running the athlete does not have to communicate with his competitors, and he does not hamper them in any way. He competes simply by perfecting his own actions and lets the others alone. This is also so in the demand-supply scheme of a free market. The producers compete for customers by lowering the price. Those who produce most effectively survive, the others go bankrupt. Intense competition is likely to increase the number of manifest conflicts as, in practice, the potential/manifest border is often easily crossed. Some elbowing in the field of runners could be promptly repaid, changing competitors into enemies. Producers struggling for survival might be tempted by industrial espionage or advertisements placing competitors in an unfavourable light, possibly transforming competition into fight.

It is not clear what should be reckoned as 'personal conflict behaviour' in the table. Greater precision on this point is attained by introducing the distinction between fight, game, and debate from Rapoport (1960). The division is based on different attitudes towards the adversary. In a fight he is seen as an enemy and met with feelings of fear and hatred. The presence or existence of the enemy threatens one's own sovereignty. In a game the opposite party is conceived more neutrally as an opponent. As oneself, the opponent knows the rules of the game, follows them, and chooses the most beneficial strategy on the basis of rational analysis. In a debate one tries to win the other contenders for one's own ideas, one's own way to see the situation and the environment. The debaters are, thus, potential allies. In fights, games, and debates one aims to render harmless, outwit, and convince the adversary, respectively. In my exposition personal conflict behaviour encompasses fight, game, and debate. Even a debate would be classified as a manifest conflict in Table 6.1. This is in contrast to Coser, as games and debates are not included in his definition of conflict cited earlier in this section. Analytic technique and communication are both frequently applied to keep the controversy on the level of debate or game. The actors may be urged to await a technical analysis, or they are kept apart and persuaded to enter a mediation process.

Deutsch (1973) has proposed a distinction based on the possibility that the actors misconceive elements of the conflict situation. In a 'real' conflict the important elements are correctly conceived by all the actors. In other cases there may be misunderstandings concerning what the conflict is really about, who is the adversary, and which means are applicable for managing the conflict. Communication can transform the conflict in both directions. Distorted communication may cause displaced conflict. Information and debate may put things right. Technical analysis can have the same two effects of misleading and informing.

When a conflict is system-dependent, the social system has to change if the foundation of the conflict is to vanish. Change may be brought about by a revolution or by decisions made in the collective political organs. Even if the concept of a 'system' is applicable on several levels, I refer here to social systems in which such organs have the formal right to decide. Collective actors like a government or a county council are often part of the conflict. This is because all social systems are man-made, and it is up to the collective to change or defend them. The management of such conflict is usually facilitated by well developed communicative channels between the lay people and the elected political councils (Bergh 1983). In system-dependent conflict there does not have to be personal conflict behaviour, but the system functions so as to produce 'structural violence' in Galtung's terminology. One could call it systemic conflict behaviour; and such behaviour is hostile in effect, if not in intent. According to this, system-dependent conflict may or may not be manifest.

Zero-sum conflicts are easily transformed to fights. The room for communication is larger in variable-sum conflicts, because conversation can make clear which strategy will maximize the common benefits. It may be possible to negotiate a result in which both parties get more than they would obtain under a smaller total gain.

Nonco-operative conflicts offer no possibilities for communication, by definition. This may apply to some games where mutual information is forbidden by rule, or to fights where mental blocking prohibits communication with the enemy. Under these circumstances analytic techniques may take on increased importance, in an attempt to predict the operational goals and the strategy of the enemy.

Conflict over values can be distinguished from conflict over material resources. However, I will not give this difference further attention. Conflict over values corresponds to what I have called goal-oriented conflict. But instead of contrasting the immaterial with the material, I juxtapose ends and means. Goal-oriented conflict is about what one tries to achieve; means-oriented conflict is about how best to accomplish it, i.e., what is instrumentally rational. The delimitation of means-oriented and goal-oriented conflict is based on a clear-cut distinction between means and ends, assuming that preferences are attached to the latter only. In public planning, then, goals should emerge as the result of a communication process. Choosing and applying means would be a purely technical matter, instrumental optimality being secured by analytic technique alone. In reality the means-end distinction is blurred, and so the means-oriented and goal-oriented conflicts are not pure types.

When the parties do not accept each other, as in informal conflict, they often refuse to communicate directly. Sometimes an indirect contact via one or more external persons is nevertheless accepted. The role of the planner as an intermediary takes on particular importance in informal conflicts.

In institutionalized conflict it is predetermined how the communication process will run and, by and large, what kinds of technical analysis are to be carried out. One might say that the communication, having once been informal and ad hoc, has been refined, structured, and formalized into a procedure as a result of experience with recurring conflicts of a similar kind. Communication has been turned into a technique.

'Scale' and 'intensity' are not brought to the fore by the dichotomies in Table 6.1. There is a parallel to the domain and scope of a power relation. The scale can be described, for example, by the width of the field affected by conflict, the number of people involved, or the extension of the controversy in time and space. When the scale is reduced to zero, the conflict is by definition terminated.

Intensity can be given a directly observable and an only indirectly observable dimension. The first concerns the means - e.g., violence and other tools of power - deployed by the parties. The second describes the depth of their emotional involvement. The polar situations with regard to intensity may be designated 'extreme' and 'unconcerned'. These contrasting degrees of intensity denote the end-points on both the observable and emotional ordering. The intensity mirrors the actors' stakes in the conflict. When the parties approach the unconcerned state, they lose interest in the conflict, and personal conflict behaviour ceases. Unconcern is also found when conflict is latent, and potential conflict is marked by unconcern along the observable dimension. Intensity and scale are indispensable notions in the study of conflict dynamics, escalation, and management strategies. Varying intensity along the observable dimension is vital to the classification of fight, game, and debate.

Conflict management: pacify, settle or solve

The section starts with the identification of the main categories of outcome from conflict management. Pacification, settlement, and solution link stages of resolution to different kinds of conflict and to the power relations (force, manipulation, persuasion, and authority). This lays the foundation for a discussion of the relationships between concepts of conflict resolution and planning theories in a later section. The advantage to the construction of a comprehensive picture of power, conflict, and planning theories makes up for the inconvenience of having to get used to slightly unfamiliar concepts of resolution.

The main outcomes of conflict management:
pacification, settlement, and solution

The term 'conflict management' is used to designate all efforts to reconcile the challenging parties, reduce intensity or scale, mitigate the conflict - whether manifest or potential - and dissolve the conflict matter. Conflict management can aim at transforming the controversy from informal to formal, and from ad hoc to an institutionalized status. If these transformations are successful, an agreement might be easier to arrange. Conflict management can lead to a conditional and tentative halt in personal conflict behaviour or to lasting restrictions on the use of force. In planning disputes a truce is sometimes accepted while the stakeholders await a technical report or a mediation proposal. However, none of the above results are included in the categorization of negotiated resolutions below. Negotiation

151

is a broad term here, encompassing any kind of communication to reach a peace-arrangement with or without intervention from a third party. When 'conflict' can point to very different phenomena, it should not be expected that 'negotiated resolution' can be attributed the same meaning for all of them. The main outcomes of managing manifest conflict are:

Pacification,   implying a state of manifest conflict in which the exercise of force has ceased.

Settlement,   implying a state of manifest conflict in which force and manipulation are not in use.

Solution,   implying potential conflict, i.e., a state in which force, manipulation, and persuasion have stopped.

Even with the weakest resolution category much can be achieved, as pacification precludes violence. A 'settlement' has more desirable qualities, as it excludes both types of power relation usually considered to imply intrinsically malevolent conflict behaviour. It marks the transition to a state in which all acts of power are reciprocal in principle, and restricted to various techniques for more or less biased exchange of arguments. A 'solution' is reached by a transformation from manifest to potential conflict. Actors are no longer coerced or fooled by their contenders, and arguments are exchanged not to have one's way, but in search of agreement. With a behaviour-defined concept, implementation of a solution means that the conflict is ended. The above definitions deviate somewhat from the customary meanings of 'settlement' and 'solution' in sociological conflict theory.[2]

For groups recently involved in manifest conflict over an issue, avoiding persuasion will most likely mean not talking about the issue. When this is so, a solution implies that the conflict matter is withdrawn from the agenda of both contenders. Some tension may linger, but the parties choose to ignore it and shift attention elsewhere. Under a condition-based definition of conflict, the passivity following a solution does not necessarily mean the end of conflict. There are three possibilities:

a) The conflict is perceived but the contenders remain passive. Authority may conduce acceptance of the situation.

b) The conflict is latent; i.e., the parties are unaware that the conflict matter still exists. Authority may be in use to keep it that way.

c) The conflict matter is dissolved and there is nothing more to argue about. The conditions causing the conflict have disappeared.

Structural influence can be present under a) and b), so a smaller or larger change of the social system may be required to reach c). Settlements and solutions may be marked by structural influence. One should, therefore, not presume without reservation that the results of conflict management are fair.

The suppression caused by structural influence can be as hard to bear as the effects of most other power relations.

We are now in a position to see that negotiation does not guide us beyond situation a). Authority is hard to avoid or regulate by formal arrangements, because its exertion requires no action. Moreover, unconsciousness of the conflict matter cannot be a negotiation result. Surely, one can continue the efforts towards a dissolution of the conflict matter by integrative method, but the removal of conflict matter from the political agenda is as far as negotiation can take us.

Negotiation does not have the same contents in all conflict management. Pacification often requires an outside intervener because communication between the fighting parties is perverted or cut off. A deterioration of communication can be assumed when force is the prevalent power relation between the actors. They may have to be coerced into accepting the terms of armistice. Solution, on the other hand, must be a self-determined negotiation result - with the reservation that authority may influence the outcome. The quarrellers cannot be coerced to drop the conflict matter from their agenda because it is not the question of a formal act. It requires a mutual will to shift the attention to other issues. Settlement is a case in between, sometimes largely based on voluntary arrangement, sometimes including the pressure of an arbitrator or another intervener. Some co-operation on the side of the adversaries is needed, as manipulation cannot be prevented by decree alone. To sum up: pacification is often coerced, settlement may be partly coerced and partly self-determined, solution must be self-determined, not coerced. This suggests that the scope for integrating method increases as the parties work their way from pacification towards a solution. The procedures should increasingly be based on communicative rationality, and to a diminishing degree on instrumental reason, as the aspiration level rises in conflict management.

Liberation is enhanced by the development towards more lenient types of power relations. Progression from pacification to settlement and on to a solution would normally constitute such a process. Exceptions exist because liberation requires consciousness of the domination, which is not self-evident under structural influence. Latent conflicts may have to be transformed to perceived ones and often to manifest ones in order to get on with conflict management facilitating liberation. One can expect no fair settlement if one party is unaware of the systematic inequalities at the core of structural influence. The unmasking of authoritarian relationships giving ideological accounts of systematic social inequalities as 'natural' in some sense, is often the starting phase of an emancipation process.

Fight, game, debate, and the power relations

If it seems sensible to interconnect resolution types with power relations it should not be less so to define categories of conflict by means of the same power relations. Rapoport's (1960) tripartite classification into fight, game, and debate provides terms with useful connotations. Nevertheless, I redefine the concepts and place them in categories that he did not use:

Fight	is a conflict in which the actions of the combatants entail the use of force and can involve other power relations as well.
Game	is a conflict in which force is not present but manipulation always is.
Debate	is a conflict in which persuasion is present and authority is the only power relation that may be found in addition.

Authority can be part of all the three types of manifest conflict. The above classification is complete only when presupposing a behaviour-defined concept of conflict. With a condition-defined concept, the categories of potential and latent conflict can be added as before.

The definitions of the main outcomes of conflict management and the manifest types of conflict have the following implications:
- Pacification is logically possible only as an outcome of managing fights.
- Settlement is logically possible only as an outcome of managing fights and games.
- Solution is a logically possible outcome of managing all manifest conflicts.

As is frequently the case in tripartite classifications, the first and last types are extremes and as such quite easily grasped. The category in between needs further explication, which warrants a lengthy but illuminating quotation from Rapoport, spelling out the characteristics of a game:

> A game is characterized by an analysis of a *situation* and of *other situations* foreseen as outcomes of *decisions*, both one's own and those of an opponent. The distinction between an enemy and an opponent is crucial. Whereas the enemy is defined by associated emotions and attitudes (for example, as someone who is hated or feared), the opponent in a game is not. The attitude toward the *person* of the opponent may be neutral or even entirely friendly. The focus of attention is not on the presence of noxious stimuli in the person of the opponent but on the situation, which the opponent partially controls. It is desired to bring about another situation, but the outcomes of one's actions are determined only partially by one's own decisions. The decisions of the opponent also influence the outcomes. Consequently, rational analysis is an

indispensable feature of game behavior. The elimination of the opponent is not a central issue; the opponent is constrained by the rules of the game just as oneself is. A more desirable situation can be brought about by adopting a *strategy*, that is, a plan of action contingent on what the opponent can do in following his own interest. The type of conflict just described is, of course, typical of so-called games of strategy - chess, bridge, etc. The opponent in such a game is not typically a personal enemy who must be eliminated or constrained in order to safeguard one's autonomy. In fact, the opponent is more often a personal friend. The opponent *cooperates* in keeping the game going, and the process of playing the game is typically a pleasant experience. The pleasure of the experience derives from the struggle itself. Since victory in this case is meaningful only if the rules of the game are adhered to, the player's resources are mobilized toward rational analysis. The task is to bring about a desirable situation (to 'win') *within* the constraints imposed by the rules of the game, among which is the fact that the opponent is trying to frustrate one's efforts. The opponent is therefore a *necessary* feature of the environment and of the satisfaction derived from it.

(Rapoport 1974:181-2)

It is enlightening to juxtapose Rapoport's description with the prototype of manipulative behaviour demonstrated by Kierkegaard's seducer. A comparison reveals striking similarities between the specification of a game and the seducer's conceptualization of the stratagem he has figured out to conduct his affair with Cordelia. This suggests that the redefinition of Rapoport's categories in terms of the power relations preserves essential aspects of his original conceptional contents. I also think that the dissimilar views of the contender in fight, game, and debate support the idea of attaching each kind of conflict to different permissible power relations. Destroying the opponent would spoil the stimulating competition, it would be imprudent to eliminate a potential ally, etc.

Communicative distortions and bounds of varying seriousness are produced by the different types of conflict. Some of the communicative techniques listed beneath are applicable in more than one type of conflict. Nevertheless, I suggest that the following techniques are among those typically applied in fights, games, and debates, respectively:

In fights   (intending to hurt or coerce): censorship, threats, interrogation, backbiting, scolding, scorn, defamation, and informing against another (delating).

In games   (where the real intention is concealed, trying to outwit or misguide): lies, keeping secrets, spreading unfounded rumours, flattery, tapping or listening in on, and misinformation.

In debates   (where the intention is well known and one tries to fulfil it by inducing sympathy for a certain point of view): propaganda, advertising, education, agitation, rhetoric, indoctrination, and bragging.

By associating types of conflict with forms of communication, the power relations and resolution types are also related to communication. The main outcomes of conflict management are seen to imply the elimination of different communicative distortions. A conclusion is that planning, functioning as conflict management, should adjust to the communicative setting as a consequence of being contingent on the type of conflict and power relations predominant among the participating groups. The use of technique, being an intrinsic characteristic of planning, is contingent on the same kinds of variables, as will be shown.

Fights are not wholly rational; in fact, they are regarded by Rapoport (1960) as fundamentally irrational. Analytic technique takes no precedence over other means of forcing the enemy to disappear or give in. In a fight the communication is entirely instrumental, it is technique only. The role of analytic technique is to investigate which bag of tricks has the most destructive effects on the enemy within 'acceptable' limits. In contrast, the behaviour in a game has a rational character. Communication is designed as part of a rational strategy or stratagem. In other words, communication in games is subordinated to the analytic techniques of constructing strategies and choosing the optimal one. A debate in my sense is never fully communicatively rational, in that the search for truth and mutual understanding is never the only interest of debaters. There is room for rhetoric, and this is widened as the conversion of the other disputants is seen as more important than shared understanding.[3]

Conflict in types of planning theory

This section delineates how the sociological consensus-conflict debate is reflected in planning, and indicates how conflict and conflict management fit into synoptic and incremental planning theory. I explain why synoptic planning is logically compatible with a small part of the fights only, and with no other kind of manifest conflict. It is clarified why the synoptic process only has a modest conflict-reducing potential, and I point out the properties that may be useful after all.

Disjointed incrementalism is compatible with most kinds of conflict, and the features of learning and loops are conducive to negotiation. I examine how disjointed incrementalism can facilitate the attainment of pacification, settlement, and solution. There are increased opportunities for conflict management under incrementalism as compared to synoptic planning.

The consensus-conflict dimension in planning theory

The phrase 'consensus-conflict debate' is commonly used to describe a controversy that arose in sociology in the 1950s. It refers to a tendency to divide social theories into two contrasting groups on the basis of their descriptions of social processes. 'Consensus theories ... include those social theories that emphasize the persistence of shared values and norms as the fundamental characteristics of societies' (Bernard 1983:1). Conflict theories emphasize the dominance of some groups over others. Most of these theories regard conflicts between groups in society as natural and inevitable, often because humans are assumed to be naturally aggressive.

The consensus view of society is consistent with the idea of conflict being due to social anomalies, to abnormal or pathological conditions. It is seen to be caused by factors such as bad will, exaggerated egoism or inability to see the common good. Conflict is something superficial that is based on misunderstanding, misconceptions, insufficient information, and deficient communication. Those who hold a conflict view of society regard conflict as fundamental. It is seen as a normal form of human interaction, which might even have positive functions in the society (Coser 1956).

It is to be expected, then, that consensus and conflict theories correspond to very dissimilar views of planning. Advocacy planning is perhaps the purest expression of the conflict perspective on society. Economic planning based on welfare theory often exemplifies the harmony-approach. It is usually phrased in aggregate terms - the common good, the welfare of society - neglecting opposing groups and competing interests. Friedmann's (1973) transactive planning takes for granted a basic harmony and precludes the view of man as naturally aggressive. His Utopia is a society where no group dominates others.[4] It is acknowledged that conflict will arise, 'but conflict can be overcome by a mutual desire to continue the life of dialogue' (ibid.179-80). Conflict should be accepted as an inevitable part of dialogue and not be seen as a reason to terminate it. Dialogue will survive conflicts of interests because it fills a fundamental mutual need to discover oneself and strive for authenticity (ibid.178).

Elements of the consensus-conflict debate are recovered in the prevailing main dichotomy of planning theory. This is clear from Faludi's (1984:157) discussion of the principal modes:

> (R)ational-comprehensive planners desire a government to be an organization with centralized decision-making and a common purpose which

mirrors the common (or public) interest of the community. On the other hand, incrementalists perceive government as a collection of agencies, each having its own clientele, with perpetual conflict between them reflecting the ongoing struggle between groups in society, each with an interest of its own.

In synoptic planning there is an optimal solution despite power relations, and even if conflict should occasionally occur. Incremental planning assumes that conflicts are always present, restricting the politically feasible set of plans. What is finally implemented, is carried out because satisfactory agreement on that policy is attained, not because of any properties of optimality disconnected from the political situation.

Conflict in synoptic planning

Conflict in synoptic planning cannot be caused or kept up by misunderstanding, false consciousness or insufficient information. One will see that some of the conflict categories in Table 6.1 are incompatible with synoptic planning. If there is a conflict to be conscious about, the participant in synoptic planning will perceive it, so latent conflict is not a meaningful category. With information equalling that available from hypothetical dialogue, the conflict will be correctly conceived, so displaced conflict is out of the question. The occurrence of means-oriented conflict would mean that the knowledge of data or analytic technique is incomplete, which excludes such conflict from the synoptic process. Furthermore, nonco-operative conflict is not in harmony with synoptic planning, as all information can be acquired from the planners.

To many people, the synoptic procedure of option seeking, impact analysis, evaluation, and choice in itself possesses an intuitive appeal, that gives it some qualities as a conflict managing strategy. The parties of a potential fight may decide to accept the planning proposal, because the data processing and the algorithms leading to it seem impartial and reasonable. Perfect information provides some advantages in the handling of conflicts. The players do not run the risk of being misunderstood or manipulated. The preferences, intentions, and social perceptions are mutually known to all parties and can be used by negotiators to ascertain salient issues, to locate areas of possible trade-off, and to assign meaning to their opponents' actions. This is of significance as social judgement analysis has shown that distorted perceptions of goals, attitudes, and opinions of adversaries (stereotypes) are important impediments when working for a satisfactory conflict management result in practice (Brehmer and Hammond 1977).

I recall from Chapter 5 that manipulation and persuasion have no place when perfect information is assumed for all actors. Furthermore, conflicts involving force can be expensive, and most potential fights will not get off the ground when the actors know their relative strength and usually can predict the outcome of the conflict. One can conclude that the synoptic conditions rule out games and debates and minimize the number of fights. Integrating qualities are not decisive in managing fights, so the procedures of synoptic planning may be helpful. The algorithmic synoptic plan-making does, however, presuppose an accepted substantive notion of the public interest. Such a notion exists when an arbitrator's idea of the common good is given priority to the partial interests of the fighting actors. It also exists in a very different situation, namely when a solution to the conflict has been reached. Both manipulation and persuasion are then ruled out, which is in line with the synoptic conditions. In the conflict situations in between, instrumental reason is bounded by communicative rationality, and conflict management requires a planning process embracing both rationalities. Elements of dialogical incrementalism are helpful when working out settlements.

Synoptic planning theory is based on the assumptions of ample calculating capacity and knowledge of all issues that would hypothetically gain consensus, were the matter to be discussed in Habermasian dialogue. There would be agreement on facts, but not necessarily on future events. Even in dialogue, there might be different opinions of the likely outcome of a future conflict. An actor does not always know, then, whether he will win or lose if entering a conflict. Hence, the concept of fight is logically compatible with synoptic planning theory.

Even when the outcome of the fight is known beforehand, the prospective loser entering the conflict may be rational. He may be convinced that his qualities as a human being are determined by his actions: you are what you do. Then it is not enough for the actor to *know* that he has everything it takes to bear a fight against a stronger enemy; he will in fact have to endure it. The point is that he has to behave a certain way to be the kind of person he wants to be, regardless of material loss and gain. For instance, certain ideas of honour can render it practically unthinkable to comply with a demand perceived as unfair or insulting. I conclude that there is a case for manifest conflict even under perfect knowledge.[5]

There is also a case for potential conflict. This is especially so when the controversial question is not the only common concern of the parties. In some cases all parties benefit from a peaceful relationship because of future common business, and they therefore choose to abstain from action (Fisher and Brown 1988).

Conflict and disjointed incrementalism

The incremental process is designed as a search for agreement among stake-holders with viewpoints close to the existing policy. Allowance for the omnipresence of controversy is made already in its basic design. Conflicting interests and diverging perceptions of reality are seen as the normal situation in public planning. Disjointed incrementalism shuns conflict on goals and concentrates instead on being remedial, to build on (preferably common) experience of what is worth getting away from.

The weaknesses of the incremental strategy are the minor consideration for groups advocating substantial change, and the vagueness regarding which power relations can legitimately be established to keep such groups in check. Support is often most easily won for policies close to already familiar ones, and disjointed incrementalism may all too willingly bow to this fact. Incremental planning can motivate conflict because only a constricted range of alternatives is considered, and only a few impacts are predicted. Some groups may feel excluded, although incrementalists might argue that what is ignored at one point in policy-making becomes central at another point. Therefore, regard will be paid to most interests before the process is concluded. Still, groups in sharp opposition to the prevailing policy will have difficulties in squeezing their issues and proposals onto the agenda.

The pursuit of compromise may easily lead to excessive pragmatism and prohibit the many small steps from adding up to something desirable in the end. When the test of good policy is the achievement of agreement on policy itself, consensus may be ranked too high. The question of justifiability of the terms of consent is pushed into the background. Besides, the lack of a vision guiding the numerous small steps can make the stakeholders uncertain. What does a compromise really mean? What direction will the next few increments take? Will the compromise have lasting significance, or will it be undermined by the subsequent moves? Whether the agreement should be voluntary, forced or legitimate, and what should be meant by these terms, have been debated too little (Forester 1981). Surely, in principle one can go back and correct steps yielding untenable results for a group. But what would make powerful stakeholders accede to such a request? Even if the ideal of the mutually counterbalancing pluralistic democracy is attractive, the problems of power in incremental planning practice are not satisfactorily solved.

Force, manipulation, and persuasion are compatible with incrementalism, so no main type of outcome of conflict management is ruled out. An agreement under disjointed incrementalism may be a settlement or even a forced pacification. This planning mode may be used whether there is a fight, a game or a debate going on among the stakeholders. However, throughout fights it may be useful to introduce synoptic features, as already mentioned. The learning approach of incrementalism does not come into its full advantage under the stereotyping, the distortions of social judgement, and the breakdown of communication often observed during fights.

Under a settlement on the way towards a solution the aspect of the incremental strategy aiming at 'getting something done', the practical competence of muddling through, does not seem to be pertinent. The point now is that the disputed matter must be shown to be less important after all. The means-end structure of the challenging parties will gradually have to be rearranged to transform the conflict matter into a non-issue. And it must all be accomplished without manipulation. The integrative facet of communicative rationality must be exploited to the full. It seems appropriate to include elements of dialogical incrementalism when organizing a process aiming at the solution of conflict.

All the kinds of conflict in Table 6.1 may logically be present in incremental planning. However, the occurrence of zero-sum conflict and noncooperative conflict indicates that the incremental strategy has not been successful. The searching, pragmatic, small-step procedure is designed to avoid zero-sum situations because these easily result in an impasse. Compensation schemes are usually needed to create negotiation results that are fair enough and will be honoured by the participants. Furthermore, the exchange of information is the foundation of learning, and coalitions are usually required to reach sufficient agreement. Nonco-operative conflict is therefore atypical in incremental planning. Finally, in settings where preferences are attached to means, and ends are adjusted to the means at hand, means-oriented conflict will not be found as a pure type.

Communicative procedures in conflict management

The section treats the pro and con arguments of citizen participation in a consensus-conflict perspective, and considers whether communicative involvement procedures are likely to have a mitigating effect on planning conflicts. The conclusion is that the opposite effect may be just as likely. The opportunity to talk is not enough; the communicative negotiation process has to pay respect to certain principles to result in effective conflict management. A set of recommendations for structuring the process is discussed and compared to communicative rationality. Mediation is also considered from this point of view. Finally, a role as facilitator of dialogue is sketched.

The case for citizen participation can be developed along four main lines. When the process is the process is seen as the most important, the first two arguments can be used:

(1) Improve the process by making the product better:

   Citizen participation will increase the value of the process through demonstrated improvements of the plans. Personal growth depends on a feeling among the participants of having substantive influence.

(2) Improve the process directly:

   Citizen participation provides the planning process with independent qualities. There is value in a fair and educating process regardless of the outcome (the plan).

When the product is considered crucial, the below arguments are pertinent:

(3) Improve the product by making the process better:

   Citizen participation leads to more efficient planning and implementation of the product (the plan).

(4) Improve the product directly:

   Citizen participation causes increased efficacy, that is, plans more in accordance with the goals of the constituency.

The above survey is not necessarily based either on a purely conflict-oriented view of society or a purely consensus-oriented one. On the one hand, the acknowledgement of conflicting interests among affected groups forms much of the basis of the claims for open planning processes. On the other hand, the idea of exploiting this openness to the common advantage by participating in a collaborative effort organized by the planners, reveals a harmony-oriented belief in the existence of a common foundation for mutual understanding and reasonable compromise.

An opponent holding a strict conflict-view of society could easily reverse the four statements above. For instance, he might be convinced that, contrary to the assertion of statement (1), the process will be rendered valueless, because it will be clearly demonstrated that the lay participants have no influence on the important features of the plan after all. Since the consensus/conflict dichotomy has great bearing on how to argue for and against public involvement, I list some further pros and cons from a technocrat's and a lay participant's point of view:

Technocratic pro-participation consensus-view argument:

   A co-operative effort in which the planners will have the opportunity to present and explain their point of view properly, will vindicate the plans of the experts and show that they are also in the interest of the lay participants.

Technocratic pro-participation conflict-view argument:

It is easier to handle the conflicts before every aspect of the plan is worked out in detail. Techniques of authority, manipulation, and co-optation can also be used more effectively when the conflicting views are presented in an orderly manner.

Technocratic con-participation consensus-view argument:

It is unnecessary to involve lay people in the planning process, as the experts take care of their interests in the best possible way. Citizen participation would yield the same result after extensive idle chatting.

Technocratic con-participation conflict-view argument:

There are, indeed, deep conflicts of interest which cannot be solved, not even by all the talking in a citizen participation process. Public involvement would most likely give advantages to the strong and most articulate interest groups. The involvement of lay people should therefore not be encouraged. When the planning is conducted by the experts, one can at least ensure a technically and economically sound solution, and limit the costs of the planning effort itself.

Lay people pro-participation consensus-view argument:

We should participate to give information about how we want our physical environment to be.

Lay people pro-participation conflict-view argument:

We should use all the channels open to us, to press the experts to take our point of view into account and give us fair treatment.

Lay people con-participation consensus-view argument:

Participation is not worthwhile. The planners know how we feel about the plan anyway, because they are informed by the politicians. They will provide the planners with a more representative picture of social reality than would result if each of us were to state his or her claims directly. Our views will be duly considered and built into the public interest.

Lay people con-participation conflict-view argument:

They want us to participate to involve us in a discussion on their terms. They want us inside the decision-making system to make us 'responsible'. Protests and actions arranged by ourselves are more effective.

It should be evident by now that one can argue both for and against citizen participation from a conflict-view of society as well as from a consensus-view. Hence, citizen participation as such is not specifically linked to either the consensus-side or the conflict-side of the debate.[6]

Citizen participation as a harmonizing device

Citizen participation is consistent with a disjointed incremental planning process in which the information on preferences is imperfect. Politicians and public officials usually hope that the participation of lay people will bring a reduction in the scale and intensity of planning conflicts. This is also a common assumption in the planning literature, e.g., Amir (1972), Bruton (1980), Irland (1975), and Priscoli (1975). However, others have accentuated that the lay participants often focus on controversial aspects of the plan, and that involvement makes the preferences of the local public more stringent:

> The conventional wisdom holds that 'more and better' technical information will make it easier for decision-makers to determine the 'best' course of action. In practice, this is rarely the case. Putting more information into the hands of interested stakeholders often complicates their claims and guarantees that better documented statements are put before the decisionmakers.   (Susskind 1983:154-5)[7]

I think that Beesley and Kettle (1979:522) extract quite general experience in the following comments on the proposal of a British committee on trunk road planning:

> Clearly, the greater the time and ingenuity devoted to tracing the distribution of prospective welfare gains and losses, the more are conflicts likely to be uncovered and brought to life in argument over the choice to be made.

The ambiguous expectations concerning the net effect of citizen participation in controversial planning mirror a more generic dilemma registered in communication research: the more two individuals communicate, the more they agree. On the other hand, however, the closer they are, the more a statement of disagreement intensifies conflict (Hawes and Smith 1973). Alexander (1977) set out to provide a more definite answer to the question of what is the net effect, by undertaking a comprehensive examination of the research in the field. He distinguishes 'conflict of interest' and 'perceptual conflict'. The conclusion is that communication helps to manage conflict of interest. With respect to perceptual conflict, however, the effects of communication are equivocal. It seems to be less effective in reducing conflict over how a phenomenon is to be understood, than it is in mitigating conflict of interest (ibid.302).

Communication can be structured in various ways so as to be more effective in a process of conflict management. Among the most well-known structured group processes are the Delphi technique and the nominal group technique (Delbecq et al. 1975). Rohrbaugh (1976) has undertaken a comparative study of the conflict reducing effects of Delphi technique and social judgement analysis. Groups using the last technique reduced existing conflict significantly more and arrived at decisions that were significantly more accepted by their members than groups using the Delphi technique. The structured group processes imply learning and attitude change, which make these communicative techniques most at home in incremental planning.

Negotiation in participatory planning can benefit from adapting to a set of precepts that are also apposite in dialogue. They are set forth in *Getting to YES* (Fisher and Ury 1981), which is a (paradigmatic) strategy for resolving disagreement without resorting to coercion or domination. Fisher and Ury discuss five maxims for guiding the communicative search for mutually acceptable negotiation results. Below I exhibit the distortions resulting when the recommendations are not observed.

Do not bargain over positions: The stand one takes, one's attitude, always reflects underlying interests. The problem is attached to these interests while the ego is usually associated with the attitudes. The more I explicate and adhere to my attitude and my initial opinion and defend it against attack, the more I am bringing the dealings towards a deadlock. The harder I try to convince the other parties that it is impossible for me to relinquish my attitude, the more difficult it is to do so. Attitudes are confused with ego. I end up with arguments intended to save face, which is a distortion of the mutual interest in finding tenable arguments or negotiating an agreement attending to generalizable interests.

Separate the people from the problem: A problem in a certain area is frequently identified with the person being responsible for that area. Pointing out the problem - 'this housing estate pollutes the lake', 'the municipal properties are decaying', 'the main road is jammed again due to digging' - may be interpreted as a personal attack. When the problem is confused with the person, the relationship between the parties easily gets involved in the discussion of the conflict matter. If we do not succeed in counteracting this, the problem-oriented communication is distorted.

Focus on interests, not positions: Opinions may be directly incompatible, even though the underlying interests are not. The opinions are symptoms of interests that need protection, but they are usually not identical with these interests. Communication in conflict management should aim to uncover the concealed interests. It is essential to ask 'why' when the contenders take up certain standpoints. The real problem to be solved is one between conflicting interests, not one between irreconcilable opinions. When opinions are confused with interests and the argumentation turns away from the conflict of interest, it is a distortion of the problem-solving communication.

As an example, the inhabitants of a dwelling-area may want a speed limit of 30 km/h to improve traffic safety for the children. The police disagree because they have experienced that such low limits are neglected by many motorists. They do not have the capacity for sufficient control, and thus they fear that the proposed traffic signs will impair the respect for traffic regulations in general. The antithetic opinions refer to traffic signs, while the interest of the inhabitants concerns traffic safety. Conflict management can direct their attention towards speed-reducing traffic humps and narrow passes in the roadway.

Invent options for mutual gain: Failure to search for alternative possibilities indicates that one is catering for other interests than the creation of agreement on a mutually satisfying way out of the problem in question. Then it is no longer only the power of the best argument that counts. The search for solutions to one problem is hampered by concern for other problems. When these are not openly presented, the communication is distorted in the sense of being unduly limited, confined to only a subset of the possibilities for constructive action. As a rule, such a restriction makes it seem like all the useful answers are situated on a straight line between the opinions of the negotiators.

Insist on objective criteria: Fisher and Ury form this point as an appeal that the negotiation result should not be based on a demonstration of will, on stubbornness or repressive power relations. It is a plea not to relegate communicative rationality to the advantage of force and manipulation. These are distortions of the common search for a result that both parties judge to be reasonable and fair. One should insist on identifying objective criteria reflecting principles of social justice instead of risking a result determined by the clash of two isolated wills. The parties should bow to just standards, precedence, and normal practice, not to threats.

Critics claim that the strategy of *Getting to YES* is best suited for an unaggressive bargainer who is in a relatively weak position. It offers no comprehensive analysis of how to exploit or deal with the various kinds of force and manipulation in negotiation (McCarthy 1985:64). The problem of how to negotiate with people who do not feel committed to follow the above principles, is discussed in Ury (1991).

Mediation

Like the strategy of *Getting to YES*, mediation dissociates itself from coercion and brings communicatively rational elements into the negotiation process. An unequivocal standpoint is taken regarding the use of instrumental power. The mediation process recommended by Cormick and discussed by Amy (1987) is reasonably clear as to how an arrangement should be negotiated, what should be meant by an agreement, and what kinds of influence technique can be tolerated. Cormick (1982:3) describes mediation as follows:

> Mediation is a voluntary process in which these involved in a dispute jointly explore and reconcile their differences. The mediator has no authority to impose a settlement. His or her strength lies in the ability to assist the parties in resolving their own differences. The mediated dispute is settled when the parties themselves reach what they consider to be a workable solution.

According to process-oriented planning theory, the conflict management process is as essential as the terms of the agreement. This is in agreement with the mediation approach of Cormick. His ideas on intervention in environmental planning disputes are also in full harmony with the personal growth rationale, and self-determination is underlined: 'The basic ethical principle that the intervener should espouse is self-determination for all parties to a conflict' (ibid.1). This requires a pursuit of mutually derived and acceptable outcomes. Note that self-determination can result in the decision not to proceed with the attempt to negotiate a settlement or a solution.

Cormick's guidelines for mediation can be read as a specification of how agreement should be built in incremental planning. Three elements promoting self-determination are (1) information, (2) capacity for intended influence, and (3) opportunity for involvement. They are also needed for the functioning of the incremental process. The claim (1) is not for perfect knowledge but for dissemination of important information to all stakeholders. Point (2) says that each party to a dispute must have an independent source of power. Inviting individuals and organizations without a developed power base to participate in a 'joint' process, can be an effective strategy for preventing self-determination, e.g., by co-optation. Benevolence, patronage, or charity will not give self-determination. The third point is essential to make the parties honour the commitments made by those 'at the table'. Not only should all affected groups participate, but the representation should be effective. This is particularly a problem for groups that are inexperienced in negotiating and do not have an organizational structure conducive to developing, correcting, and ratifying positions.

The ideal self-determination strategy for intervention cannot be used in all circumstances. For example, when parties demonstrably at interest oppose an intervention process, it cannot proceed and still claim to pursue a mutually acceptable outcome. This may be the case for a challenging party not yet strong enough to negotiate an acceptable outcome. The time for mediation is not right until a power base is built warranting a strategy change from protest and confrontation to a co-operative mode of interaction.

Advocacy planners conceive it as their duty to assist groups lacking a power base. The question is whether it is possible to simultaneously negotiate interests on behalf of weak groups (or as a representative of public interests) and mediate between disputing parties. Forester has studied empirically how planners in local land use conflicts try to reconcile the different considerations by adjusting the negotiator and mediator roles. The tasks appear to collide in two fundamental ways:

> First, the interestedness of a negotiating role threatens the independence and presumed neutrality of a mediating role. Second, although a negotiating role might allow planners to protect less powerful interests, a mediating role threatens to undercut this possibility and thus to leave existing inequalities of power all too intact.   (Forester 1989:82-3)

Nevertheless, practical planners 'make do', and they have developed several strategies identified and explicated by Forester. When these are successful, some problems of power in incremental planning may be solved. Forester's strategies are not specifically designed to assist weak groups, but may nevertheless be used for this purpose. One may imagine a building permit case, in which the stakeholders are the local planning agency, the private developer, and the neighbours. I present the key words Forester uses to signify the strategies, and a few explanatory sentences:

1. The facts! The rules! - the planner as regulator: The planner works as a fact-finder preparing for the assessment and the institutionalized sanctioning process for plans. However, he also applies the facts for judging what is legitimate protection for the neighbours.
2. Pre-mediate and negotiate, representing concerns: The planner acts before manifest conflict arises. He anticipates and articulates 'the concerns of affected residents and changes the informal staff recommendation accordingly to search for an acceptable compromise with the developers' (ibid.89-90).
3. Let them meet - the planners as a resource: The planner arranges for the developer and the neighbours to meet on their own in an informal way at an early stage of the planning process. He prepares the neighbours' representatives for the meeting but seldom meets jointly with the two parties. The planner stands back but is accessible as a resource for both to draw on.
4. Perform shuttle diplomacy, probe and advise both sides: The planner mediates actively, although mostly dealing with one party at a time. He

applies this 'shuttle' technique to obtain a freer role as a professional. It enables him to be frank to the neighbours without having to worry about how the developer can cash in on remarks and advice given.

5. Active and interested mediation - thriving as a non-neutral: The planner is invested both professionally and emotionally, in that he wants the process to be credible and the product to be successful. He knows that emotion and substance are interwoven, and tries to build trust by careful listening and by acknowledging and respecting thoughts and feelings. Real evidence is not ignored, but introduced by letting the parties anticipate each others' arguments and prepare a defence.

6. Split the job; you mediate, I'll negotiate: 'When local planners feel they cannot mediate disputes themselves, then, one strategy may be to search for informal, most likely volunteer, mediators ... (T)heir facilitation of meetings between disputing parties can allow planning staff to participate as parties professionally interested in the site in question' (ibid.96).

I will leave it at this, only adding that since negotiations always involve questions of relative power, they depend heavily upon the parties' pre-negotiation work of marshalling resources, developing options, and organizing support. Thus, 'planners will need both organizing and mediated negotiation skills if conflicts are to be addressed without pretending that structural power imbalances do not exist' (ibid.102).

Facilitation

There are several forms of assisted negotiation. Susskind and Cruikshank (1987) deal with facilitation and nonbinding arbitration besides mediation. I conclude this chapter with a few comments on facilitation, because this conflict management technique can be given new contents in a planning process aiming at dialogue.

The facilitator focuses almost entirely on process and 'uses whatever tools are available to create and foster an environment conducive to joint problem solving' (ibid.152). The task is not only to take care of the practicalities, like arranging meetings and ensuring that notes and minutes of the meetings are kept. The facilitator establishes contact between the parties, gets them to the table, and sometimes even acts as a moderator.

Susskind and Cruikshank state that the facilitator's emphasis is on monitoring the quality of communication. The facilitator intervenes with questions designed to enhance mutual understanding. Discussion approaching Habermasian dialogue is very demanding, and it is probably necessary with an impartial intermediary checking that commonly agreed rules are observed. Are all parties given the same opportunity to set forth their points of view? Are the real goals and intentions openly stated? Are arguments backed by reason or power? The facilitator has the difficult task of looking after the ideal role taking: he should find ways to make the disputing parties show empathy towards the problems and worries of their contenders. This is at the core of dialogical planning.

Notes

1 Pondy (1967:299) provides a clarifying classification, which covers the gap between the definitions of Coser and Boulding, and which is in accordance with concepts to be introduced later. The first four stages of a conflict episode as he sees it, are
  1 Latent conflict   (conditions)
  2 Perceived conflict   (cognition)
  3 Felt conflict   (affect)
  4 Manifest conflict   (behaviour)
  The notion of conflict is gradually given a more restricted content as one proceeds down the list. For a discussion of behaviour-defined versus condition-defined conflict definitions, see Fink (1968:433-40).

2 Usually the term 'settle' is used when a manifest conflict is transformed so that personal conflict behaviour no longer takes place. A conflict is commonly regarded as 'solved' only when the cause of the controversy is eliminated. In bringing together the resolution concepts and the power relations the way I do, the distinction between settle and solve becomes somewhat less decisive. There has been a debate in peace research between proponents of the settle-approach and the solve-approach to conflict management (Wiberg 1975:201).

3 Rapoport (1960:273) emphasizes the distinction between 'debate' and 'argument'. In his terms, a dispute over verifiable facts is an 'argument', and this is, thus, a kind of means-oriented conflict. A 'debate' is not resolvable by rational procedures alone; it results from a clash of (partly) incompatible images. Both kinds of dispute may be debates in my sense. When a debate cannot be terminated by facts (Rapoport's debate-category), rhetoric will have priority to technique. When the debate can, in principle, be brought to an end by appropriate facts (Rapoport's argument-category), analytic technique can play an important role.

4 The position of Etzioni (1968) is more ambiguous. He seems to consider disagreement the natural or basic situation, stating that 'dissensus is the entropic state of societal nature; consensus is not found but must be produced' (ibid.470). However, he also states that even if societal actors

tend to 'resist' each other in the sense of hampering each other's actions, 'this is not to imply, as has been suggested, that conflict is the prevailing mode of societal relations' (ibid.317). Etzioni thinks it is possible with a high degree of consensus in society. His vision of 'the active society' requires both extensive control and consensus-building:

> The level of societal activeness affects the extent to which consensus-building is required: The more a society 'gets done', the more the differences in the values, interests, and viewpoints of the members 'need' to be resolved. (Etzioni 1968:468)

5 There is an additional reason for actors to enter a manifest conflict although sure to be defeated. In some cases both winner and loser will gain from the fight. A trade-off can exist between disadvantages as measured in instrumental terms and advantages as assessed by communicative rationality. An economic loss may, e.g., be offset by strengthened group identity and improved solidarity fusing the group into a unit more capable of resisting pressure from the surroundings (Coser 1956). However, entering a conflict over economic matter knowing that the only gains to be hoped for are improved group identity and solidarity would be paradoxical. If the members of a group are willing to be involved in a fight on these terms, it means that they already possess the group qualities aimed for, and the entire struggle is deprived of rationality. The desirable integrative effects have to be realized as by-products of entering a fight to acquire other gains. For the mechanism to work, there must be some possibility to win whatever is disputed. (The enigma encountered here is reminiscent of the Rosa Luxemburg paradox mentioned in Note 10 of Chapter 5.)

6 Sager (1990a:Ch.3) deals with legitimation of planning in a consensus-conflict perspective. I discuss the relationships between citizen participation and legitimizing concepts like equality and the public interest.

7 Susskind (1983) offers recommendations for negotiation in a hybrid process sometimes met in the planning literature. The feature of a rather comprehensive impact assessment is inherited from the synoptic process. The telos of his negotiation approach, namely that the purpose of impact assessment should be consensus building, is more at home in incremental planning.

Part three　Neither command nor chaos: responsiveness and flexibility in planning

Part three discusses how the communicatively ideal planning model can be modified to form a practical problem-solving mode in a society replete with conflict and structured for a large part by asymmetric power relations. The part deals with four types of attempts to plan in a context of controversy. (1) The effort may be opportunistic, meaning that the endeavour to introduce change is not conducted according to principles or criteria. (2) The planning may be rigid so that it does not adapt to significantly changed circumstances. (3) Input to the process may clash with planning system resistance and produce threatening conflict. Attempts to handle the conflict can pervert the planning effort and cause serious bounds on rationality (parapraxis). (4) Planning may be organized so as to adjust to pressure and changed circumstances in a principled though flexible fashion not leading to irrationality.

The ensuing chapters clarify the notions above and explain the meaning of responsiveness and reflection-in-action. Some reasonable demands are made on planning in light of the critical theory of communicative action. Planning should be questioning in order to direct attention to mismanagement and social distortions. It should, however, also be answering, since planners have to be responsive if dialogue is to be approached.

The conceptual analysis lays the foundation for critical pragmatism. This planning mode accentuates responsiveness and flexibility without renouncing the critical social consciousness of Forester's 'questioning and shaping attention' approach, and without abandoning the commitment to dialogue at the core of dialogical incrementalism. Responsiveness is close at hand when searching for strategies that can relieve the strain caused by the control aspect of planning. Flexible and reliable planning seems to be the proper response to an environment aiming at conflict solutions, insisting on persuasion instead of force and manipulation, favouring fairness and democracy in collective choice processes, and legitimizing by appealing to equality and community.

It may prove helpful at this advanced stage to recapitulate how the three parts of the book contribute to the discussion of the major themes already introduced. First, there is the perspective of mainstream planning theory. The synoptic/incremental distinction is made clearer by the introduction of communicative rationality in Part one. The dichotomy is deepened in Part two by showing that different concepts of power and conflict correspond to synoptic planning and dialogical incrementalism. Part three explains that the two planning modes exhibit very different characteristics of flexibility and rigidity. The second theme is the communicate/calculate distinction. Part one clarifies the role of dialogue and analytic technique in the planning theories. Part two examines how communication and calculation enter the power relations of force, manipulation, persuasion, and authority, as well as the types of conflict management. Part three spells out the meaning of flexibility under instrumental and communicative rationality.

7 Striking a balance between opportunism and rigidity

Manifest conflict can profoundly affect the succeeding development of the planning process. Three inferior directions are defined in this chapter. They are opportunism, rigidity, and parapraxis. The last mentioned outcome is a compromise characterized by irrationality. Flexibility in planning is described as an attractive compromise, a principled-adjustment outcome of conflict. It is argued that planning should be responsive, and such practice has an answering aspect and a flexibility aspect. Donald Schön's concept of reflection-in-action is treated as a background condition for responsiveness. In the appendix I maintain that posterior reasoning is a type of bound on instrumental rationality that has relevance for responsiveness. This is illustrated by the difficulties created by posterior reasoning when it comes to deciding what is flexible behaviour and what is opportunism. The discussion also shows the relationship between posterior reasoning and the 'backward mapping' approach to implementation. Posterior reasoning and reflection-in-action promote responsiveness by adjusting preferences to experience.

Outcomes of conflict between the planning system and defying impulses

The purpose of this brief section is to clarify the relations between the main concepts in this part of the book. These concepts relate to the ability of the planning system to adjust and to be rational. It will be shown that there is a link between the degree of success and the power and conflict themes of Part two.

The object of analysis is the public planning effort, for instance the planning of a new airport, regarded as a system. The system requests protection in order to maintain and improve the quality of process and product, and to secure the working conditions and the personal integrity of the planners. Protection is required because the system is constantly challenged by impulses questioning or disobeying its principles, goals, etc. The potentially harmful impulses spring from needs, wishes, and ideas reflecting the partial interests of actors inside and outside the system. The encounter between the recalcitrant impulse and the resisting system breeds conflict. The outcome is attempts to plan that are of widely varying quality. Four main types of planning endeavours are listed in the right column below.

$$\left.\begin{array}{c} \text{Impulse demanding satisfaction} \\ \updownarrow \\ \text{System requesting protection} \end{array}\right\} \rightarrow \text{Conflict} \rightarrow \left\{\begin{array}{l} \text{Opportunism} \\ \text{Parapraxis} \\ \text{Flexibility} \\ \text{Rigidity} \end{array}\right.$$

Opportunism and rigidity are outcomes marked by extreme reaction to the impulse. In the first case the safeguarding needs of the system are ignored, and the particular interests have their way in full measure. The second case reverses the situation, and even reasonable input, suggestions, etc. are rejected by the system. Rigidity wards off danger in the short run, but a non-adapting system may be less viable in the long run. Something between is clearly called for. However, a compromise is not by definition a good solution. When the conflict is sufficiently menacing, the planners may be unable to face it in a rational manner. They can use tricks and make analytical and procedural short-cuts to keep clear of the conflict. Planners can try to gloss over or sweep the controversial material under the carpet, acting as if the conflict did not exist. Bounds on rationality can add up as a result. A compromise based on conscious or subconscious efforts to evade the sight of danger can be highly suboptimal, and the subsequent planning may suffer from aggregated irrationality - or parapraxis, as it will be called here. Flexibility characterizes a compromise that does not imply significant bounds on rationality. The conflict must be acknowledged by the actors involved and be managed openly and communicatively to maximize the likelihood of finding a rational outcome. The power of the system relative to the power of those backing the impulse determines if the outcome will be planning characterized by opportunism, compromise, or rigidity.

The question now is what can be done to prevent that the outcome of conflict is planning belonging to one of the three unsatisfactory categories. Important concepts of Part three help to provide an answer. 'Reflection-in-action' and 'responsiveness' are ways of thinking and acting to avoid the extremism of opportunism and rigidity. Consensual approaches to resolving public disputes, like the mediation described in Chapter 6, also point towards a resolution of the problem (Susskind and Cruikshank 1987).

'Critical pragmatism' is the last of the central notions. It is a planning approach designed as a 'questioning talking cure' with the purpose of counteracting parapraxis. Aiming at dialogue is meant to loosen the bounds on communicative rationality. Working along the lines of investigative journalism, action research, and critical questioning is meant to relax the bounds set on instrumental and communicative rationality by illegitimate power relations.

How to distinguish opportunism and rigidity from flexibility

The main purpose of the section is conceptual clarification. I want to determine the meaning of the flexibility-rigidity distinction and assess its usefulness in defining responsiveness and analysing theories of planning. The concept of 'reflection-in-action' is presented, and I use it to mark out flexibility from opportunism on one hand and from rigidity on the other. It is claimed that reflection-in-action is a requisite for flexibility, and that opportunism is irreconcilable with planning. The contents of the thought process of reflection-in-action are outlined.

The concept of reflection-in-action

'Reflection-in-action' is delineated below by using phrases from the works of Donald Schön (1983, 1986, 1987). A related idea, 'review while implementing', was set forth by Etzioni (1968:287) as an element of his mixed scanning. Reflection is a process of turning thought back on a surprising phenomenon and, at the same time, back on itself. Reflection is at least in some measure conscious, although it need not occur in the medium of words. Much of our knowledge is tacit, implicit in our pattern of action and in our feel for the stuff with which we are dealing. What distinguishes 'reflection-in-action' from other reflection is its immediate significance for action. 'The performer reflects in action in the sense that his or her thinking occurs within the boundaries of ... a stretch of time within which it is still possible to make a difference to the outcomes of action' (Schön 1986:243). Reflection-in-action establishes an interaction between understanding and change. The problematic situation comes to be understood through the attempt to change it, and changed through the attempt to understand it.

Reflection-in-action is a thought process with an inner logic according to which reflection on the unexpected consequences of one action influences the design of the next one. Below I quote the six points used by Schön (ibid.) to describe the process. Each point is supplemented by an example from the planning of the Trondheim toll ring dealt with in Chapter 4.

1. In the context of the performance of some task the performer spontaneously initiates a routine of action that produces an unexpected outcome.

When planning the toll ring in Trondheim, hearings were arranged on where to situate the toll stations. Written statements were invited from all the local communities.

2. The performer notices the unexpected result that he or she construes as a surprise - an error to be corrected, and anomaly to be made sense of, an opportunity to be exploited.

Some communities were slightly in favour of the ring because of the improved main road system to be built. Others argued against based on principle or because they feared increased through traffic in their neighbourhood. These kinds of statement were expected. What surprised the planners was the massive resistance expressed by one particular community named Trolla.

3. Surprise triggers reflection, directed both at the surprising outcome and the knowing-in-action that led to it. It is as though the performer asks 'What is this?', and at the same time, 'What thoughts and strategies of mine have led me to produce this?'

Trolla is situated on a steep, north-oriented hillside sloping downwards towards the fjord. This suburban village is rather isolated from the rest of the populated areas around Trondheim, except for the road leading into the city. Would Trolla be particularly disadvantaged by the toll ring? Do the people there have especially little use for the planned roads, cycle tracks, etc.? Was the idea of a toll ring conveyed very inadequately to the inhabitants of Trolla?

4. The performer restructures his or her understanding of the situation - his or her framing of what is going on, or the strategy of action he or she has been employing.

It turned out that the foundation of the uncompromising protest is the isolation of Trolla. There is little supply of local service in the community, so people have to go outside Trolla for nearly everything. And in contrast to people in other suburban areas, the people of Trolla would not be able to escape the road tolls by changing the destination of their trips. They would have to pass the ring even if the destination was located outside of it.

5. On the basis of this restructuring, the performer invents a new strategy of action.

The planners were aware that the Trolla community had an important ally in the visitors to Trondheim from the hinterland on the other side

177

of the fjord. The road from the ferry landing passes through Trolla. People crossing the fjord objected to the toll ring, claiming that they had enough expenses already, paying the car ferry tickets. The planners suggested to the politicians that the future revenues from Trolla and the ferry traffic might not compensate for the political trouble that could be raised in a critical phase for the toll ring.

6. The performer tries out the new action, running an on-the-spot experiment where he or she interprets the results as a solution, an outcome which is generally satisfactory, or else as a new surprise that calls for new reflection and experiment.

The thought of dropping the planned toll station between Trolla and Trondheim was aired. Could the adjustment be made without stirring up a torrent of objections from other communities? If some pay less, then of course others have to pay more. Finally, the toll station on the road to Trolla was cancelled.

These reflections were made while they could still make a difference to the outcome of action. They are reflections-in-action made before the toll ring was implemented.

A surprise always catches our attention. Reflection-in-action can be viewed as the mental activity enabling us to exploit the initial surprise. It works to unite the expository questioning improving our understanding and the mobilization of attention necessary to achieve change. Reflection-in-action has a critical function, questioning the assumptional structure of the sorts of (partly tacit) knowledge revealed in our intelligent action (Schön 1987:28). This line of reasoning integrates reflection-in-action with the view of planning as questioning and shaping attention.

Assume, now, that politics is the action we have in mind, and that planning is conceived as consisting of both plan-making and implementation. Public planning itself may then be seen as future-oriented reflection-in-politics. Planning is part of the political process, not prior to it; therefore, it is not only reflection but reflection-in-action.

Critics have argued that simple forms of incrementalism do not answer to this description. When incrementalists argue that, by thinking small and constantly reacting to feedback, they can manage without recourse to any theoretical understanding of the system, Goodin and Waldner (1979) call it 'muddling through black boxes'. They regard such incrementalism not as reflection-in-action but as 'unreflective reaction'. 'Whereas the ordinary decision maker who is confronted with new data feels obliged to try to understand it, the incrementalist needs only to react to it' (ibid.3).

Flexibility as the principled-adjustment part of the opportunism-rigidity continuum

The range of responses to changed circumstances stretches from no adjustment, through adjusting while keeping an eye on principles, to the acceptance of any adjustment serving the immediate self-interest of the actor. In my terminology behaviour of the first kind is rigid, the second is flexible, and the third is opportunistic. I go on now to say some more of what characterizes rigidity, flexibility, and opportunism. And I use the terms not only to describe behaviour, but also a plan, an implemented product, or a planning process (a strategy).

Rigidity implies unwillingness or a lack of ability to adjust to a changing situation. The inadequate adjustment may be caused by resistance to change, because the actor does not see that the new conditions require that things are done differently. Or the actor may feel stuck and without opportunities to improve his or her position. Rigid behaviour follows certain patterns which the actor might not be able to break away from; as when a person refuses to relinquish stereotypes even when faced with information contradicting it. When characterizing plans etc., rigidity means that it is very costly or in other ways hard to alter them sufficiently.

Opportunism is at the opposite end of the continuum. *Webster's New Twentieth Century Dictionary* defines opportunism as the policy or habit of adapting one's actions, thoughts, and utterances to circumstances. One may be an opportunist in politics, in order to further one's immediate interests without regard for basic principles or eventual consequences. In Faludi's words it means putting expedience before principle, and it implies a failure, or unwillingness, to recognize the wider implications of decisions. In his setting, opportunism implies a failure 'to think simultaneously on the level of the overall land regime and the individual plot of land' (Faludi 1987: 209).

In institutional economics opportunism is self-interest seeking with guile. Opportunism is used to describe the market-behaviour of consumers and producers who are dishonest, disguise intentions or preferences, distort data, obfuscate issues, and otherwise confuse transactions (Williamson 1981:554). Guile is, however, no necessary feature of opportunism as I use the term.[1]

We will now see how opportunism is linked to some of the central concepts of the study. One can calculate what is sensible to do provided that one or more goals are given and some principle of rational action is attended to. But opportunistic behaviour neglects principles and deviates from goals in order to cater for the felt needs of the moment. Calculation of solutions requires rules, while opportunistic action breaks them. Besides, when there are two or more parties, the choice of an opportunistic action cannot be the result of communicatively rational deliberation. In a free discussion one will not agree to behaviour serving the myopic self-interest of one of the actors. Hence, opportunistic action follows neither from dialogue nor from analytic technique.

Banfield once commented on the difference between planning and opportunistic action:

> A plan (unless we depart very far from customary usage) is a decision with regard to a course of action. A course of action is a sequence of acts which are mutually related as means and are therefore viewed as a unit; it is the unit which is the plan. Planning, then, as defined here, is to be distinguished from what we may call 'opportunistic decision-making', which is choosing (rationally or not) actions that are not mutually related as a single means. (Banfield 1959:362)

There is an element of strategic thinking in planning which is wanting in opportunistic decision-making. 'Opportunistic planning' is a contradiction in terms according to Banfield. This inference can be combined with that of the last passage. Since synoptic planning is a largely calculative process, it is not compatible with opportunism. And since the kind of incrementalism I have identified as its most worthy opposite implies communicative rationality and dialogue, this cannot be opportunistic either. Even when opportunistic decision-making is compared with very short-range incremental planning without operational goals, there is a marked difference in that disjointed incrementalism observes some principles or rules. For instance, change is to be brought about by steps which are so small that failure can be easily corrected. And there is to be sufficient agreement on whichever action is taken. No such rules are obeyed in opportunistic decision-making. If it makes sense to use the term 'collective opportunism', disjointed incrementalism can be characterized as rule-bound with respect to procedure and collectively opportunistic with regard to direction. Dialogical incrementalism dispenses with this collective opportunism.

I have now pinned down the poles of the opportunism-rigidity continuum and am going to characterize some states in between, which will be called flexible. The core of the 'flexibility' concept is that something (A) can be easily adjusted if something else (B) changes unexpectedly. Here we may think of A as a phenomenon or object that is partly under our control, e.g., a plan. B may be influenced by us to some extent or be entirely outside our control. It is not enough, however, that A can be changed. It is conceivable that change in A might occur without steering from the planners, and in a way resulting in very low goal achievement. The concept of flexibility implies a *controlled* alteration of A by which satisfactory goal achievement is maintained. Houses and other built structures should be adjustable, as they have long durability and their functions change over time. They are flexible when they retain their functionality in changed circumstances.

Furthermore, flexibility implies a capacity for *future* change. There must be opportunities to adjust A in the future if B changes in the meantime. Accordingly, flexibility should be defined within a dynamic scheme comprising end-states and stages of intermediate decisions, rather than within a static means-end scheme. For instance, substitutability among the input factors of production is not in itself flexibility. Neither is the ability to reach several goals or to employ numerous means at the same time. Thus, the essence of flexibility is not that we have many options in a fixed state of the planning environment, but that we can preserve a number of satisfactory options under changing environmental constellations.

There is no contradiction inherent in the term 'flexible planning'. Flexible decisions are different from opportunistic ones in that they respect some principles and values, and do not necessarily convey self-interest. Concordance with principles and values does not, however, come of itself. Reflection on one's own practice is requisite to prevent losing sight of values and thus to hinder adjustment from being short-sighted and unprincipled. Reflection-in-action is a line of defence against opportunism.

Reflection-in-action is also a bulwark against rigidity. Reflections on one's own way of thinking, one's role frame, conflicting goals, unintended consequences, and other puzzles and dilemmas furnish the mind with the impulses necessary to reinterpret and reformulate the problem in situations where one is about to get stuck. The ambition is to obtain a sort of flexibility, to adjust in a manner creating future opportunities when the old ones are closed. This is illustrated by Schön (1983) with case studies from a number of professions.

Through reflection-in-action one achieves flexibility by entering what Schön (1987:31) denotes 'a reflective conversation with the materials of a situation'. 'Conversation' is here used in a metaphorical sense, and some of the important 'back talk' of the situation comes as the display of unintended effects:[2]

> Each person carries out his own evolving role in the collective performance, 'listens' to the surprises ... that result from earlier moves, and responds through on-line production of new moves that give new meanings and directions to the development of the artifact. The process is reminiscent of Edmund Carpenter's description of the Eskimo sculptor patiently carving a reindeer bone, examining the gradually emerging shape, and finally exclaiming, 'Ah, seal!'   (Schön 1987:31)

Although the outcome might have been another arctic animal or some Eskimo artifact, a seal did probably not come as a big surprise. After all, when the problem-solving is flexible, one always asks whether the found procedure and solution are congruent with one's fundamental values and theories.[3]

The task of reflection-in-action is not to make the search for a better solution go on forever. Reflection must comprise the balance between the quality of solutions found so far and the likely costs of improving them. One never escapes the shift from embracing freedom of choice to acceptance of implications, from exploration to commitment (Schön 1983:102-3).

Responsiveness

The aim here is to define the concept of responsive planning and discuss the role of responsiveness in various theories of planning. I do not embark on a general discussion of the place of responsiveness in democracy, or responsiveness as a criterion for deciding what is an improvement of public policy. It should be kept in mind throughout that the planners in many cases work according to a mandate drawn up by elected politicians. Democracy is not necessarily improved if the planners strain the mandate in an effort to please interest groups.

A conceptual discussion

According to Getter and Schumaker (1978:249),

> (m)ost scholars agree that responsiveness occurs when citizen concerns and activities, treated as input variables, are reflected in public policy, treated as output variables. A lack of responsiveness occurs when policymakers adopt and implement policies which are independent of, and contrary to, citizen concerns.

A more narrow definition of responsiveness in planning emerges when only the answering aspect in point (1) below is taken into account. A broad concept like that above will also include the flexibility aspect.

(1)   Communication: A minimum content of responsiveness is that the planners are in fact answering complaints, enquiries, requests, proposals, etc. The result is two-way communication, but not necessarily in accordance with the dialogical ideal. Answering is a kind of symbolic responsiveness. This is public gestures meant to create a sense of trust and support in the relationship between the planners

and the populace (Eulau and Karps 1977:246). Responsiveness as answering goes beyond the purely critical perspective: planning should provide answers as well as questions, and this emphasizes planning as problem-solving.

(2)   Flexibility: Adequate response beyond answering can be given only when there are possibilities for satisfactory solutions other than the one initially chosen. However, just providing the possibility does not give a broader concept of responsiveness. Flexible planning and thus responsiveness require both the possibility and the willingness to make concessions. The opportunity for adjusting the process and the product must be seized to some extent.[4]

The last section made clear that flexibility refers to the future choice among satisfactory alternatives. Responsiveness based on flexibility implies adjustment in accordance with principles and criteria, which excludes opportunism. This means that democratic planners would not be required to fully reflect profoundly antidemocratic or racistic sentiments if such values are held by the public. Adjustment can be made, e.g., when the commonly accepted view on fairness requires so. Or when the adjustment does not detract from the plan as a tool serving the public interest. The answering aspect is procedural, while the adjustment aspect concerns both process and product.

Responsiveness can alternatively be seen as preference-policy congruence. Eulau and Karps (1977:249) point out that with this definition, 'responsiveness' and 'response' are not the same thing. The congruence is not obtained only by the planners responding. They are sometimes supposed to be active as well as reactive. The planners can take the initiative and use their technical competence to suggest projects catering for community needs. And they can influence public opinion by giving the project an attractive design.

When such initiatives are supported by citizens, policymakers should not be labeled unresponsive merely because the initiative does not come from the people ... (C)itizens seem better able to generate meaningful preferences in response to policymaker behaviour than to articulate policy initiatives ...   (Schumaker 1981:230)

One advantage of the congruence approach to responsiveness is that it does not require the disentangling of the causal processes in the citizen-planner relationship. By responsiveness I shall nevertheless mean points (1) and (2) above if not otherwise specified.

I will not go into detail on the question of to whom or what the planners should be responsive. One possibility is that the planners should give answers in a manner furthering the principle of equal regard. The principle implies that the planners must not only treat people with concern and respect, but with equal concern and respect with regard to the distribution of goods and opportunities (Dworkin 1977:272-3). Even if the concept of equal regard is still quite indeterminate, it is common to the different interpretations that some sacrifices of one person for another are permissible, but that a limit is imposed by everyone's equal status as moral persons (Griffin 1985:152).

One could also assert that planners should be responsive to the public interest. The idea is problematic, however, since this would allow the planners to claim responsiveness without adjusting to the viewpoints of any group at all. The problem does not arise with the definition of responsiveness as answering. With the broader definition, however, goal conflict can turn up between responsiveness and pursuit of the public interest (Saltzstein 1985:291-2). A weak kind of responsiveness is usually assumed by social choice theory. The individual preferences are decisive, and if each person wants a shift of policy from x to y, the device aggregating the individual preferences must rank y above x (Arrow 1963). The Pareto principle says that y should be chosen if at least one person wants the shift and nobody is against it.

Principled response requires that the planners reflect on the requests for change. Reflection-in-action has an inner logic according to which reflection on the unexpected consequences of one action influences the design of the next one. It is a mental treatment of surprising input to the planning process. Reflection-in-action takes place while it is still time to influence the result, i.e., during the process of acting. To lay the basis for responsiveness, it is necessary for reflection-in-action not to be afterthought or retrospection.

Responsiveness has its costs. The planners will find it more difficult to make credible commitments the more people expect them to be responsive. That is, a reputation for responsiveness restricts the current strategies available to the planners. They lose the possibility of committing themselves not to respond (Rodrik and Zeckhauser 1988), and so flexibility bites its own tail. The general public often demand that the government take action when a threatening social problem arises. The demand may be, e.g., to clear up pollution from a large number of sources. When a public agency is expected to act responsively and it engages to solve the problem (often) created by private actors, the last mentioned will have weaker incentives to abstain from the detrimental behaviour in the future. Hence, the dilemma is that government responsiveness may foster private opportunism (ibid.).

Synoptic planning, although based on comprehensive information, gives some room for learning and adjustment. Thus, it is logically possible to be responsive, but the planners have no obligation to be so. On the contrary, the synoptic planner is loyal to the impact assessment (IA) and not to any interest group. The plan is adjusted only if it improves its score in the IA, and the alternative ranked first by the IA may be taken to express the public interest. However, the IA does only evaluate the product, and it may still be asked how synoptic planners react to suggestions about changing the process. Recall, then, that the planning process has no value of its own under strategical rationalism. The process is arranged so as to maximize the probability of establishing a correct IA and to assist in the implementation of the alternative ranked number one. There is no room for yielding to interest group pressure for setting priorities in conflict with those above.

Disjointed incrementalism is opposed to the idea of being responsive to the public interest. Pluralists demonstrate the production of democratic plans from responsiveness to those citizens having such intense preferences that they take the time and trouble to join political groups. The searching process, taking a small step as a trial and interpreting political opposition as strong indication of planning error, is at the core of Lindblom's incrementalism. Nevertheless, disjointed incrementalism is only responsive within limits, as demands for radical change are ignored. When no conditions are imposed on the reasons for the protests, incrementalists may comply with opportunism. This is avoided in dialogical incrementalism. There, the planners must be responsive, but they yield only to suggestions serving generalizable interests in Habermas's sense.

Etzioni (1968:518) asserts that both overly incremental and overly synoptic decision-making lead to unresponsiveness. When the claims of interest groups are strongly contradictory, attempts to please everybody may result in low responsiveness in the sense that nobody appreciates the chosen strategy. Although incompatible wishes cannot always be prevented, the planners can make responsiveness more manageable by increasing the predictability of the other actors' conduct and thus facilitate the anticipation of proposals and complaints. According to Heiner (1983), this effect can be produced by increasing uncertainty to the extent that people fall back on simplified patterns of behaviour. Hence, the incremental planner has a motive for complicating the decision situation of the other actors in the planning process.

Advocacy planning is primarily a means of forcing a (planning) bureaucracy to act responsively. When the government is not monolithic but rather polyarchical and disjointed, some public planners may find the opportunity to take on the role of advocates for under-privileged groups, against the interest of other governmental agencies. This does not make the public planning generally responsive. It can be hard to distinguish responsiveness from partiality in the advocacy model. Working closely with a group to defend its interests, it can be difficult for the advocate planner to insist that adjustment of the plan should be based on principle and criteria.

The approach to planning as questioning and shaping attention generalizes the advocacy model. It is based on a critical attitude towards authorities and biased power relations rather than commitment to a particular group. Listening, as spelled out by Forester (1989:Ch.7), is a requisite for responsiveness. Putting emphasis on listening is another way of saying that planners should be answering as well as questioning. These functions are intertwined, though. 'To listen well inevitably means to ask questions about deeper interests, future possibilities, and reformulations of the problems we seem to face' (ibid.109-10). The listening provides the planners with information of the needs and the anxieties of those affected by the plan. The planners acquire a knowledge base for posing fruitful questions.

The influence of biased power relations on planning efforts can be reduced by exposing the communicative distortions produced by the wielding of power. Controllers can affect responsiveness by distorting the answering. It can be done, e.g., by refusing to address the protesting group, pretending not to have heard the objection, ridiculing the competing proposal for lacking realism, or intimidating the opponent by answering in inaccessible technical jargon. Communicative distortions can also upset the flexibility aspect or responsiveness. Those against alterations may convey a distorted picture of what changes are desired, or try to conceal the need for adjustments. Controllers can give the false impression that possibilities for adjustment are being examined and that change will be made. Etzioni (1968:518) set forth his mixed scanning approach to planning partly to counteract sources of unresponsiveness.

Responsiveness is presented here as a means of preventing that conflict leads planning into opportunism, rigidity, or parapraxis. Rigidity is counteracted by responsiveness per definition, and my appeal to principled adjustment rules out opportunism. Furthermore, Etzioni (1968:8) strongly suggests that responsiveness interferes with development towards parapraxis:

> Providing the conditions for mobilization of its members (the other side of increased responsiveness), is to society what psychoanalysis is to a person. It is an attempt to unlock the combinations formed under the impact of past events, to remove distortions thus accumulated, and to make for a less costly accommodation to the environment. Such mobili-

zation serves to increase spontaneity within the limits of the constraints of society in its particular historical stage.

The allusion to the psychoanalytic theory of neurosis is particularly apt as a transition to the next chapter. There, this theory inspires a model explaining the cumulative bounding process leading to parapraxis.

Appendix:
posterior reasoning and the flexibility/opportunism distinction

The appendix demonstrates that posterior rationality is a type of restriction or bound on instrumental reason and has relevance for responsiveness. Such behaviour is more plausible within a model accounting for changes in the preference structure. With posterior reason the planners learn from experience and adjust their preferences accordingly. In the following, unanticipated consequences as the cause of posterior reasoning is briefly discussed. Then the relationship between posterior reasoning and the 'backward mapping' approach to implementation is used to illustrate the difficulties created by posterior reasoning when it comes to deciding what is flexible behaviour and what is opportunism.

Unanticipated consequences

Throughout this book we have met unanticipated consequences when discussing self-altering forecasts, personal growth, the master and bondage paradox, Hayek's reasoning on planning and serfdom, and the Machiavellian emancipation/freedom paradox, just to mention some of the themes. Additional examples are supplied by Boudon (1982) and Sieber (1981), for instance.

'In some one of its numerous forms, the problem of the unanticipated consequences of purposive action has been treated by virtually every substantial contributor to the long history of social thought' (Merton 1936:894). Nevertheless, Merton's own article, opening with the quoted sentence, seems to be the first theoretical text by a sociologist on the unintended consequences in social life. The phenomenon is not made interesting by the obvious fact that we occasionally fail to foresee even first and second-order impacts of poorly planned actions. What makes the theme an essential one to planning and social theory is the far stronger claim made by Sartre (1982:38-9): in the dialectic inherent in the interrelations between individuals, the consequences of our actions always finally escape us.[5]

Vernon (1979:57) states that for Sartre as well as for Popper, '(u)nin-tended consequences figure as an explanatory bridge between the "human" character of action and the "alien" character of history'. Giddens (1984) shares the Sartrean insight that the consequences of activities chronically escape their initiators. He uses this to explain the relationships between individual agency and social structure. Most individual actions have the indirect effects of strengthening institutions. For instance, correct talk reproduces the language in question - effectively although wholly unin-tended.

Prominent scholars have singled out the unintended consequences as the main target for social research. Merton (1957:66) suggests that 'the *distinctive* intellectual contributions of the sociologist are found primarily in the study of unintended consequences ... of social practices, as well as in the study of anticipated consequences ...'. He goes on to say that there is some evidence that their major contributions have been made at the point when the sociologists shifted their attention to consequences which were neither intended nor recognized. Popper (1972:124) has put the matter more squarely:

> (I)t is one of the striking things about social life that *nothing ever comes off exactly as intended*. Things always turn out a little bit differently. We hardly ever produce in social life precisely the effect that we wish to produce, and we usually get things that we do not want into the bargain. ... To explain why they cannot be eliminated is the major task of social theory. ... The characteristic problems of the social sciences arise only out of our wish to know the *unintended consequences*, and more especially the *unwanted consequences* which may arise if we do certain things.

To the extent that planning is accepted as a social science, the declarations of the above authors place it in a peculiar position. Planning is the study of anticipated and primarily intended consequences of deliberate action, and hence there is a contrast to social science in general. The formulations of Merton and Popper indicate an ex post approach; unanticipated effects have to be studied after the event. Planning is essentially an ex ante activity preparing for the event.[6]

'Public planning' sounds to many as a meaningful phrase despite the preceding assertion that the consequences of our actions always end up by escaping us. This indicates that there may be counteracting mechanisms enabling us to approach some of our goals after all. Several processes may be behind this kind of flexibility, for instance:

- The planned action has the intended effects, but also additional ones which, however, do not distort those predicted.
- The goals are short-term, while the unanticipated effects are long-term. Insofar as it is conceivable to protect against the unanticipated, this might be done in the meantime.
- There are means in planning that work towards the goals in multiple ways, of which some causal chains include by-products and productive unanticipated effects as links.
- Planning creates publicity and interest in a problem and is a learning process. In favourable circumstances, it stimulates creativity and makes it possible to exploit some of the unanticipated effects to our own advantage.

The point to be made here is that flexibility tends to be underestimated because creativity is always underrated. Albert Hirschman (1967:13) puts it this way:

> Creativity always comes as a surprise to us; therefore we can never count on it and we dare not believe in it until it has happened. In other words, we would not consciously engage upon tasks whose success clearly requires that creativity be forthcoming. Hence, the only way in which we can bring our creative resources fully into play is by mis-judging the nature of the task, by presenting it to ourselves as more routine, simple, undemanding of genuine creativity than it will turn out to be.

This is what Hirschman calls 'the principle of the hiding hand'. Planners tend to underrate both the difficulties caused by unanticipated consequences and the creativity and flexibility helping them to cope with unexpected problems. So planners are 'tricked by these two offsetting underestimates into undertaking tasks which we can, but otherwise would not dare, tackle' (ibid.13).

Posterior reasoning, implementation, and opportunism

When a decision proves to have unanticipated effects, which is always the case to some extent, the ex ante preferences for the decided action were based on more or less unrealistic expectations. It seems rational, then, to adjust them ex post when adequate information is available.[7] Such posterior rationality is a pre-condition for a particular type of flexibility: it enables us to gain acceptance of some end-states that can be reached despite the occurrence of failure in the system. This kind of flexibility requires that failure causes a reconsideration and adjustment of preferences. When it proves impossible to attain the announced goals, one will have to look for new ones. If end-states formerly judged unsatisfactory are now found acceptable (or vice versa), this implies that posterior rationality is at work.[8]

I have already shown posterior reasoning to be an integrated part of disjointed incrementalism. Now it will be shown to generate an important view of implementation denoted 'backward mapping'. It is introduced to launch a second attack on the problematic distinction between flexibility and opportunism (in a way similar to Faludi 1987:Ch.13).

The point of view that implementation is the realization of projects, plans, or policies in accordance with goals and objectives determined in advance, was challenged by Pressman and Wildavsky (1973). To Majone and Wildavsky (1978:104) it is no longer clear '(w)hat comes first, the chicken of the goal or the egg of implementation'. The authors assert that old patterns of behaviour are often retrospectively rationalized to fit new notions about appropriate objectives. The consequences of this perspective for the study of implementation have been spelled out most fully by Elmore (1979-80, 1985). He contrasts backward mapping to the traditional view. This 'forward mapping' begins with an objective, elaborates an increasingly specific set of steps for achieving that objective, and states an outcome against which success or failure can be measured.

> The logic of backward mapping is, in all important respects, the opposite of forward mapping. It begins not at the top of the implementation process but at the last possible stage, the point at which administrative actions intersect private choices. It begins not with a statement of intent, but with a statement of the specific behavior at the lowest level of the implementation process that generates the need for a policy. Only after that behavior is described does the analysis presume to state an objective; the objective is first stated as a set of organizational operations and then as a set of effects, or outcomes, that will result from these operations. Having established a relatively precise target at the lowest level of the system, the analysis backs up through the structure of implementing agencies, asking at each level two questions: What is the ability of this unit to affect the behavior that is the target of the policy? And what resources does this unit require in order to have that effect? In the final stage of analysis the analyst or policymaker describes a policy that directs resources at the organizational units likely to have the greatest effect.   (Elmore 1979-80:604)

Opportunism means allowing undue weight to circumstances of the time in determining policy, putting expediency before principle. The traditional view of implementation makes us less vulnerable to accusations of opportunism as long as we stick to a strategic scheme worked out in advance to serve the predetermined goal. Problems of distinguishing flexibility from opportunism only emerge if new situations develop which were not anticipated when designing the scheme.

With backward mapping - and with posterior reasoning in general - we are more vulnerable as we cannot employ a preconceived strategic scheme. This is because we do not know how preferences will change throughout the decision process. The procedure, as experienced by the 'street level' implementing agency closest to the problems, appears much like an incremental trial-and-error process. This makes it hard to demonstrate that we are not deviating from our principles. When the concept of strategy has gone and it is conceded that implementation shapes policy, the distinction between plan-making and implementation is blurred. If we are not committed to any plan, not even one disguised as guide-lines, instructions, principles, etc., the difference between flexibility and opportunism is hard to discover (Faludi 1987:208). Adjustments deserving the term flexible have to be measured against some preconceived path, direction, or end-state.

One might wonder whether backward mapping is bound to result in opportunism. At the lowest level of the implementation process, in the 'street level' organization first affected by the specific behaviour generating the need for a policy, the wider implications of such a policy are not likely to be adequately considered. However, as we ascend the hierarchy of organizations, we will find that the agency funding the street level organization looks at the measures proposed by it in a wider perspective. The organization on the next higher level might broaden the perspective further, aiming at consistency with other plans and judging the expenses required in light of the overall budget. This outline shows that backward mapping is not necessarily opportunistic.

The problem of adjustments of and deviations from plans is a recurring theme in planning due to what Luban (1985:414-5) calls the paradox of compromise:

> Commitment to a principle means commitment to seeing it realized. But in practice this means compromising the principle (since all-or-nothing politics is usually doomed to defeat) - and compromise is partial abandonment of the principle. Conversely, refusal to compromise one's principles means in practice abandoning entirely the hope of seeing them realized.

In our case we are committed to a plan that we wish to see realized, and compromising the plan raises the question of flexibility versus opportunism.

I see no general criterion for resolving this problem, which can avoid the commonplace and somewhat perplexed appeal to good judgement.

Notes

1   The most detailed discussion of opportunism and its economic consequences seems to be presented by Williamson (1975). Standard economic models treat individuals as playing a game with fixed rules which they obey. They do not buy more than they know they can pay for, and they do not rob banks. Williamson introduces opportunism as a lack of candour or honesty in transactions in order to explain why internal organization has attractive properties. It permits the parties to deal with uncertainty and complexity in an adaptive, sequential fashion without incurring the same types of opportunism hazards that market contracting would pose (ibid.25).

Elster (1989:263-72) presents arguments in favour of opportunism. He refers to literature about specific types of opportunism, such as corruption and bribery. Elster (1988:98) discusses opportunistic actions which can be tempting to industrial co-operatives, such as issuing shares to people who do not work there, in order to attract new investment capital. In Elster (1987:74-6), opportunistic behaviour is discussed in a social choice perspective. One example is to express preferences other than the true ones in order to manipulate the collective choice.

In a choice among assured, familiar outcomes of behaviour, Ainslie (1975) regards impulsiveness as the choice of less rewarding over more rewarding alternatives. Opportunistic behaviour does not imply impulsiveness; it is nevertheless often impulsive. Both types of action will easily give specious reward. There are similarities in the way of thinking about opportunism and impulse action, and in the theories of the control mechanisms needed to prevent such behaviour.

2   One can get an idea of the relationship between Schön's reflection-in-action and Forester's questioning-and-shaping-attention approach to planning by comparing their views on design. The chapters I have in mind are *Design as a reflective conversation with the situation* (Schön 1983:Ch.3) and *Designing as making sense together* (Forester 1989: Ch.8).

3   The anecdote of the Eskimo sculptor illustrates an ancient concept of efficiency according to Sennett (1970:92):

In pre-industrial factory systems, the experience of making a product was more important than a standard image, a clear picture, of the 'whole' to be made; those craftsmen conceived, therefore, that to define in advance what a thing should look like would interfere with 'efficiency', that is, with the freedom of the craftsman to exploit his materials and forms during production.

This stands in contrast to the peculiarly modern concept of efficiency demanding that the parts be made in keeping with the preconceived picture of the whole. Addressing urban planners, Sennett contends that 'when this mentality of production, this image of machine efficiency, becomes transferred to the production of cities, in the designing of social parts from a predetermined, previsualized urban whole, the results become inhumane' (ibid.93). It seems to me that Schön, with his 'reflective conversation with the materials of a situation', aims for a revival of the pre-industrial notion of efficiency.

4   Saltzstein (1985:286) shows that the concept of responsiveness is still problematic:

> Those who define democratic responsiveness in terms of 'reflecting and giving expression to the will of the people' ... face difficulties in operationalizing the 'will of the people'. Is it reflected in articulated demands ..., general public opinion ..., or some combination of the two ...? If articulated demands reflect the people's will, which of those must be met? All of them, even if contradictory ..., or only the most intensely felt ...? Similarly, if responsiveness is owed to general public opinion, which opinions are relevant? Are only strongly felt majority opinions relevant? What response is owed to uninformed opinions, strongly felt minority opinions, or situations in which opinion is evenly divided? Is responsiveness a winner-take-all proposition, or does it require some attempt to balance competing claims and provide something for everyone? What meaning does it have when the public is apathetic or has no opinion?

5   Ricoeur(1981:206) reinforces this basic insight by drawing an analogy between an action and a text (e.g., between planning and a plan):

> In the same way that a text is detached from its author, an action is detached from its agent and develops consequences of its own. This autonomization of human action constitutes the social dimension of action. An action is a social phenomenon not only because it is done by several agents in such a way that the role of each of them cannot be distinguished from the role of the others, but also because our deeds escape us and have effects which we did not intend.

The autonomization of the text is more fully explained in Ricoeur (1976). The classic Greek tragedies are examples showing how good intentions are transformed to unintended and catastrophic results, an idea exploited, for instance, by Olsson (1991) in an essay on *Oedipus Rex* (Set Your Mind at Rest).

6   It should be noted that the omnipresence of unanticipated consequences contradicts the entire idea of planning according to some authors. This is so when the definition of 'planning' hinges on the capacity of the planner to control his environment, as is the case in Wildavsky's (1973) celebrated essay *If planning is everything, maybe it's nothing*. He asserts that '(t)he determination of whether planning has taken place must rest on an assessment of whether and to what degree future control has been achieved' (ibid.129). '(P)lanning is the ability to control the future by current acts' (ibid.128).

7   Posterior rationality is treated in economics under the heading of endogenous changes of taste (Weizsäcker 1971). Habit formation is one of the mechanisms guiding such changes (Pollak 1976, Camic 1986). Cohen and Axelrod (1984) propose a decision process that incorporates a controlled form of preference change. Adjustment is a function of the difference between experienced and expected utility. Besides, a drag is used to retard excess value change. The conditions of synoptic planning can be approached by assuming that individuals know that their present choices influence their future preferences (Strotz 1955-56). This gives rise to a variety of problems of consistency, existence, and stability of plans and choices over time (Peleg and Yaari 1973).

8   This type of flexibility is denoted product-resilience in Sager (1990b). Leon Festinger's idea of 'cognitive dissonance' is closely affiliated with the notion of posterior reasoning. Akerlof and Dickens (1982:309) hold that 'persons who have made decisions tend to discard information that would suggest such decisions are in error because the cognition that the decision might be in error is in conflict with the cognition that ego is a smart person'. Due to the strain of cognitive dissonance posterior reasoning tends to overstate the attractive features of past action. The mechanism tends to narrow the gap between ex post and ex ante preferences. An informative account of the theory is offered by Janis and Mann (1977:Ch.4), who find similar mechanisms at work in the pre-decision phase.

8   Towards a theory of parapraxis: a case study of cumulative bounds on rationality

Deficient means-end rationality is found to set bounds on the communicative rationality - and vice versa. This gives rise to a theory of how bounds on instrumental and communicative rationality cause and sometimes reinforce each other and thus arrange for aggregated irrationality in planning - i.e., parapraxis. Inspiration is drawn from Freud's psychoanalytic theory of neurosis. The factors provoking accumulation of bounds on rationality can, e.g., originate in moral dilemmas and in paradoxes and conflicts studied in previous chapters. The case material consists of integrated transportation and land use plans for the ten largest urban regions in Norway. Mechanisms of limiting and misrepresenting information and thus distorting the communication between planners, politicians, and populace are discussed. The planners make modest reference to the impact assessment (IA) when building an argument in support of their choice, so the link between recommendation and IA-results is weak in many cases. Observations and impressions from the ten planning processes are adapted and rearranged in order to construct an archetypal example of a cumulative bounding process.

The setting and the problem

Comprehensive transportation and land use plans were made for the 10 largest urban regions of Norway in the period 1990-92 (denoted TP10 for short). Road construction programmes are an important part of the plans, and the TP10 will be co-ordinated with the Norwegian Road and Road Traffic Plan for 1994-97. The TP10-process was initiated by the Ministry of Communication and Transportation and the Ministry of Environment. The process was guided by the Central Advisory Group, with a majority of

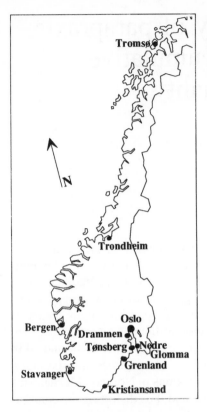

Figure 8.1 **The location of the TP10-regions in Norway**

its experts coming from the Public Roads Administration. Important guide-lines for the TP10-planning are:

- A comprehensive transportation system should be planned for the urban region, i.e., it should be outlined how accessibility can be improved for all transport modes.
- Integrated transportation and land use strategies should be worked out.
- Improvements of the road system and the public transport system should be co-ordinated.
- Improvement of the natural and social environment should be a premiss for the local plans. It should not only be passively forecast how the environment will be affected.
- The plans should take into account environmental effects both on the local and the global level.

The population in nine of the urban regions varies from 50 to 300 thousands. In addition there is the Oslo-region with 880 thousand inhabitants in 1990. Each of the ten regions was asked to develop strategies leading to three preformulated scenarios called Trend, Public transport, and Environmental. In the guide-lines from the Central Advisory Group, the scenarios were briefly described as follows:

Trend: - Individual mobility is maintained on the present level or increased. The transport system is improved to cater for predicted traffic. This implies extensive road construction schemes.

Public transport: - Considerably expanded public transport is supplied to stem the increased private driving. New restrictions on the use of cars are not accepted.

Environmental: - Specified environmental goals are fulfilled. A more restrictive policy towards car driving is implemented.

Each urban region was asked to present an impact assessment (IA) of the strategies T, P, and E corresponding to the scenarios. The TP10-plans have much in common with the British urban transportation plans published recently (see May 1991).

This chapter is not concerned with the *making* of the IAs. The case material is used to (1) show how differently the results of the IAs were applied in forming a recommendation, (2) illustrate how various forms of misinformation distort communication related to the IAs, and (3) exemplify the process of cumulative bounds on rationality. The critique is based on Jürgen Habermas's (1984, 1987) theory of communicative action, and on John Forester's (1989) approach to planning as questioning and shaping attention.

Use of impact assessment results to support the recommended plans

The IA is meant to inform the subsequent decision-making. The reasonable procedure would seem to be that the planning document recommends a strategy suggested by the IA, and that the recommendation is substantiated by reference to the IA. In case the recommended strategy is not suggested by the IA, one would expect an explanation of the overruling of the IA-results. The decision-making in TP10 does in most cases deviate significantly from this argumentative process.

Table 8.1 juxtaposes the recommendations and some main results of the IAs, and the last column characterizes the correspondence between the two. It is briefly stated if the strategy indicated by the IA is in fact chosen, and I describe to what degree assessment results are used to back up the recommendation.

From the first column of Table 8.1 it is clear that the Environmental strategy is never dominated. That is, in none of the TP10-cities are the other strategies better than E on all indicators or all main goals. The IA does not point strongly in the direction of T or P in any of the urban regions. The typical situation is that the IA points towards E, although T is usually considered best on accessibility for motorists. Table 8.1 reveals six types of recommendation:
- Only implicit recommendation (Bergen)
- Only projects included in all strategies are recommended (Drammen)
- Recommending that a compromise strategy is developed (Oslo)
- Recommendation of the strategy judged best by the IA (Grenland, Kristiansand)
- Recommendation of a compromise judged inferior by the IA (Tønsberg)
- Recommendation of a compromise without assessment of its impacts (Nedre Glomma, Stavanger, Trondheim)
The recommended compromise does always comprise more road projects

Table 8.1
Degree of correspondence between recommendation and impact assessment (IA)

TP10-cities	Undominated and reasonable strategies according to the IA	Recommendation	Correspondence and argumentative connection with impact assessment (IA)
Bergen	T and E(protection of agric. and recreational land), →E	Implicit: E(concentration of built-up areas)	Inconsistency within the E strategy. Weak link with IA
Drammen	E best on most goals, no strategy dominated	Implement projects common to T, P, and E	Neither inconsistency nor full acceptance of IA
Grenland	E dominates T and P on main goal level	E with concentrated land use	Full correspondence and strong link with IA
Kristiansand	All T, P, and E variants are undominated on indicator level, →E	Similar to E	No logical inconsistency. Partial analysis of recommendation, but only implicit links with IA
Nedre Glomma	All strategies undominated, →E	Compromise of T, P, and E; primarily P/E	Corresp. and explicit link with IA, although recom. is not analysed
Oslo	The reasonable choice is between P and E	Compromise strategy should be developed	Weak link with IA
Stavanger	Analysis of T and a P/E combination; P/E best except for car accessibility	Compromise of T and P/E	Compromise is not analysed. Recom. and IA are linked, although not strongly
Tromsø	E(moderate) better than T and P on most indicators and avoids serious disadv. No strategy dominated	E(moderate) with modified restrictions on use of private cars	Correspondence. Strong link with IA on the land use aspects. Much weaker on transport aspects
Trondheim	No dominated strategies. P is middle on most indicators, →E	Compromise with basis in P	No logical inconsistency, but recom. is not analysed. Weak link with IA
Tønsberg	E dominates other strat. on goal level, included recom.	Compromise of T and P, deviating significantly from E	Clear inconsistency, IA is set aside

→E means that most indicators point to E as the preferable strategy.
Grenland includes the towns Skien and Porsgrunn.
Nedre Glomma includes the towns Fredrikstad and Sarpsborg.

198

than in E. The compromise is said to give higher goal achievement - frequently even on the environmental indicators - but it is not demonstrated by IA to have this effect. In one case the recommended compromise is even demonstrated *not* to have positive effect on goal achievement. In most cities the pure E-strategy would imply saying 'no, thanks' to classified road projects paid for by the Central Government. Like other people, local politicians are apt not to reject what they can have for nothing.

Some mechanisms in the TP10-process pulled the recommendation away from a fully developed Environmental strategy. In nearly all the cities at least one of the following stratagems was applied:

- The road system was identical in all strategies (two cities), or E included not all but at least two-thirds of T's road investments (two cities). In all these cases the road construction schemes are extensive.
- E is suggested only implicitly, boiled down to a common base alternative, or simply repudiated due to financial difficulty or other political motives external to the IA (three cities).
- Road building is added to the E-strategy without founding this supplement on arguments backed by the IA.

Most TP10-cities do either make an initial Trend-adjustment by requiring extensive road construction in all strategies, or they move towards the recommendation in a way not sustained by professional planning argument. Only in one city is E analysed, found best, and consequently recommended. It is possible that this procedure is too simple when the preferred future state is not among the preformulated scenarios. Nevertheless, it is straightforward, honest, and transparent. Hence, deviations from it should be more strongly supported by impact calculations and political arguments than is the case in TP10.

There are few logical inconsistencies between assessment results and recommendation, meaning that one solution is found to have the best consequences, while another one is chosen. Possible incongruities are hard to pin down when the impacts of the recommendation are not, in fact, analysed. A puzzle frequently met is the modest use made of the IA when giving reasons for the recommendation. The IAs are applied very differently:

- Recommendation explicitly based on the IA (Grenland)
- Recommendation in line with the IA, but weak argumentative link (Kristiansand)
- IA referred to when arguing for a compromise strategy (Nedre Glomma, Stavanger)
- IA scantly or not at all referred to when proposing a compromise or base alternative (Trondheim, Drammen, Oslo)
- IA ignored or repudiated (Bergen, Tønsberg).

The rickety bridge connecting IA and recommendation would be particularly hard to explain if it could be assumed that the TP10-planners made the recommendations without interference. As it is, political influence on the recommendation varied considerably among the cities. Four suggestions why the recommendation is only loosely connected with the IA are offered here, and the reader is referred to Sager (1993b) for an extended discussion.

(1) The IA rarely selects one alternative as the unambiguously best solution. A choice will most often reveal that some effects, goals or groups are given higher priority than others. Politicians do not always consider it wise to make these priorities clear to the general public. (2) Moreover, were the IA of T, P, and E to be emphasized in the decision process, it would be evident that the recommended compromise deserved the same detailed treatment. This might not be wanted due to time pressure or a wish to suppress potential conflict material. (3) It might even be that some politicians see the answers of the transportation planning as given in advance, and thus prefer a downgrading of the IA-presentation. The TP10-process may be regarded as a prescribed exercise necessary to ensure extra funding from the State. (4) In a number of the cities, the prominent politicians have been struggling for years to gain accept on a radically improved network of main roads. Simultaneously with the TP10-process, they are preparing their list of proposed road investments for the Norwegian Road and Road Traffic Plan for 1994-97. Since the local transportation plans and the national road plan will be co-ordinated, the choice of a low-investment E-strategy means that their favourite road projects may be excluded from the national road plan.

Forms of misinformation and other communicative distortions can be specified on the basis of Table 8.1 and the four points above. This theme is further developed in the next section.

Forms of misinformation

The section contains a critique of some aspects of planning practice, which are manifestations of 'distorted communication'. This term designates all forms of restricted and prejudiced communication that by their nature inhibit a full discussion of problems, issues, and ideas of public relevance. There is communication in talk and in writing, and it takes place between numerous actors in the planning process. The observed distortions mentioned here concern information primarily written by the planners to be read by bureaucrats, politicians, and the general public. My aim is to show examples of distortions that seem to be typical when using IAs.

The transportation plans are part of local politics, and they should provide a foundation for informed public debate. The ideal is an open and unconstrained communication among planners, politicians, and populace. In the terms of Jürgen Habermas, dialogue requires that each party in the conversation has equal possibility to set forth arguments and be listened to. Dialogue is achieved in the ideal speech situation when no power relations interfere with the interlocutors' aim for mutual understanding. In practice the communication will not be without distortions, because of external political and internal psychological constraints on the participants. Habermas's concept of dialogue is nevertheless important as a yardstick against which actual discourses can be judged (Kemp 1985:188).

It would of course be misconceived to aim at an analysis of the entire communicative process in TP10 by studying only the final reports from the 10 cities. My more modest task here is to comment on the quality of the reports regarded as argumentative input to that process. One should bear in mind that misunderstandings can be unravelled, concealments can be revealed, etc. in other parts of the communication process. It is likely that the reports are followed by, e.g., local newspaper debates and open meetings on the transportation plans. Nevertheless, the main reports can be more or less fruitful starting points for the ensuing public debates. I focus on the negative features, applying the critical and communicative approach of Forester (1989) to transportation planning.

In some cities, the planners analysed, concluded, and recommended with minimal interference from the politicians. In other cities the politicians were more active throughout the TP10-process. They are, in exceptional cases, said to have been dictating the recommended transportation/land use strategy. Hence, the planners are not necessarily the sole source of the misinformations exemplified in Table 8.2 and 8.3. Nevertheless, when they have to change their analysis or conclusions according to political pressure, efforts should be made not to deceive the reader. For instance, when the IA suggests one strategy while another one is recommended for political reasons, it is invidious to leave this in silence. The planners should call the reader's attention to the incoherence and present the reasons for it as far as possible. Then, the reader can at least spot the anomaly and judge if the arguments offered are convincing.

Table 8.2 classifies examples of misinformation according to the planning phase in which they occur and the typical motive behind each type of distortion. Habermas claims that dialogue rests on the comprehensibility, sincerity, legitimacy, and truth of the utterances of everybody involved. Forester (1989:36-9) interprets distortions of these 'validity claims' as managing comprehension, trust, consent, and control, respectively. These are the forms of misinformation listed in the head of Table 8.2.

Table 8.2
Classification of misinformation in the decision process

Planning phases revealing the examples of distortion	Forms of misinformation			
	Managing comprehension (problem framing)	*Managing trust (false assurance)*	*Managing consent (illegitimacy)*	*Managing control (misre-presentation)*
Identifying problems and generating alternatives	Causing confusion on what is to be clarified by the planning; e.g., emphasizing that T, P, and E are not the choice alternatives, while still restricting IA to these alternatives.	Announcing scenario planning covering a wide range of policies, yet analysing (1) the same extensive road scheme in all alternatives, and (2) land use strategies too similar to cause significant differences in traffic.	Avoiding strategies that, if chosen, make previous political decisions look foolish or make implemented projects a waste of money.	Formulating alternatives only to exclude them at some stage of the impact calculation without comment and explanation.
Impact assessment	Each alternative may be undominated on single impact level. By manipulating the aggregation level and the implicit weights of impact importance, one can give the impression that one alternative dominates the others. Hence, the presentation of aggregate results may conceal important trade-offs.	Including an introductory caveat on uncertainty in general, while presenting all calculated impacts as if they were accurate.	Excluding information on how specific groups and segments of the population are affected by the plan.	Using averages to conceal important impacts. A public transport strategy may give shorter journey times for each group of travellers, while only the increase in total average journey time is reported. This increase is due to a transfer of travellers from private car to slower modes.
Application of assessment results in decision-making	No comments on the connections between recommendations and IA-results. Making comparison of recommended and analysed alternatives difficult.	Developing an elaborate goal hierarchy, but letting the choice of strategy be significantly influenced by goals which are not part of that structure.	Presenting all strategies as environmental strategies, since 'environmental improvement' is the current buzzword.	Recommending a strategy different from the one (implicitly) ranked highest in the IA - without comment or explanation.

Table 8.2 shows mechanisms of communicative distortions that are fairly widespread in the TP10-process. Examples are found for each planning phase, and nearly all the distortions apply to several cities.

There will always be bounds on the instrumental (means-end) rationality in a collective decision process. The question of interest here is to what extent this affects the possibility for an open political communication where arguments are exchanged on equal terms. Table 8.3 is designed to indicate an answer as far as TP10 is concerned. The hypothesis is that the planners try to conceal flaws, to the extent that they become aware of the limited means-end rationality, by misinformation distorting the public communication. The table deals only with the presentation and use of IA-results, while the examples given in the text relate for a large part to the planning phases of generating and analysing alternatives. The types of distortions in the head of Table 8.3 are somewhat more concrete and specific than the corresponding categories in Table 8.2. However, the stub, classifying types of pressure causing means-end rationality to deteriorate, needs some explanatory comments.

One can imagine various kinds of pressure biasing or short cutting deliberation. Resource pressure is the only kind that is experienced even when making decisions alone and unaffected by other people. By 'resources' is meant intellectual capacity as well as time and money needed to produce data and theory. Cognitive limitations are studied by, e.g., Elster (1984) and Hogarth (1980). As a consequence of resource pressure in TP10, cost-benefit analyses were not carried out, and so the economic net effects for the society were hardly discussed. Another example is that the limitations of analytical planning models can be seen as causing and being caused by cognitive limits. One of the TP10-reports states that a decisive criterion for choice of policy was the possibility for using the traffic model to forecast the impacts of the policy. Hence, the set of traffic calming measures discussed is partly determined by available analytic technique. Technique affects what the planners are talking about and thereby, in the end, our physical surroundings. Table 8.3 mentions that debate on evaluation can be confused by double-counting. Several of the TP10-cities list an increased share of public transport trips as an indicator of higher achievement of both the 'efficient transport' goal and the 'efficient land use' goal. This procedure is liable to assign an unduly heavy weight to the indicator when assessing total goal achievement.

By 'internal integrative pressure' in the stub is meant interaction in groups of planners affected by groupthink ('t Hart 1990, Janis 1982). In groupthink the decision-making is influenced by an aim for cohesiveness among colleagues, resulting in conformity, compliance, and deindividuation. Groupthink is marked by excessive concurrence-seeking. Group norms, member roles, and peer pressure cause the debate to be narrow and to converge towards an uncontroversial standpoint, objections not being voiced or listened to. In some TP10-cities, groupthink and educationally homogeneous planning teams may have contributed to uncritical acceptance of equal road systems

Table 8.3
Connections between bounds on instrumental and communicative rationality

Types of pressure bounding instrumental rationality	Communicative distortions in the presentation and use of calculated impacts		
	Saying too little: Withholding information	Saying too much: Misleading information or judgement	Inconsistencies in what is said: Gaps in argumentative chain
Resource pressure: Cognitive limits, limits on time and costs	No IA of recommended strategy because of time constraints	1) Confusing the debate by double-counting. 2) Using goal achievem. scales where 'medium' is always the present ±10%, no matter if the situation today is good or bad	Establishing objectives on positive benefit-cost ratios for the entire plan and for particular projects, without following up in the IA - thus aborting the discourse
Internal integrative pressure: Groupthink	Not stating or discussing which strategy the IA is pointing at	1) Referring to welfare economic calculations not shown or carried out. 2) Always interpreting reduced number of trips negatively, even when land use becomes more concentrated and thus diminishes the need to travel	Cursory presentation of impacts of T, P, and E in order to play down their role, as they are not seen as the real choice alternatives - while directing attention to an unanalysed strategy closer to the centre of political opinions
Internal segregative pressure: Conflict	1) Silence on trade-offs. 2) No reasons given for recommending only the projects common to all strategies - because of potential conflict?	Emphasizing that measures improving accessibility on the road network will also let the busses go faster, concealing that the terms of competition will still be altered in favour of private cars	No explanation of the choice among the undominated alternatives, and no argumentative link from IA to recommendation
External interest-oriented pressure: 'Political' concessions	Mayor insisting on recommendation deviating from the IA-conclusion, without giving reasons	Pretending that the IA is the central tool for assessing and ranking the strategies, while letting external considerations - like avoiding conflict with existing plans - be implicitly decisive when choosing	Co-ordination of TP10 and the national road plan (NVVP 1994-97) directs the attention in the land use/transportation planning towards road construction, at the expense of land use and public transport
Structural pressure: System-generated bias	1) Lack of arrangements for increased transfers to public transport directs the discussion towards Trend and Environmental strategies. 2) There is a monolithic and strong central organization of the road sector compared to the agencies dealing with land use and public transport. Thus, integrated plans tend to accentuate the road network in analysis and conclusions, while public transport is found costly and land use is found to have little bearing on the amount of traffic.		

in all strategies. Then the strategies do not display the broad set of future opportunities, and the exercise merely pretends to arrange for the scenario approach that was expected.

The following three peculiarities observed in TP10-reports may also be caused by groupthink:

- The planners state that the Environmental strategy gives a high degree of goal achievement, although the IA shows this to be true only for six out of twenty quantified indicators. Judging from goal achievement on the indicator level, the Trend strategy might be an equally reasonable choice at least. The T-strategy is nevertheless given a lower rank without arguments being offered.

- The planners conclude that it is demonstrated that the city needs at least £100 million for transport investment. Evidence is not given beyond demonstrating that some benefits will emerge. There is no use of criteria, no comparison with costs, and no reference to reasonable standards for the quality of transport and environment that will be satisfied by the investments.

- In some cities the planners fit the strategies to a predetermined amount of investment. When the recommendation is based on the E-strategy but includes more road projects, some investments in safety, environmental improvement, pedestrian roads, etc. have to be left out. However, the reader is offered no assistance in identifying what is excluded. This may be interpreted as a groupthink procedure to protect the planners from public criticism. But it does not help in making the political trade-offs clear, and hence does not further public discussion.

'Internal segregative pressure' means that there is conflict among the TP10-planners. The insufficient agreement causes silence on some controversial questions, and occasionally leads to unbalanced statements when the weaker fraction withdraws in frustration and ceases to act as a corrective. It is often difficult in practice to know if a distortion is caused by groupthink or by conflict, since groupthink may be a counteraction to conflict. The categories are kept separate here for the sake of principle. Admittedly, I do not *know* whether groupthink or conflict in TP10 led to the examples of communicative distortions mentioned in Table 8.3. An example not mentioned in the table concerns the presentation of uncertainty, which is high for long-term traffic flow on single routes and even higher for the local environmental consequences of that traffic. Some planners think that integrity demands that the level of uncertainty is made clear to the decision-makers, whether it is high or low. Others fear that the politicians' recognition of substantial uncertainty will lead planning to an impasse. They fear that the politicians may be paralysed and even come to suspect that the planners do an inferior job - thus turning to other consultants for the next assignment (Wachs 1990).

'External interest-oriented pressure' means that the local planners sometimes have to take orders from politicians, central planning agencies or other superior bureaucrats. These external instructions may impair the means-end logic of the planners' locally adapted approach. I use *'political' concessions* as a common designation for the ways of yielding to pressure from outside actors. For instance, at least early in the TP10-process, the intention of the Central Advisory Group was to keep investments in the strategies within a ±20% deviation from the present budgets of the cities. The point was to ensure realism, while many local planners felt that the benefits from scenario planning would not be fully realized, and that politically interesting prospects would be squeezed out of the discussion.

'Structural pressure' is not exerted by a specific actor. This source of bias is generated by macro-level political-economic systems, and can be overcome only by collective political action; no single actor can do the job. For example, simultaneous fulfilment of the goals concerning efficient transport and a good environment requires economic resources considerably above the present budgets. Thus, while the TP10 is presented as a set of *local* choices among T, P, E and combined strategies, the Central Government's choice of transportation policy will strongly influence which of the scenarios will be closest to the future reality. In this matter the Parliament and the voters will have their say.

A classification of phenomena bounding instrumental rationality has now been offered. Table 8.3 indicates for all the categories that communicative bounds may follow from the instrumental ones. This train of reasoning is pursued and 'extrapolated' into a theory of cumulative bounding of rationality in the next section.

Towards a theory of irrationality in planning

In this section, a theory is constructed of how parapraxis is established by a cumulative bounding process in planning. The prevailing psychoanalytic theory of neurosis is a starting point. Examples are taken from the urban transportation planning case treated in the preceding sections. It is strongly suggested that planning theorists go beyond demonstrating that instrumental bounds lead to communicative bounds on rationality, and rather aim at identifying chains of bounding events weakening the rationality of behaviour. The ultimate goal is a critical theory of irrationality in planning.

The Freudian explanation of neurosis goes as follows: psychoneuroses are due to an inner conflict between an impulse and a defence warding off the impulse's direct discharge or access to consciousness. In the case of neurosis, the conflict has not been solved in favour of the impulse or the interconnected rest of the personality (the ego), nor by a suitable compromise, but has become unconscious through a process of repression. However, the repression has been unsuccessful, in so far as the repressed impulse has found its way back into conscious manifestations in disguised form (Greenson 1967:17).

As argued in Chapter 7, conflict and parapraxis in planning can originate in a similar collision between an impulse and a system as that sketched above. Parapraxis is an analogy to the symptoms of psychoneurosis caused by the individual's need to protect his or her own mind. One can describe the TP10 as a planning system structured by mandate, principles, methodological and procedural guide-lines, intentions and stated goals, agreements, loyalties, etc. Detrimental impulses can spring up inside the system, as when a TP10 planning team follows an impulse to seek methodologically challenging tasks and fall into internal dispute at the expense of external argumentation and negotiation of crucial issues. Impulses can also be external and contradictory to some of the system's principles, goals, etc. The impulse can be expressed, e.g., as political wishes, as yielding to the principle of least effort instead of being probing and questioning, or as ideas of 'smart' solutions that, unfortunately, break bonds of loyalty, violate planning doctrines, etc. The system needs to protect itself against such an impulse, and hence a conflict is established. A threatening external impulse can be, e.g., political wishes to promote particular interests to the extent that double-counting results. This is contrary to the assessment criteria of the system. Another example is the impulse of local politicians to induce planners to apply substituting arguments to avoid conflict and protect favourite projects. Managing trust and consent in this fashion threatens the legitimacy of the chosen strategy.

Ordinary planning practice needs protection because there are difficult goal conflicts (Cohen and Paris 1982), innate hard choices (Levi 1986, Wachs 1990), dilemmas and paradoxes (Rittel and Webber 1973). Besides, protection is needed quite simply because planners make mistakes that provoke attack. The potential for tension can be seen already in the multifaceted rationale for planning comprising aspects of personal growth, market correction, and aid for undistorted communication. There are also serious conflicts with officials, developers and others, threatening the economic security, political legitimacy, or professional integrity of the planner (Hoch and Cibulskis 1987, Hoch 1988, Dalton 1990). Double bind situations and moral dilemmas sometimes leave the planners in an untenable position no matter what they do (Baum 1983:155-6). Bolan (1983) denotes this 'Catch 22' situations or 'Hobson's Choice', a choice between a rock and a hard place. Cumulative bounding in planning springs from attempts to protect the planners and their ordinary planning practice from threatening conflict.

Repression of impulses and unconscious transformation into symptoms displaying irrational behaviour are not as central elements in the planning analogy as in the psychoanalytic theory of neurosis. There are a number of reasons for instrumental and communicative bounding events in planning. Freudian theory is usually not necessary to explain the provoking factors, i.e., the initial bounds. It will be seen from the archetypal example in this section that causal connections between bounds can be rather obvious and do not call for explanations based on covert psychological reactions. Sometimes, however, the mechanism linking the bounding events does not lie in the open. The analogy to the theory of neurosis is useful for explaining how bounds that do not seem to have significant consequences, may eventually give renewed impetus to cumulative processes which, to all appearance, had stagnated. The theory makes it easier to see that cumulative bounding may be going on where, on the surface, there are no causal links. It also helps to explain that the accumulation process can be complicated, containing cumulative subprocesses, long slack periods and sudden flourishing of bounding events. Following from this, the psychoanalytic model facilitates the understanding of why the cumulative bounding process may be hard to terminate.

Threatening themes tend to disappear from the discussion and from the agendas. Secrecy is often sought for the fragile and intimate, the shameful, the dangerous, and the sources of power. The consequences of secrecy are among the most important factors arranging for irrationality.

> Secrecy ... can debilitate judgment ... whenever it shuts out criticism and feedback, leading people to become mired down in stereotyped, unexamined, often erroneous beliefs and ways of thinking.
> ...
> These risks of secrecy multiply because of its tendency to spread. Aware of the importance of exercising control over secrecy and openness, people seek more control whenever they can, and rarely give up portions of it voluntarily. In imitation and in self-protection, others then seek more as well. The control shifts in the direction of secrecy whenever there is negligence or abuse to cover up; as a result, as Weber pointed out, bureaucracies and other organizations surround themselves with ever greater secrecy to the extent that circumstances permit.
>
> (Bok 1982:25)

The effects of secrecy strongly suggest that questioning can contribute much to preserve the rationality of planning. In an open planning process one cannot be sure that nobody will bring up the sensitive and covered material. More or less unconsciously the planners establish a bulwark against attacks there are not yet any sign of. Unconsciously or 'out of awareness', small groups like planning teams try to strike a balance between work and solidarity (Bales 1953) and to co-ordinate control of group defences with deepening of involvement and capability (Gustafson and Cooper 1979, Hirschhorn and Krantz 1982). Defence techniques for avoiding anxiety 'illustrate compulsive, repetitive, security-oriented, error-inducing and self-sealing human behaviour' (Diamond 1986:544). Self-protective processes and their adverse effects on organizational goal achievement are studied by Baum (1987), Diamond (1984), Kets de Vries and Miller (1989). The defence usually implies shaping of attention and organizing of bias, thereby bounding instrumental as well as communicative rationality (Baum 1987:5):

> Hierarchical authority relationships make bureaucratic workers especially anxious about being shamed by superiors for poor performance. In efforts to defend themselves against shame, workers may avoid taking initiative, attempt to confuse others about their responsibilities, ritualistically recite rules, and even doubt their own competence to act.

Baum goes on to say that '(b)ecause practitioners do these things unconsciously, generally they are unaware of their own 'hidden agenda' and have little opportunity to control it, even when it leads them to act in conflict with their conscious intentions' (ibid.5).

The main elements - impulse, system, conflict, and repression - have now been introduced. It was done without involving the distinction between instrumental and communicative rationality. This distinction is nevertheless at the core of dilemmas often encountered in planning. The contrasts between instrumental and communicative rationality help to demonstrate that planners face commitments which can hardly be simultaneously satisfied. I therefore make use of the competing rationalities in what follows.

The simultaneous striving for instrumental and communicative rationality can provoke conflict among values or ends that are not readily traded off. Communicative rationality is closely associated with communicative ethics, a commitment to the promotion of dialogue free from the influence of egoism and power relations (Habermas 1990). The competing rationalities are reflected in dilemmas relevant to planning, like:
- Democracy vs technocracy
- Participation vs efficiency
- Dialogue vs technique (Sager 1990a)
- Product-orientation vs process-orientation; e.g., planning as production vs planning as politics and integration.

Assume now that value conflict is present, and that it is not possible to decide by calculation which goal or value to yield on. Even after action, then, uncertainty will linger as to whether the right balance was found. There will be continuing tension, as the conflict is not resolved. On the one hand, experience shows that there is a psychological mechanism tending to give priority to action offering quick satisfaction.[1] This favours increased use of power to enhance objectives concerning production. On the other hand, there is a resistance against sacrificing ethical norms in order to reap material gains. Sometimes one is more likely to yield when it costs a few pounds than when it violates a few principles. This favours commitment to a planning process promoting democracy, autonomy, personal growth, etc. at the expense of implementing the best product at the preferred time.

Inter-rationality conflict of the above type can obstruct the exertion of power in pursuit of product-oriented planning goals. In such cases, the search for agreement and the mediation and negotiation among the involved parties become extensive. Even so, with limited instrumental power and a low threshold for what is accepted in terms of communicative distortions, projects may be delayed, and their design reveals the need to compromise as much as what is instrumentally rational. Frustration in the planning teams spreads and eventuates in a state of being dammed up. The planners are frustrated because they lose the feeling of doing their work well. Politicians and the populace are frustrated because they do not seem to get value for money.

The dammed up state can, e.g., manifest itself in sudden shifts of priorities, serving the urge to build *something*, even if it neither tops the ranking list nor has a satisfactory benefit-cost ratio. There will be impromptu discharges or uncontrolled attempts to end the dammed up state, usually revealing an increased willingness to wield power in order to have projects accepted and implemented. Such attempts imply irrationality, as for instance: the process is not designed in a way that can achieve procedural ends, analysis is carried out but the results are not utilized, public participation is encouraged but the citizens are not listened to, tasks granting the rationality and legitimacy of the planning effort are skipped, or communication is distorted in order to sweep sensitive material under the carpet - or more generally: in order to shape attention. Discharges like these prove the repression causing the dammed up state to be unsuccessful. The mechanisms protecting against the impulses bringing the inherent hard choices, dilemmas and paradoxes of planning to surface, do not succeed in laying them dead, but merely in transforming the problems, which reappear in planning practice in disguise.

As the symptoms of irrationality become conspicuous, the planning team becomes progressively less able to cope with the mounting tensions. For example, the conflicts related to product-orientation/process-orientation are transformed to group conflict within the agency. Fractions of the agency staff search for outside allies, making the problems externally visible. Obvious deficiencies in the rationality of the plan-making process multiply: certain people are not invited to meetings, some subjects are avoided, etc. There is a pressure on time-honoured democratic procedures in order to support partial interests. The result is inefficiency in the production and sanctioning of the plan.

To recapitulate: external and internal impulses bring to the fore dilemmas and paradoxes inherent in public planning and generate conflicts that cannot be solved in a way satisfying the involved parties. Tension lingers on and causes inefficiency and thus growing concern for the legitimate production of plans. In a modern society few decisions on public policy are made without preceding planning. As political rationality (Diesing 1962) is of paramount importance, one is not ready to accept that the decision-making system is impaired. Hence, planning as seen by the populace must appear to be legitimate, and to be thus perceived it must seem instrumentally rational. This effect can be obtained by actually restoring instrumental rationality or by concealing the irrationality resulting from bounds. Attempts will usually be made in both directions, and so the initial instrumental irrationalities are succeeded by communicative distortions as was shown in Table 8.3.

Too little is said in planning theory about what goes on from here. Will the communicative irrationalities simply be added to the prevailing instrumental ones? Or is there a possibility that communicative bounds can replace instrumental bounds? Does the bounding process bring us ever further from the original purpose of the planning? If so, why is the chain of irrationality-producing events not broken? Will a new situation emerge, in which actions are encouraged that *appear* to be rational in light of the preceding counterproductive attempts to cope with the initial dilemmas, yet tend to reinforce a pattern of behaviour continually defeating its own aim? What remedial mechanisms exist inside and outside the planning system, which can help to finally restore its reasonableness? Even though there are interesting contributions describing a number of psychological and sociological patterns causing regressive outcomes of intervention, a comprehensive approach addressing planning seems to be lacking (Boudon 1982, Sieber 1981).

Here, I shall only be able to comment on the first two questions above. Both inter-rationality bounding and replacement of bounds are conceivable. For instance, concealment and misleading information can keep potential conflict material covert and thus increase the likelihood of setting forth plans that are widely supported. However, communicative bounds reducing the chances for internal conflict may well foster groupthink. Concealing unfavourable effects of known planning alternatives may lead to premature interruption of the option seeking. And misleading information may prevent the risks attached to projects suggested by prominent staff members from being duly considered. This points to an ambiguity when it comes to the question of communicative bounds weakening or strengthening instrumental bounds. Consider also the following example concerning external conflict, that is, controversy involving people outside the planning agency. Prominent politicians sometimes insist on solutions that seem to be inferior according to the examinations made by the planners. Even when failing to give reasons for the decision, they might get away with it without scrutiny of their reasons and motives. The politicians may have anticipated protests were the planners' advice to be followed, and tacitly choosing another direction of development may help to forestall the dissent. On the other hand, it might not. Making a second-best choice without explaining why, is apt to be interpreted as arrogance and provoke groups preferring the planning alternative ranked highest by the IA. Hence, withholding information and avoiding debate may escalate external conflict and thereby reinforce some instrumental bounds.

An example is now offered in order to demonstrate how bounds on rationality accumulate. A number of cumulative patterns are conceivable. The bounds on rationality do not have to accumulate through simple and regular cycles, like every other bounding event being instrumental and communicative. And several smaller accumulation processes may be terminated within the overall on. That is, every one of the bounding events in the overall process does not have to cause new bounds.[2] Table 8.4 below shows the progression in pairs in order to clarify the degree of mutuality between instrumental and communicative bounding events. The points can be read in pairs (I1)(C1), (I2)(C2), etc., and there is one-way or two-way causal connection between the bounds in each pair. Here, the accumulation of irrationality requires that at least one of the bounds set in one pair is caused at least partly by a bound set in a preceding pair. The table illustrates an accumulation process resulting in parapraxis.

Table 8.4 is inspired by the TP10-process, but the bounding events listed are not collected from one single city. Furthermore, several points are exaggerated in order to make the progression in the table more like an archetype. Nevertheless, a paradigmatic example would give a more prominent place to conflict and repression. The strategies leading to the scenarios recommended by the Central Advisory Group - Trend, Public transport, and Environmental - are denoted 'standard strategies' in the table.

Table 8.4
Example of a planning process setting cumulative bounds on rationality

Instrumental (I) actions and bounds	Communicative (C) actions and bounds
(I1) Co-ordinated transportation and land use planning was initiated in the city. The planners were uncertain what political assumptions would be the platform of the plan, although it was clear that environmental concerns were to be taken into account more fully than before. The mandate given by the State to the local planning agencies was unclear, e.g., on extra funding and co-ordination with other plans. This generated uncertainty on ends and thus on means.	(C1) The local planners aimed at some citizen participation, and an information meeting was held. The planners raised the expectations of the local public too much and invited input of a too basic character, because the purpose of the plan and the conditions set by the Central Government were diffuse.
(I2) The basic assumptions for modelling and calculations were deficiently specified. Regional growth implies need for roads, public transport, and environmental protection, which in turn means increased grants. Growth rates for population, private cars, etc. were exaggerated in local analysis, as the planners submitted to political pressure.	(C2) Deliberately biasing the forecasts is a strategic deployment of facts, and stands in contrast to giving information for mutual understanding. The political ordering of particular forecasts made the planners suffer a value conflict, and made the co-operation between them and the politicians more difficult. The possibility for informed public debate on the need for new transport facilities decreased.
(I3) The TP10-analysis was meant to give long-term strategic choice of transportation and land use system and at the same time provide a four-year project catalogue for investment in classified roads. Both overview and detail were needed. Due to the dual purpose of TP10, the road projects were described in greater detail than the other elements of the plan. The road projects gave the impression of being more concrete and more carefully prepared, and this caused bias when setting priorities.	(C3) Because strategic overview as well as detail were required, the debate tended to develop on different levels of generality. This, and the controversial forecasts, made arguments shoot off in divergent directions instead of focusing on salient problems. The discussion of strategic choice was affected by quarrels about details in the classified roads sector.
(I4) Because of the two-level planning task and the disorderly discussion, political preferences made a confused impression with respect to future transportation and land use. Something had to be done to group the preferences and help the planners towards a	(C4) The important role to be played by the scenarios in the TP10-analysis nourished a conflict between the road-lobby and the environmentalists, that lasted throughout the entire process. The first group disliked that environmental improvement was - already in the names of the scenarios - associated with one scenario only, and even one to be reached by a strategy they considered hostile to road building. The environmental-oriented politicians and the Central Advisory Group

problem formulation. The scenarios recommended by the Central Advisory Group were adopted locally.

It turned out to be unclear on the local level what is meant by scenario planning and by strategic choice with the dual purpose of TP10. Doubt on the difference in status between a scenario, a strategy, and a choice alternative rendered the collection of input inefficient.

(I5) Due to some influential local politicians, the contents of the three standard strategies could not be laid down without intervention.

The planners had to take existing plans and political commitments into account to a degree that seriously impeded the option seeking. This led to strategies that were too similar, all of them comprising more or less ambitious construction programmes for classified roads.

(I6) For political reasons, the overall differences needed between the standard strategies could not be created by varying the road investments. They had to be generated by dissimilarities in land use and in the grants to public transport.

One was not able to generate interesting differences among future transport situations by varying the land use within the 15 years horizon. Furthermore, expectations of new criteria for subsidizing public transport operations were not held out by the State, so a radically increased supply of local transit seemed unrealistic. Hence, the strategies to be studied remained too similar.

(I7) The alternative strategies generated do mainly redistribute traffic within the urban area, while the total number of vehicle kilometres varies only slightly.

Contrary to stated intentions, the potential effects of co-ordinated transportation and land use plans on global pollution and national and international environmental commit-

wanted the City Council to make a choice among clearly distinct directions of development, as the scenarios were designed for.

Adoption of the centrally proposed scenarios was not discussed in advance locally. The road-oriented politicians regarded Public transport and Environmental as threats to the implementation of long desired road projects. As conflicts over road building were about to polarize the populace, this was not always said openly, but concealed behind the arguments that P was too expensive and E was too restrictive towards motorists.

(C5) A local Political Steering Group was established. Part of the purpose was to protect plans already made, in accordance with point (C4).

Planners were encouraged to ignore input arguing for drastic cuts in road building to the benefit of public transport or global environmental improvement. This limited the communication with radical opponents already at an early stage.

(C6) Because the differences between the alternative strategies were not sufficiently provoking, attention was directed elsewhere.

Much of the public debate shifted from the design of the future local transportation system to secondary issues, e.g., the traffic forecasts for private cars, the realism of assuming increased state transfers to public transport, and the choice of technology for collecting road tolls.

(C7) With the narrow range of alternative strategies, environmental groups felt they were not listened to. Important questions about the future environmental gains from decreased supply of road space remained unanswered.

Among the planners, interest shifted from public discussion on questions of substance to internal dispute on questions of method within the profession. They focused on model features affecting the accuracy of the answers to the questions analysed. E.g., the traffic forecasting model was criticized for not being sensitive to policy design. It does not allow calculation of the changes in traf-

ments remained unclarified. Environmental analysis was pushed into the background.

(I8) There was a political need to create the impression that environmental concerns were well catered for despite the road building profile of the strategies. One tried to achieve this by listing a considerable number of environmental objectives in the goal hierarchy. Each of these was reflected in a particular indicator included in the IA.

The indicators overlapped, because the planners tried to take account of all the crazes pursued by the politicians. The resulting double-counting affected the strategies to a varying degree and hence had a potential influence on the ranking of alternatives.

(I9) As the local politicians flinched from the thought of exploring a broad range of *local* options, the planners drew on hypothetical choices to be made by the *State* in order to generate alternative transportation strategies.

The planners pretended to formulate planning alternatives, yet central components of them could not really be chosen on the *local* level. The basic difference was, e.g., that one alternative required £30 million and the other £60 million of state grants, but such grants are beyond local control. Instrumental rationality suffers when it is not fully taken into account that the alternatives are partly chosen and partly assigned.

(I10) From the viewpoint of the majority of the local politicians, none of the preformulated scenarios looked attractive. Each of them - and the strategies leading to them - implied too one-sided pursuit of subsets of goals. Therefore, the planners designed a compromise of the standard strategies. The recommendation is something between the three strategies for which the impacts had been assessed. The basis was the E-strategy, to which some road projects were added.

fic following from each of the political measures meant to influence the demand for public transport, like improved convenience or more information about routes, bus stops, and departure times.

(C8) All groups want to make sure that the impacts they are prejudiced in favour of are analysed. Thus, the IA included indicators of virtually everything the politicians had stated an interest in. Furthermore, politicians express themselves in the language of ideologies that describe the same phenomena in different terms.

The result was double-counting in the sense that identical arguments were used without this being realized by the interlocutors. One argument was that 'P gives the greatest increase in the share of travellers using public transport'. However, increasing this share was no independent goal. Politicians wanted the increase mainly in order to reduce noise and pollution from cars, which was a separate argument. So the share-argument should not be given independent weight in evaluation.

(C9) It was attempted to make the planning alternatives seem interesting by arguing for the realism of even the most expensive of them. The debate was detached from the question of how to allocate municipal resources among projects and modes of transportation. Local political conflict on this issue was glossed over by common argumentative efforts to attract more state grants. The arguments of the planners were to an increasing extent addressing the Central Government instead of the local constituency.

(C10) The Political Steering Group did not want the public's attention to be attracted to the undesired scenarios adopted from the Central Advisory Group.

Thus, the IA of the standard strategies was superficially presented in the main report. As seen from (I10), this means that the readers were not really acquainted with *any* of the planning alternatives. Very little was done to facilitate overview of the IA-results.

A special IA was not carried out for any compromise, so the extra road projects lacked analytic support, and the consequences of the recommendation were merely sketched. That is, the only attractive strategy was not properly assessed. If analysed, the deviations from the E-strategy might not have been found to improve the calculated goal achievement. Extra road investments have to come at the expense of other desired projects when the state grants are fixed. However, the compromise was appropriate from an implementation point of view. Adjusting the road investment to the level planned in advance of the TP10 reassured the motorists. This was needed to prevent manifest conflict, since car drivers would have to pay road tolls whether the E-strategy or the recommended compromise was chosen.

(I11) The standard strategies had their impacts assessed as if they were real choice alternatives. However, they were not treated as such in the local decision process.

Nevertheless, except for the recommended compromise, no new options were identified. This means that real alternatives to the recommended compromise did not exist.

(I12) The results of the IA were used to a very low extent when giving reasons for the recommendation. The overall conclusion is that 1) there was no IA of the recommendation, 2) it did not have real competitors, 3) the construction of the recommendation was not sustained by the IA of the three standard strategies, and 4) there was no feedback from the politicians to the IA, so that it could be supplemented and take account of additional factors which might otherwise cause inconsistency between IA-result and recommendation. This impaired the instrumental rationality.

It was difficult to assess how the recommendation differed from the standard strategies. No explanations were offered on points where the recommendation deviated from the alternative found to be most attractive in the IA.

(C11) All the standard strategies were too unattractive to be reckoned as choice alternatives. How can it be, then, that the recommended compromise is so close to them that it does not warrant an IA? Why were new and attractive options or compromises not identified, so that a real choice situation could be established? Were competitors to the recommended compromise quite simply unwanted? How come, in the first place, that the local planners accepted without protest to assess the impacts of three strategies they did not intend to choose among?

Answers or comments to these questions were not given, even though they strongly affect the instrumental rationality of the planning process. An interpretation of this is that power relations affected and constrained the communication on identification and analysis of strategies.

(C12) Due to the fear of generating conflict, there is 1) silence on the trade-offs inherent in the choice among planning alternatives. Consequently, it is 2) not discussed which strategy the IA is pointing at. A recommendation has nevertheless to be made. 3) There is, however, no explanation in the final report of the recommended choice among the undominated alternatives, and no argumentative link from IA to recommendation. Still, 4) one pretends that the IA is the central tool for ranking the strategies, even if political considerations foreign to the IA turn out to be decisive. 5) These external political motives are not clarified. They may or may not improve the legitimacy of the choice of plan. This sequence of bounding events shows that the communicative rationality was seriously impaired.

The five-link chain of communicative distortions concluding the communicative column of Table 8.4 strikes back at instrumental rationality in different ways. Firstly, because the decision-makers fail to inform the planners of what they take to be important and unimportant. The political priorities should be reflected in option seeking, evaluation, and implementation. Secondly, means-end rationality is harmed because the unexplained political considerations affecting the decision can be counterproductive from the point of view of finding solutions to planning problems. The political motive may be, for instance, to avoid inconsistency between the present decisions and those of the recent past, as a loss of prestige is suspected to result from an implicit admission of defective judgement on preceding occasions. Reduced instrumental rationality follows when there are sound reasons for change of policy, while the politicians do not trust the constituency to approve it. In this case, new decisions will aim at supporting the former resolutions, even if conditions have changed so that higher goal achievement would result from parting with the outdated policy.

In the archetypal example, the TP10 as a rational planning system is challenged by both internal and external impulses. The first type comes from the TP10-planners themselves and accounts for nearly half of the impulses bounding rationality in the example. The behaviour of the planners causes the bounds in the last four pairs of Table 8.4 and threatens the credibility of the local planning effort. In the ninth pair, for instance, there is an impulse to argue vis-à-vis the State instead of mediating local conflicts. The tenth pair reveals an impulse to secure the recommendation by dropping the IA. External impulses threatening rationality come mainly from the local politicians. Their impulse to exaggerate the potential for local growth in the second pair threatens the planners' integrity and the realism of local plans. The fifth pair points to an impulse for protecting favourite projects, which hampers the option seeking. The impulses impede the planning process by giving rise to conflicts. Most of the conflicts probably do not arouse strong feelings, and there is little need to repress emotional material. There are exceptions, however. Below I draw attention to a couple of conflicts in the archetypal example and examine if the psychoanalytic approach helps to assess their influence on the accumulation of bounds.

The second pair of bounds in Table 8.4 deals with a conflict between the planners and the local politicians. It initiated when some politicians tried to persuade the planners to produce forecasts holding out expectations for substantial regional growth. On the surface, the conflict does not seem to contribute much to the cumulative bounding process, except for being among the factors causing unfocused debate (C3). However, the political threat against their integrity may well implant an anxiety in the planners. They may fear repeated attempts to manipulate their professional calculations and judgement to fabricate support for political goals. The ordering of forecasts may be followed by orders for special IA-results or by instructions to fall into line with a predetermined recommendation. The planners' anxiety may motivate their behaviour in the last three pairs of the table. If the planners know that the politicians have ready-made answers, it will seem meaningless to make a special IA of the recommendation and to work out additional compromise strategies.

Another conflict is identified in the fourth pair (C4) of Table 8.4. The controversy between the road-lobby and the environmentalists over the use of scenarios and the design of strategies is important even when taking only easily noticeable causalities into account. The succeeding pairs disclose the compromise of compensating for use of the scenarios by accepting considerable road building in all strategies. Also in this case, the acknowledgement of psychological mechanisms can reinforce the causality of the cumulative process. The conflict may affect the behaviour of the planners in the last three pairs through a process of anticipated reaction. While not quite happy with the recommendation, they would be even worse off having to support a similar recommendation after first casting serious doubt on it by conducting a more comprehensive and critical analysis. Furthermore, the questions of (C11) may remain unanswered because neither planners nor politicians want to risk disturbing the balance laboriously established between the road-lobby and the environmentalists. Repression might even make the planners unaware that there were important questions of this type to be answered. I conclude that the analogy with the psychoanalytic theory of neurosis helps to provide a more complete picture of the causal structure of the cumulative process.

When, as in Table 8.4, the types of rationality do not correct each other, parapraxis may be established. In cases where instrumental and communicative rationality mutually sustain a set of irrationalities or bounds, the parapraxis can be more or less chronic, and the analogy with neurosis is all the more suitable. Ineffective behaviour can be difficult to unlearn, because there may exist hidden reinforcements of the persisting conduct. Besides, there are barriers to the planners carrying out 'extinction trials'. By this is meant trying out the ineffective behaviour under circumstances that could demonstrate its inappropriateness to the planners. Little effort has been made so far to examine these phenomena in planning contexts. The study of build-up and de-escalation of parapraxes seems to be a meaningful future task for a critical theory of planning.

Notes

1 The effectiveness of a reward is reduced the longer the reward is delayed. The effectiveness of a punishment in attaching fear to the cues produced by performing a response is reduced more the longer the punishment is administered after the performance of the response. Thus, if a reward for a response comes immediately but a punishment for the same response is long delayed, the reward will control the subject's response, and the punishment will have little impact. Accordingly, when a person makes a response that has very damaging effects on his or her achievements, but the damage (the punishment) occurs after considerable delay, it may well occur that this maladaptive response will persist. The mechanism may induce an actor to wield unacceptable power in order to have his way now, at the expense of maintaining a good relationship with the respondent to the advantage of future co-operation.

2 The causal structure of cumulative bounding in the archetypal example is shown in Figure 8.2. The arrows run from cause to effect. Bounding events often have causes in addition to those indicated by the arrows. The figure displays several partial and terminated bounding processes, for example the one from (I1) to (C1), and the long subprocess ending with the ninth pair. The example could have terminated with this pair. However, the inclusion of the last three pairs reveals an overall process of cumulative bounding where the threats against the TP10-system are clearly becoming more serious towards the end.

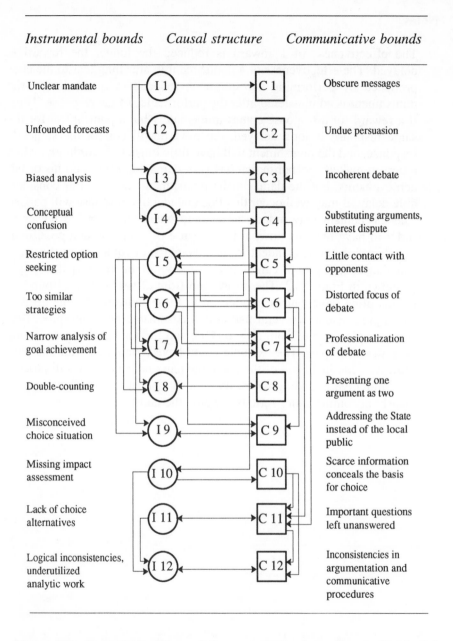

Figure 8.2 Causal structure of the cumulative bounding in Table 8.4

9 Flexibility in planning: between blueprint and garbage can

Introduction: the blueprint and 'garbage can' models

Blueprint planning forms the rigid end of the spectrum of planning theories. It presumes that preferences are stable and fully known in advance of planning, and that nothing is learned on the journey that will make us change the destination. One constructs a model of the future society or a segment of it, and implements it in full scale despite of the objections encountered on the way. Blueprint planning is strategical rationalism with the assumption of a linear process added.

In blueprint planning nothing is left to chance. The planning product is realized exactly as initially conceived by the planners. The popularity of the outcome is an entirely different matter. By giving a brief outline of the 'garbage can' model, it can be shown that chance seems to decide nearly everything at the other end of the spectrum of planning theories. Here, the outcome of planning is not determined by the will of a powerful actor to realize something figured out in advance. On the contrary, the outcome depends on which actors happen to run into each other in the arenas where plans are set forth, prepared, financed, and carried out.

The garbage can model of organizational decision-making in ambiguous contexts describes a decision situation in which instrumental reason is limited by inferior information, conflict, and ambiguous preferences. The model treats a choice opportunity as a garbage can into which participants dump various kinds of problems and solutions. The essence of garbage can models is spelled out in March and Olsen (1986:17):

> In pure form, the garbage can model assumes that problems, solutions, decision makers and choice opportunities are independent, exogenous streams flowing through a system ... They are linked in a manner determined by their arrival and departure times and any structural constraints

on the access of problems, solutions and decision makers to choice opportunities. In the absence of structural constraints within a garbage can process, solutions are linked to problems, and decision makers to choices, primarily by their simultaneity.

In its pure form, the garbage can model substitutes a temporal order for the consequential (causal) order usually taken for granted by planners. This is the central idea of the model (March and Olsen 1989:11-14). Intention is lost in context-dependent flows of problems, solutions, people, and choice opportunities. Their timing of arrival and disappearance from the scene are what make decisions happen as they do. In the citation above, 'independent streams' means, e.g., that the solutions drawn to our attention are not determined by the problems on our agenda. 'Exogenous streams' means that the planner or decision-maker cannot create or control the flow of problems, solutions, etc. By 'structural constraints' is meant (1) restrictions on access, requiring or not allowing a particular problem, for example, to be attached to a particular choice opportunity, or (2) constraints on the decision structure, e.g., a hierarchy determining who is permitted to participate in the making of a particular choice.

Would it be meaningful to specify a planning process corresponding to the pure garbage can decision situation? The ability to plan disappears when all the elements making up the decision are beyond the influence of the decision-maker. Moreover, events within a pure garbage can process may be understandable and even predictable, but they are not dominated by preferences. Planning, on the other hand, implies volition and attempts to realize preferences. The task of the 'planner' in a pure garbage can situation would be to sort out problems and action alternatives that fit together. Choice opportunities should be provided when promising combinations are identified. The planner might create such arenas for choice. This notwithstanding, the planner is reduced to a process facilitator without influence on substantive matter. Even problem identification and option seeking exceed his capabilities. A 'planning theory' founded on the garbage can concept might result in the most clear-cut contrast to the synoptic model that can be achieved by nearly eliminating instrumental reason without introducing an alternative form of rationality.[1]

We certainly want planning processes that are something between the blueprint and the garbage can models. Plans should be products of knowledge and human will. If their design is arbitrary, their correspondence with the preferences of the affected public will be arbitrary too. On the other hand, the myopic implementation of the blueprint, the blindness to everything but the preconceived picture, can bring us as far from the preferences of the affected public as the arbitrariness of the garbage can solutions. This provides the motive for elaborating the flexibility theme introduced in Chapter 7.

Flexibility can be a characteristic of planning, of a plan, a planning product (meaning an implemented plan), a decision, a system, a process, etc. Part of my analysis will be general, but I will specify the object when required. It is not discussed here how much flexibility is rational, or under what conditions it is so. The exposition can be supplemented on these points by a couple of other contributions. Pye (1978) treats 'keeping opportunities open' as a way of trading off flexibility against expected value as estimated under foreseeable uncertainty. An optimal level of trade-off is interpreted as rationality. Bratman (1983) investigates the circumstances in which stability of plans is rational or reasonable, i.e., when it seems sensible not to change them.

Most definitions of flexibility presuppose uncertainty. As Pearman (1985: 313) notes, '(u)ncertainty is a double-edged sword for the planner. Without it society's need for strategic planning would be much reduced, but its existence is often at the root of much of the criticism which public perceptions of the planning profession induce'. However, the emphasis here is neither on linking the concept of flexibility to the various notions of uncertainty and risk, nor to the principal analytic techniques for handling these phenomena.

In broad outline the sections of this chapter contain the following: the next section presents robustness, resilience, and stability as the three main forms of flexibility, and it is explained what is meant by flexibility in communicative rationality. The various facets of flexibility are helpful when assessing plans and planning processes under conditions of uncertainty. Then follows a section relating flexibility to substantive planning theory. Redundancy turns out to be the generic means for working out flexible solutions, and it is shown how redundancy may be obtained. The connections between flexibility and reliability and between rigidity and efficiency are explicated. In the last section I investigate whether synoptic and incremental planning are compatible with robustness, resilience, and stability. Furthermore, the two modes are contrasted from a new angle by means of the notions of reliability and efficiency.

The main concern is future opportunities

The section distinguishes three aspects of flexibility, viz., robustness, resilience, and stability. The preservation and creation of future opportunities for action are shown to be central features of them all. The notion of flexibility is shown to be applicable both under instrumental and non-instrumental rationality. The inquiry gives the background for relating flexibility to the planning modes in a later section.

Robustness, resilience, and stability

'Robustness' is probably the aspect of flexibility most often treated and applied in the planning literature. (References are given in Sager 1990b.) Gupta and Rosenhead (1968) define the robustness of a decision as the ratio of the number of satisfactory end-states which remain as open options after a decision is made, to the number of satisfactory end-states possible to reach prior to that decision. In the planning process reported in Chapter 8, robust decisions were made in a couple of the urban regions when choosing among transportation strategies. For instance, Oslo recommends simply that a compromise strategy be worked out, and Drammen's preliminary recommendation is to implement only the projects common to all the standard planning strategies.

One should not infer from the robustness concept that no options will be closed and maximum flexibility will result if no decisions are taken. As already mentioned, opportunities are actively created as well as closed through decisions. Note also that the closing of opportunities may have useful effects. For example, focusing on fewer action alternatives may enhance efficiency. Robustness places emphasis on planning as a decision-making process. The point is always to decide in such a way that several end-states can be reached. This is desirable because unexpected events may occur which block some end-states or make them inferior.

'Good' or acceptable end-states may be difficult to define, as there are most often competing interests involved in the planning process. Robustness to one party may sometimes mean restriction of opportunities to others, or mean that end-states that are threatening to others are nevertheless not discarded.[2]

Objections to the robustness concept are discussed by Rosenhead (1989), and an obvious one is illustrated in Figure 9.1, where decision II is far more robust than I. A, B, and C are decision-points and d-k are acceptable end-states. The robustness does not say anything about the internal difference between the end-states still accessible after decisions I and II. It might be that all the end-states which can be decided upon in decision-point C are extremely vulnerable to the same unexpected event. If II is chosen and that event occurs, the plan may be completely blocked. Rosenhead's concept of robustness states only that six out of eight good options are kept open by decision II. It does not consider how events beyond the control of the planners influence the relative likelihood of their implementation. The measure is designed for games in which we lack information on the moves of nature and the other actors.

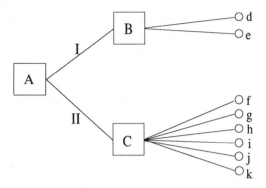

Figure 9.1 Decisions with different robustness

It should be kept in mind that robustness is not proposed as the one and only criterion for making decisions. Other criteria can take into account relative probabilities of implementation and the relative net advantages from each end-state.

Strictly speaking, Rosenhead's measure of robustness is only defined for decisions. The idea of robustness as keeping options open can, however, be applied to related phenomena, e.g., planning. Robust planning keeps alternative solutions to the planning problem open throughout the process. Different versions of the planning product should be implementable. The final design depends on the new information collected during implementation.

'Resilience' is the next aspect of flexibility to be dealt with. Hashimoto, Stedinger, and Loucks (1982:16) say that resilience describes 'how quickly a system is likely to recover or bounce back from failure once failure has occurred'. The resilience is measured as the inverse of the expected time elapsing from a failure occurs to the output of the system is again satisfactory. In the transportation and land use planning outlined in Chapter 8, a resilient strategy was proposed for the Stavanger region. The planners contend that 'it is the sum of many different actions and projects that will lead to the desired results, not the one-sided promotion of a few elements'. When this recommendation is followed, one can use some of the other means to correct failure if one measure does not give the expected results.

If failures are prolonged events and system recovery is slow, this may have serious implications for plan or system design. One would like to design plans that can make the system return to a satisfactory state rapidly. Imagine, for instance, that a new arterial road link is built on the basis of predicted traffic. However, the traffic forecast turns out to severely underestimate the real volume. As a result, the transport system does not function well, and there are queues at many junctions. Resilience denotes the inverse of the time needed to correct the plan, possibly by increasing the capacity of the new link so that the objectives of the plan are achieved.

Resilience can be defined within a strategic scheme, giving a closer correspondence with robustness. System failure may then occur if the planner makes a wrong decision. Failure is manifest when the actor is prevented from continuing the advance towards an acceptable end-state. For instance, an airport planning process may have to be reversed as detailed investigation shows the most promising sites to be far more vulnerable to fog than expected. The decision not to search for other promising sites may have to be reconsidered. Failure, in the sense I employ the term here, occurs when the robustness is zero, and only then.

If decisions are reversible, as is likely in the airport example, it may be possible to correct the failure.[3] Within the strategic scheme, resilience is the inverse of the time needed to 'undo' the unfortunate decision. This means making a new decision setting the process on the right track towards satisfactory end-states. It may be necessary to go back several decision-points to identify the set of decisions that has to be altered. One can infer from the last paragraphs that resilience is defined for processes as well as products.

Now, recall Hirschman's (1967) statement that our ability to be creative is always underestimated. When this is true, our skill to improvise and to remedy the harm done by unanticipated events is systematically underrated. Accepting the argument of Hirschman, one can deduce that the resilience of plans and projects tends to be higher than expected. It may nevertheless be expedient to plan for increased resilience by developing public-sector crisis management strategies. Crisis response planning aims to foster the development of adaptive strategies before a crisis strikes (Kartez 1984).

'Stability' is the third aspect of flexibility to be described. Stability renders the plan useful even if the conditions change significantly. As for robustness and resilience, one has to determine what is and what is not a satisfactory outcome. The two other concepts tell, respectively, how large a part of the satisfactory outcomes is retained, and how long an outcome will be unsatisfactory in case of failure. Stability says to what degree and how frequently the key variable can deviate from its predicted value before the plan is judged to be less than satisfactory (Sager 1990b:18). Suppose that the key variable of a plan for public transport in a sparsely populated area is the number of passengers per trip relative to the capacity. A dial-a-ride system operating vehicles of varying size would be stable over variations in travel demand compared to scheduled transit with buses of uniform size. The idea of stability is readily applicable both to a planning process and a planning product.

Concern for stability was observed in some of the cities during the transportation planning dealt with in Chapter 8. In Nedre Glomma the stability of the recommended planning strategy was tested by working out the economic programme for action under several alternative financial assumptions. In Trondheim the planners argued that the land use strategy filling in the open spaces of the existing built-up area and increasing the population density close to the city centre, would be stable with respect to prospective restrictions on the use of private cars.

'Staging' is a procedure aiming at stability, and frequently used in road construction (Norgaard and Dixon 1986:310). Staging means that a project is divided into shorter links in such a way that the first links fit into the existing network. These links will then yield benefits even if the later stages are postponed, altered, or cancelled. The prime advantage is that financial expenses can be adjusted to changed budgetary conditions, and more easily fit the limited annual grants. To some extent, staging permits adjustments to be made in response to unanticipated environmental, social, and technical problems or opportunities. This is flexibility during the implementation of project or plan, and it is an incremental practice.[4]

Keeping future options open is the crucial concern when flexibility is aimed at. This is obvious for robustness, but indirectly it is also behind the search for resilience and stability. When there is resilience, there are possibilities for adjustments. Adjusting means doing things slightly different from what was firstly planned. So, in fact, we have kept some options open, although they are most often quite close to the one initially chosen. When aiming for stability, there is a specific future action alternative one wants to keep open: one wishes to retain the possibility of holding on to the original plan. A stable plan is rarely in need of correction.

Notions of flexibility can be defined by the application of the social science concepts dealt with in previous chapters, e.g., conflict. A plan could be called flexible when it can be adjusted so as to be politically feasible no matter which party wins some particular political conflict in the community. Coser (1967:32-3) uses conflict to characterize a flexible social system. It is able to readjust itself and prevent the accumulation of conflict. This indicates that the idea of flexibility is so general that it can be specified in relation to numerous social concepts and variables.

Flexibility and communicative rationality

For the sake of 'the beauty of symmetry', this section should have dealt with flexibility in instrumental as well as communicative rationality. However, the applicability of robustness, resilience, and stability to the characterization of a means-end scheme does not seem problematic. I have spelled out elsewhere how the notion of flexibility is used in economics and planning where such a scheme is valid (Sager 1990b). Here, I explain what it means to be flexible in an integrating process on the personal or the small-group level. An extra gain from this subsection is that the conception of a flexible human being gives some flesh and blood to the notion of personal growth.

When it is necessary to be precise, I use 'instrumental flexibility' when referring to means-end schemes and instrumental relationships. The term 'social flexibility' is employed when referring to the socialization aspect of communicative rationality, as in the psychological literature shortly to be quoted.

The core of the social flexibility concept is to keep open the possibilities for meaningful future interaction with other people. The emphasis is on the ability to adjust without losing integrity. Social flexibility should not be thought of as an instrument for achieving operational ends. On the other hand, as the individual (or collective) is most often able to influence its environment, social flexibility does not denote just a passive reaction to external change. It includes this aspect but is more typically the capacity for mutual adjustment of the self and its environment in a way maintaining the potential for growth and integration in the individual. Thus, social flexibility is a property of a living and viable system, not of a thing or a process.

In psychology, flexibility is not the most common term used to designate the elasticity of mind ensuring the beneficial modifications that are necessary to meet external demands. Other words describing much the same quality are adjustment, adaptability, and ego-resilience.[5] Nevertheless, Coan (1974) and Boelen (1978) apply the flexibility concept to characterize important qualities of the personality. It will be seen that the concept is closely connected with other notions related to the co-ordination and socialization aspects of communicative rationality treated in preceding chapters.

Growth of the self is a change in the way of experiencing the world and one's own being. However, one can speak of growth only when the changes enhance the person's ability to cope with challenges in existence. Constructive response to change and wilful initiation of change require some elasticity of mind. Coan (1974:204) infers that '(f)lexibility is both a precondition for growth and a consequence of growth'.

Coan examines the question of flexibility in the context of many aspects of personal functioning - the individual's characteristic locus of attention, cognitive skills, impulse regulation, fundamental attitudes towards oneself and the world, and basic modes of sensing, imagining, and understanding. He concludes that:

With respect to those functions that distinguish the major life styles and general attitude patterns of people, flexibility may be less essential, for a onesided life can be very useful and productive. Flexibility, however, makes possible a life of richer experience, and it is prerequisite for continuing growth.   (Coan 1974:213)

Boelen aims to describe the mature personality. This is found in adults having gone through a substantial process of personal growth. He criticizes the usual understanding of emotional maturity in terms of self-control. His stand is that:

The rigidity of the controlling will-to-power has nothing to do with the playful, flexible, and creative interplay of primordial inspiration and particular emotions that orchestrates the entire personality. Consequently, a person is emotionally mature, not when he merely controls his emotions or keeps a lid on his feelings, but rather when he is able to accept his integral emotional resources in a healthy, creative and spontaneous way.   (Boelen 1978:172)

Boelen conceives of flexibility as an inner balance characterized not by a state of perfect equilibrium or the taking of a middle-of-the-road position in every situation. On the contrary, a flexible balance holds the properties of playful seriousness, elastic stability, and creative faithfulness to the process of integration. This last feature is crucial because Boelen emphasizes the relationship between flexibility, rootedness, and integration. Flexibility is seen as a requisite for obtaining a mature balance of the personality.

Planning should arrange for social flexibility when personal growth is part of its rationale. Besides, flexibility fostering integration is required, e.g., when planning takes the form of conflict management. In fact, an amalgamation of instrumental and social flexibility is needed.

Redundancy as a means to attain flexibility

The section draws attention to an aspect of good plan design. Theories of how to make the plan flexible are part of substantive planning theory. 'Redundancy' is the general key to flexibility, and I specify ways to achieve it. Flexible plans are also reliable, and rigid plans tend to be efficient. Both reliability and efficiency are interesting properties of a plan, but they are scarcely simultaneously attainable in practice.

Posterior rationality means that experiencing the planning product may alter the preferences of the decision-makers. They might appreciate the effects of the plan more than expected in advance, or they might be disappointed. Under such conditions it is a great advantage if the planning product can be adjusted, expanded, contracted or completely replaced. In short, posterior rationality calls for flexible planning products, and this makes flexibility an interesting theme in substantive planning theory.

Rosenhead's robustness is defined for decisions and is a kind of flexibility of the planning process, not of the product. The demand for flexible planning products implies an invitation to consider the product as probationary, as something not necessarily final. When this is accepted, there is a link between robustness and the claims for adjustment possibilities. The planning product as it was first implemented is now called x_0, and the results that would emerge after alternative adjustments of x_0 are denoted x_1 and x_2. When it is assumed that the decision to implement x_0 keeps the opportunities x_1 and x_2 open, one will see the close connection between flexibility as robustness and flexibility as possibility for adjustments of the product. The idea of robustness approaches the ideas of stability and resilience as it is transferred from process to product. With a robust plan, unexpected events leave the opportunity open to hold on to the plan or to easily correct it in various ways. The above notwithstanding, keeping options open tends to be a less pressing concern as the implementation proceeds. The critical choices have been made, and the major task is now to make the chosen alternative function satisfactorily. This shifts the focus to stability and resilience, which are properties attached as much to the product as to the process.

The question is now how flexible planning products come about. When writing his theory of interpretation, Ricoeur (1976) subtitled the book 'Discourse and the surplus of meaning'. Interpretation presupposes a surplus of meaning. It is this property of the text that provides the multiple opportunities and hence flexibility. In planning for flexibility the analogue to surplus of meaning is 'redundancy'.[6] We communicate in a pleonastic manner not only to make sure we are understood, but also to escape the unequivocal rigidity of command-like messages. We also equip projects with excess capacity in various directions. They are furnished with attributes that could have been omitted for the moment without significant loss, although they expand our opportunities with respect to future use. Repetition, duplication, and overlap are general remedies to introduce redundancy and thereby cure an efficient but vulnerable and too error-prone process or plan (Landau 1969).

McLoughlin (1969:119) adopts the redundancy concept from cybernetics and information theory. When the aim is to design a flexible system, more elements and more connections are included than strictly necessary for the functioning of the system. With reference to substantive planning theory in transportation and town planning, this means that more space for certain activities and a more fine-meshed transportation network should be supplied, than needed for the functioning of the planning product under normal conditions. The link to robustness is readily seen, as that property implies redundancy by keeping more opportunities open than seem required at the time.

Lynch (1981:Ch.9) suggests the following common means for providing flexibility of human settlements which requires a match between place and patterns of behaviour:

a) Provide excess capacity.
   Excess capacity improves all three aspects of flexibility. Two examples are the construction of a framework strong enough to take extra storeys on top of a structure, and the instalment of sewers large enough to handle population growth. One reason for building excess capacity into the road network is uncertainty as to where activities generating substantial traffic will be located in the future.

b) Improve access.
   If it is easy to collect information and to bring in resources (capital, workers, expertise), then productive activity can be changed quickly and with small effort. This is requisite for quick recovery from failure. Alternative routes connecting the most important origin and destination zones provide an example.

c) Reduce the interference between parts.
   Stability improves if negative influence on any one part of the planning product will not force change on another. Staging is one way to protect the early parts of a plan from growing resistance against the later parts.

d) Standardize remedies, equipment, and input factors.
   Resilience is facilitated when constructing by means of standard units permitting easy replacement of damaged parts, and simple connections between parts arranging for uncomplicated repatterning (Cowan 1963).

The above list helps sum up how the three forms of flexibility depend on redundancy:
- Robustness implies a redundancy of opportunities, e.g., alternative future solutions to a planning problem.

- Resilience is fostered by a redundancy of capacity, access, and standardization. Redundancy may also mean spare parts or subsidiary command centres to take over the functions of those which have failed or been damaged. Other helpful features are 1) excess agreement enabling the steering system to make decisions without delay, and 2) excess power, e.g., strong potential allies to fight off resistance.
- Stability is improved by redundant capacity and independence among the parts of the plan. The parts should be designed so that they can be expanded and contracted.

The plan should be designed to promote the realization of the intrinsic values of the planning process. This implies that participants feel they have been listened to, and that their involvement has been meaningful. The task may be difficult because the participants usually represent competing interests and therefore disagree among themselves. Hence the plan design will be a compromise judged suboptimal by any partisan criterion. From this perspective, it is an advantage if a design is chosen that is heterogeneous, complex, and composite. The plan should be composed by loosely interconnected parts, so that some can be adjusted to the wishes of one interest group, and some correspond with the preferences of another. The redundancy needed is arranged for by

(1)   making the whole project more multifaceted and versatile than is functionally required;
(2)   letting the plan consist of more elements than are technically necessary; and
(3)   reducing the interdependence among the elements beyond the level suggested by economic risk analysis, to be able to tailor each part to special interests.

Another - manipulative - strategy is well known from bargaining and haggling. The planner may expect protests anyway, so he announces substantial changes, then yields on some of his initial proposals, and thus gives the local participants a sense of victory. In this case redundancy refers to the number of encroachments required by the precursory contrivance.

This subsection is concluded by reference to a theme dealt with by Landau (1969).[7] He poses the question whether one can build an organization that is more reliable than any of its parts. His answer is that von Neumann demonstrated that this could be done by adding sufficient redundancy (ibid.350). Analogically, one may ask if a plan can be more than the sum of its parts; or more specifically, if it can be more reliable than its weakest component. An example indicates that the answer is affirmative. Suppose that one is to plan the operations of an urban public transit system. On each bus there is a change of driver several times a day, and smooth and punctual operation requires that the driver supposed to relieve another does in fact show up. The table announcing who relieves who, and where and when the shifts are to take place, is one part of the plan. Another part may be to situate a ward office near the relief place and always have spare drivers present. If a reserve driver should oversleep, the buses are still likely to run as usual, and if the new driver is held up on the way to work, there will probably be someone in the ward office to step in for him or her. Due to a redundancy of personnel, the operation plan will be reliable even if one or another of its components sometimes fails. Stability is achieved even if unexpected things happen.

Reliability vs efficiency

The challenges issued by the political environment can be met by the planners in various ways. The planners can vary their responses by designing more or less synoptic or incremental processes, and by solving their tasks more or less communicatively or computatively. This chapter points to flexibility/rigidity as a third response dimension. There is something peculiar about the last dichotomy, however. The dimension is useful in a contingency approach only if both of its extremes possess attractive features. Then the planners will respond flexibly in some contexts and rigidly in others. Valuable properties of rigidity have not been specified so far. Drawing on ideas from Landau (1969), it will be done now that the concept of redundancy has been introduced.

The allegation is that rigidity implies low redundancy and therefore improves efficiency. At the same time, however, it gives more unreliable solutions. In the above example concerning public transit operation planning, redundant personnel gave rise to a stable and reliable system. It might nevertheless have been more efficient (except, perhaps, when starting in the morning) to demand that the drivers continue until they are relieved, even if the next driver is late. Assume that a missing driver always causes some delay on the route. Then, less redundant personnel would decrease the reliability of the system. It might still be the most efficient solution in terms of profit, though. The personnel-saving system would be a step closer to a streamlined organization operating with the absolute minimal number of units needed to perform a task. Such streamlining is likely to require seriality as in the case of drivers succeeding each other without overlap or spare personnel. The efficient solution above is rigid because (1) there is only one way to cope with the problem, (2) it is highly vulnerable to the particular failure discussed, and (3) it takes longer time to correct the failure than the solution based on reserve drivers.

A more abstract picture of such efficient seriality is given by a means-end chain without an excess link in it, i.e., without redundancy. It is very efficient for guiding action as long as no error occurs. But it is also very rigid and vulnerable, for when a problem-solving system consists of no more than the absolute minimal number of parts, no unit has the special task of detecting error (ibid.356). The extreme efficiency is obtained at the cost of reliability. The loss of efficiency caused by the redundancy required for reliability and flexibility leads Friedmann (1978:164) to formulate a paradox of planning: 'when you have least need of planning because nothing changes, planning works best; it is 100 percent efficient'.

It has now been shown that high redundancy brings about flexibility and reliability, and low redundancy leads to rigidity and efficiency. The link to reliability strengthens the argument for analysing flexibility as part of substantive planning theory, as the need for reliable products, I think, has an intuitive appeal. I go on to specify what is meant by reliability and efficiency of a product and a process, respectively. A planning product is reliable when it functions as preconceived under varying conditions, and if it can be easily brought back to its normal way of operating when malfunction occurs. One recognizes the ideas of stability and resilience. Reliability as understood here does not presuppose that the planners have succeeded in taking action satisfying those affected by the plan, so a reliable plan is not necessarily efficacious. A reliable process will, with a high probability, identify a feasible planning alternative of satisfactory quality. This is accomplished by working out reserve options in case of changing circumstances, i.e., by robust planning.

The most efficient planning product solving a particular problem is that with the highest effect-cost ratio. When goals are quantified, one can express this as the ratio of goal achievement to costs. As an approximation, that process is said to be the most efficient, which results in a sufficiently good plan, or implements a satisfactory planning product, at the lowest costs. Rigidity is not conducive to communicative rationality, because rigid planning is geared to the demands of instrumental efficiency.

Now that the affinities of flexibility and reliability are established, one is better equipped to see the contours of a general dilemma. Sometimes it surfaces as a tension between flexibility and rigidity or between reliability and efficiency, but it may be disguised in other terminology. Sillince (1986:169) writes about ambiguous versus specific plans, and Friend and Jessop (1969: 117-8) contrast freedom of choice and commitment. Levi and Benjamin, in discussing conflict resolution, point to the necessity of balancing focus and flexibility:

Focus is the function of exclusion and constancy, flexibility that of variety and variability. A central human paradox, which reflects itself in all applied behavioral science practice, is the simultaneous requirement for these contrasting functions.   (Levi and Benjamin 1977:405)

Flexibility requires an ability to view matters inclusively, to take as much as possible into consideration, and to change direction easily. Focus pinpoints the crucial elements and demands a degree of rigidity.

One way to alleviate the general tension of efficiency and reliability in the planning process is to design different yet intertwined subprocesses. The one should support efficiency where the other accentuates reliability, and vice versa. The subprocesses should be run parallel in order to complement each other and allow planners to unite them when special tasks require so. For instance, the solution to a planning problem may be found by discussion or by analytic technique. The communicative and sometimes unruly and conflictful citizen participation process may run parallel, yet somewhat unintegrated, with the technical experts' more streamlined analytic approach to problem-solving. The simultaneous use of both subprocesses provides a form of constructive redundancy. The planner can resort to one of the subprocesses when it comes to tasks where the other is weak. Seen in the perspective of flexibility and redundancy, there is clearly a case for communication *and* calculation in planning; it is not a matter of either/or.

Flexibility and the principal planning theories

The section deals with the relationships between the various notions of flexibility and the synoptic and incremental planning modes. I investigate how redundancy enters synoptic and incremental planning, and show that there are reliable as well as efficient aspects of both modes. Neither synoptic nor incremental planning is unequivocally flexible, and neither are they unambiguously rigid. While synoptic planning follows a rigid plan-making process, choice is made in an unrestricted manner. With incrementalism it is the other way round.

The forms of flexibility in synoptic and incremental planning

Uncertainty and risk are what make flexibility an interesting concept. Without incertitude about one's own future preferences or the future actions of the planning environment (including nature), flexibility would be superfluous. Nevertheless, omniscient and optimizing agents respond with complete flexibility to every perturbation in their environment (Heiner 1983).

So synoptic planning is flexible in that it nearly always succeeds in realizing the best possible solution no matter how conditions change. The quest for optimality makes us hunt for only one attractive but rare kind of game. If we do not track it down, we might return home empty-handed even if there was a great abundance of other game in the shoot. That is, strategical rationalism, as a maximizing procedure, aims at the optimal without systematically considering the availability of second-best solutions. This may be problematic in an uncertain world. Rosenhead (1980) and others have contrasted flexible planning with the pursuit of optimality. Sillince (1986:137) recommends that we 'opt for a flexible and adjustable plan rather than one which is "optimal" in some way, but runs the risk of being inappropriate'.

It is of no consequence that the number of opportunities is reduced as long as the best end-state is still accessible. The power of the controller is not diminished if he loses some opportunities that would not be used in any case. Hence, there is little reason for the synoptic planner to hold preferences concerning the number of open options.

The robustness concept of Rosenhead is neither strictly incremental nor synoptic. The concept requires that the number of acceptable end-states is known at the outset, which is a synoptic property. But it also assumes that an aspiration level is set, practising satisficing rather than maximizing, and this is an incremental property. In the standard formulation of Rosenhead, the probability of choosing a sequence of actions is independent of the values of the end-states as long as they are satisfactory. In some cases the qualities of the end-states may be one-dimensional, or the multiple dimensions may be represented in a linear utility function. Pye (1978) proposes a robustness concept allowing the decision-maker to take into account differences between the values of sequences of actions. This variant is more synoptic because satisficing is dismissed. One need not assume the existence of an aspiration level, but may start out from a feasible set of end-states (which does not necessarily make a big difference). The decision-maker is a maximizer, but because of uncertainty he balances the value of a sequence of actions against the number of opportunities kept open.

So long as the best possible result is reached at any time, there is nothing to correct. Even in synoptic planning, however, deviation from the best possible may occur, and resilience becomes an attractive property of a plan. Likewise, perfect foresight gives key variables equal to their predicted values, and the question of stability is irrelevant. As synoptic planning was defined in Chapter 1, however, information on the future is imperfect, and forecasts may diverge from realized values.

We now pass on to a discussion of the reconcilability of incrementalism and the notions of flexibility. With extreme rigidity or extreme flexibility, there is no need for planning - at least not the control aspect of it. In the first case the chain of events is predetermined, and planning can make no difference. In a very flexible system one simply adjusts to the stress and strain that turn up instead of figuring out strategies and solutions beforehand. This points to incrementalism with its ideal of mutual adjustment.

Whitehead (1974:35) contends that 'if we produced no plans at all, but made decisions in the spirit of disjointed incrementalism, we would have complete flexibility'. I have two objections to this statement. First, a rigid social system will not become flexible, in the sense of acquiring a high capacity for adjustment, just because we apply the incremental process when making decisions concerning the system. Rather, the logic should be reversed; it is the flexibility of a system that makes it meaningful to apply the incremental process. Second, even when incrementalism is aptly used, it does not necessarily arrange for maximal flexibility in the sense of future choice opportunities. Large steps and radically new ways to attack a problem can sometimes generate a new range of attractive solutions. This is in line with the critique set forth by Rosenhead (1980:211):

> Under incrementalism, existing social priorities would be effectively insulated from fundamental challenge - for the generation of information and of solutions would be in the hands of agencies with vested interests in the status quo or its 'natural' development. Such a process therefore offers only a different type of inflexibility in social planning, the determinism of the unhindered unfolding of existing tendencies.

The above points are in accordance with Heiner's (1983) view of the relationship between the uncertainty of the environment and the observed regularities of behaviour. Heiner contends that uncertainty in distinguishing preferred from less-preferred behaviour leads to behavioural rules 'that restrict the flexibility to choose potential actions, or which produce a selective alertness to information that might prompt particular actions to be chosen' (ibid.561). These mechanisms simplify behaviour to less-complex patterns, of which the small-steps-low-risk procedure of disjointed incrementalism is one example. The significant discord between competence and difficulty - the 'C-D gap' - under incrementalism causes the rigid kernel of that mode of planning: always opt for small adjustments creating only modest resistance. Satisficing is another simplifying response to uncertainty. In this case one sacrifices flexibility by always choosing the first alternative satisfying the aspiration level. Then the robustness measure is not operational, since we know only one useful solution when we act. Heiner states that '(n)umerous deviations from the resulting behavior patterns are actually superior in certain situations, but they are still ignored because of uncertainty about when to deviate from these regularities' (ibid.585).

Recall Hirschman's (1967) thesis that we tend to undervalue our creativity, our ability to handle unforeseen difficulties, and hence our capacity for flexibility. It suggests an additional reason why we follow rigid behavioural rules in uncertain decision contexts. Braybrooke and Lindblom's (1963:239) recommendation is explicitly risk adverse, as 'the virtue of incrementalism ... is to shun any policies whose scope is such that if they miscarry, the evils will exceed the remedial powers of existing institutions'. The rule requires that insurance be in force for each step. Especially when creativity is underestimated, this rule may well be too rigid.

Although disjointed incrementalism is permeated by the need for adjustability, Lindblom rarely uses the concepts of flexibility applied in this chapter.[8] This is also true of the following citation which is nevertheless an appeal for robust decisions:

> Sometimes policy analysts deliberately make little mistakes to avoid big ones. One can deliberately choose a policy (knowing that it is not quite the right policy) that leaves open the possibility of doing better in a next step, instead of a policy designed to be on target but difficult to amend. ... In as relatively simple a policy problem as routing New Haven traffic, to try out one-way traffic going south and stand ready, if that is unsuccessful, to try a northbound flow may be better than to gamble, through an a priori study of traffic flows, on a permanent installation of expensive controls to inaugurate southbound one-way movement.
>
> (Lindblom 1968:24)

The request is presented under the heading of 'The next chance', and robustness is regarded as a strategy or dodge for dealing with very complex problems, on an equal footing with, e.g., remediability, satisficing, and feedback. Remediability designates the practice of making efforts to break out of an intolerable situation without having decided on the characteristics of the situation one would consider most attractive. The immediate ambition is to escape from failure and reach something satisfactory - just as when resilience is called for. Resilience may be seen as a measure of the effectiveness of the remediable manoeuvres under incrementalism.

It is an inflexible aspect of incrementalism that only a certain kind of change is accepted, but it is a flexible trait that all implemented changes can be adjusted. The first property decreases robustness while the last one promotes resilience. Robustness, resilience, and stability have two incremental features in common, namely the explicit acknowledgement of uncertainty and failure, and the setting of an aspiration level (satisficing).

Much critique of disjointed incrementalism springs from a fear of too low stability (Boulding 1964, Etzioni 1967). When unexpected incidents occur, the former steps on the incremental path may be judged as mistakes, and policy may take a new direction. This may happen in any decision-making process facing uncertainty. The point is that disjointed incrementalism has no long-term strategy to help determine the new direction. There are several actors advocating different interests, there are series of disjointed decisions to be made, and there are decision-makers yielding to pressure. In these circumstances a useful long-term course would not be easily stuck to even if it did exist. No such mechanism can exist, however, because the notion of 'a useful long-term course' implies predetermined long-term goals. But goals are not predetermined under incrementalism; they are developed as one goes along.

Reliable and efficient aspects of the synoptic and incremental modes

I spell out here how redundancy enters synoptic and incremental planning. One will see that there are reliable as well as efficient facets of both planning modes. Only under perfect conditions is it possible to concentrate on reliability without being troubled by inefficiency - and vice versa. Disjointed incrementalism and the synoptic planning found in practice are modes in which rationality is bounded and attention is limited. The less than perfect conditions under which planning is then undertaken force a loss of both reliability and efficiency.

Seriality was pointed out in the former section as a way of ordering elements, units, etc. to obtain an efficient system. The synoptic planning process comes close to the serial arrangement. The problem-solving phases follow each other without overlap, and repetition is avoided as far as possible since nearly perfect knowledge makes loops superfluous. The disjointed aspect emphasized by Lindblom is not present, so duplication is not a feature of the process. The absence of procedural flexibility has to be compensated, and this is done by supplying a gross redundancy of information and computational capacity. Deficient redundancy in the process is balanced by perfect technical planning conditions. The synoptic process is rigid and efficient. Under the utopian condition of omniscient actors the process works. It does not matter much that flexibility is lacking, because things rarely go wrong.

A very different characterization can be given of the synoptic choice situation. The choice of solution to any problem is flexible and nearly unrestricted. The solution is not limited to a narrow subset of possibilities, but is the universally best one thanks to abundant information. Synoptic choice maximizes goal achievement even when a higher level of integration would be reached by other solutions. Put differently, social flexibility is given up to protect the instrumental rationality of the process. Yet, because of the ample information rendering most conflicts irrational, only small problems arise when deciding on planning proposals. Nevertheless, even synoptic planning might fail, since uncertainty is not completely eliminated. Unlimited attention cannot be directed to maximization of the difference between known benefits and costs. Some attention must be given to risk, and this introduces some rigidity because it limits the choice set. Hence, less perfect planning conditions generate a less efficient planning process and less flexible choice.

Synoptic planning gives technique and calculation a prominent place. What is meant by reliability and efficiency in a technical analysis? Reliability is improved in the following three ways:
a) Experience: increased number of observations.
b) Understanding: for instance, models including more of the variables affecting the solution of the problem.
c) Complete exploitation of knowledge: use of mutually supplementary techniques; for example, estimation from both cross-section and time-series data.

In order to utilize these three pieces of advice without further ado, there must be a redundancy of calculative capacity and of information (data). The second point recommends that many phenomena are taken into consideration to reduce the probability that unanticipated events upset the conclusions (stability). In addition, errors following from such events should be easily corrected by running the calculation again on the new data and possibly by changing the technique.

Efficiency of technical analysis is achieved when the solution to the problem is found, which is sufficiently reliable and requires least data among the solutions having this property. Efficiency means that redundant data are not processed. The number of variables and the number of observations of each variable are kept on a minimum level.

I will now consider dialogical incrementalism, which proves to be a contrast to the synoptic mode also with respect to reliability and efficiency. The incremental process contains loops and repetition of analysis, duplication of work carried out by different actors, and overlaps among the phases of the process. Hence, there is a redundancy of 'hook-ups' between actors and between tasks. The process itself is flexible and reliable. It can be trusted to produce a planning alternative that has a high probability of being implemented. In fact, the plan will be implemented, since those involved have perfect abilities for mutual understanding and agreement.

Dialogical incrementalism bounds instrumental rationality, but the conditions are nearly perfect for decision-making by dialogue. There is perfect communicative competence which is unconditionally used in the service of mutual understanding. In dialogue there is perfect suppression of communicative distortions. The redundancy of competence and abolition of 'misinformation' under dialogical incrementalism can be seen as analogues to the redundancy of, respectively, calculative capacity and information under synoptic planning. To epitomize the salient features of the process: dialogical incrementalism is reliable; and it does not matter that efficiency is lacking in the design of the process, because all parties agree about what should be done. Empathy and communicative competence make them adapt to the fact that instrumentally more satisfying solutions would cause loss of integration that is more highly appreciated.

Choice in incremental planning is restricted to a relatively small subset of possibilities. There is a rigidity in the terms of choice because of rules saying that change is to be incremental, safe in the sense of corrigible, and acceptable to most interest groups involved. There is insignificant redundancy of information and calculative capacity. Each small and disjointed decision is efficiently taken with respect to these resources. However, the effects are so unreliable that one has stopped aiming for 'the best' solution. One never knows if the implemented change will be offset by the next few incremental steps. In dialogical incrementalism a satisfactory level of integration is chosen even when a higher degree of goal achievement would be reached by alternative solutions. In other words, instrumental flexibility (robustness) is given up in order to preserve the communicative rationality of the process.

Some conclusions have to be adjusted when we consider the more practical disjointed incrementalism instead of the dialogical 'ideal type'. Instrumental reason is still bounded, and this is now the case for communicative rationality as well. The suppression of communicative distortions is no longer perfect. Even if the planning process is still flexible, relationships of domination prevent it from being fully integrative. Perfect mutual understanding cannot be presupposed. There has to be some redundancy of information and processing activities (calculation) to prepare choice. Thus, under the less perfect planning conditions, choice is not made as efficiently as under the unanimous vote of dialogical incrementalism. In disjointed incrementalism implementation problems are to be expected. They are commonplace in a pluralistic society with conflicting interests. The ability to reach agreement is not perfect, so implementation is not fully reliable. In contrast to dialogical incrementalism, however, domination can now be used to increase the efficiency with which plans are carried through.

Communication is essential in disjointed as well as dialogical incrementalism. I will now suggest what is meant by reliable and efficient communication. Dialogue is reliable in the sense that the interlocutors are sure to understand and to be understood. They talk to this purpose in a pleonastic manner, being repetitive, overlapping, and duplicating. Simultaneously,

Habermasian dialogue is in one respect rigid. The concept does not denote chat or small talk. In a one-track fashion it concentrates on mutual understanding and agreement. The conversation is structured by the urge to identify generalizable interests.

If dialogue is left out of account, a reliable communicative process is one in which messages are likely to be received and understood despite distortions. Misrepresentations reinforce the need for a redundancy of signals. The communication is efficient when messages are received and understood by transmission of as few signals as possible. There shall be no redundancy of transmitted signals.

To sum up: reliability and efficiency are relevant concepts for characterizing both communication and calculation. They are thus germane in an analysis of incremental modes as well as in synoptic planning. The plan-making process itself is rigid and efficient in strategical rationalism and flexible and reliable in the incremental modes. In the actual choice situation, however, the synoptic mode gives up integration to gain instrumental flexibility, while incrementalism renounces goal achievement for the sake of social flexibility (integration). All boundedness implies that restrictions are introduced and hence that an element of rigidity is present. Therefore, there will be some rigidity in the instrumental functioning of disjointed incrementalism, and the communicative and integrative functions of practical synoptic planning will be rigidly performed.

Notes

1   What follows is a comparison of the garbage can decision-making model and Lindblom's model. In the synoptic model the causal order rules, while the garbage can implies temporal order. Disjointed incrementalism does not completely abandon causal order, but the main principle is 'consensual order'. That is, problems and tentative solutions are chosen, on which there is sufficient agreement. The association of incrementalism and the search for agreement presupposes a society of risk-adverters believing risk to increase with the difference between the proposed policy and the existing situation.

What makes disjointed incrementalism useful as a planning model despite the extensive substitution of causal order by consensual order? The important feature is the connection between agreement and preferences. Moreover, well-known planning alternatives are most likely to gain support, so there is a link between agreement and deliberation of consequences. Hence, the problem with the garbage can model from the point of view of planning theory is not the substitution of causal order by another order in itself. The salient point is that the principle of temporal order is too dissociated from preferences and from the idea of human agency (Giddens 1984:Ch.1) - which in turn is a pre-condition for planning.

The pure garbage can decision model can be modified by admitting a compromise between temporal and causal order. The scope for planning increases when we can decide on an action because we think it will contribute to the solution of our problem, and not only because the problem and the action possibility happen to be present at the same time. However, when the temporal order becomes less conspicuous, the garbage can model approaches the kind of decision situation in which disjointed incrementalism is appropriate. This is demonstrated by the similarities of the columns in Table 9.1.

Table 9.1
Comparison of the assumptions of the 'garbage can' model and disjointed incrementalism

Garbage can	Disjointed incrementalism
Limited rationality	Constraints on information and data processing
Conflict	Multiple interests very likely to oppose each other over potential goal statements and to disagree on what means are efficient and proper
Ambiguity of preferences	Lack of stated goals, adjustment of ends to means, revising preferences after experience from action
Loose couplings	Remediality, disjointedness, fragmentation, partisan mutual adjustment
Temporal order	Lack of knowledge about cause-effect relations, no accepted means-end scheme, consensual order

The survey shows that a modified garbage can model accepting a mixture of temporal and causal order has much in common with main traits of Lindblom's model. This may explain that planning models claiming to be based on a garbage can approach, so far have done little else than adopting the garbage can terminology and applying it to a process with disjointed incremental features. My conclusion is that there is little room for a garbage can planning model with characteristics so notably different from disjointed incrementalism that it is likely to revise, not to say replace, this existing planning paradigm.

2 The 'debility' concept of Caplin and Kornbluth (1975) deserves mentioning. A strategy with a high measure of debility is defined as one which leads to many bad options. We are interested in two affiliated properties of a decision: high robustness keeping good options open, and low debility keeping bad options closed. In a conflict-ridden planning process, some options are good for one group and bad for another. The objectives of robustness and debility are then contradictory, as low debility for one group implies low robustness for another.

Debility is of special interest when information is incomplete and, at the same time, decision-makers use information imperfectly. This situation is analysed by Heiner (1985, 1988). He concludes that higher robustness implies higher probability of choosing inferior alternatives.

3 'Reversability' is sometimes used in the literature of planning theory to cover much of the same ground as resilience, see Cowan (1969) and Lynch (1981:172-4).

4 'Staging' is close to what Rosenhead, Elton, and Gupta (1972:419) named stability. They see stability as the ability of the system to perform well should the subsequent stages of the investment plan be delayed or cancelled. This is a special case of my stability concept.

5 Ego-resilience refers to the individual's ability to adapt to environmental demands by appropriately modifying his or her habitual level of ego-control. Ego-resilience allows functioning with some 'elasticity'. Ego-control refers to the degree of impulse control in such functions as delay of gratification, inhibition of aggression, and planfulness. Together, these two constructs represent the core qualities of 'ego' from a broadly psychodynamic perspective (Mischel 1986:168-9).

6 Cyert and March (1963) have developed an affiliated notion which they denote 'slack'. Organizational slack is the difference between total resources and total necessary payments. It consists in payment to members of the coalition in excess of what is required to maintain the organization. Cyert and March found the organizational slack concept useful in dealing with the adjustment of firms to gross shifts in the external environment (ibid.36-8).

7 Landau (1969) discusses the concept of redundancy in public administration theory. He holds that redundancy is important to achieve stability (suppression of error in spite of unexpected events), and he criticizes those 'who seem to make zero redundancy the measure of both
   economy and efficiency' (ibid.347).
8 Braybrooke and Lindblom (1963:160-67) use the phrase 'thematic flexibility'. They hold that choice is most flexible when interesting themes
   are identified, discussed and compared across the alternatives without
   any specified rule to guide the comparisons. Contrary to my claim in
   this subsection, they seem to conceive of their strategy as not sustained
   by rules: 'the strategy is more flexible than any method of evaluation
   that depends on the use of rules' (ibid.161). The passage just quoted in
   the main text telling incrementalists to shun any policy with low resilience, is in my opinion an example of an incrementalist rule.

10 Critical pragmatism

I owe the term 'critical pragmatism' to John Forester, who uses it occasionally to describe his own approach to planning (Forester 1989:211, 1990: 45). The dialogical incrementalism of Part one has to be modified in face of the conflicts and power relations analysed in Part two. Critical pragmatism denotes a practical mode of planning. Here, the term combines the critical theory of communicative action - also at the core of Forester's approach - with an explicit concern for flexibility and responsiveness in public planning. Some features of the critical and the pragmatic sides of the planning mode will be spelled out shortly.

Dialogical incrementalism is mainly a tool for theoretical analysis and a distant guiding light for planning; it is no practical planning approach. It is not even obvious that Habermasian dialogue is desirable in all public interaction (Rorty 1989), although my analysis is grounded on the assumption that we ought to move in that direction from where we stand today. The purpose of this final chapter is to delineate a few facets of a more practical approach - critical pragmatism - and to conclude the analysis. I accentuate important features complementing the picture of critical pragmatism already drawn, while at the same time highlighting its critical and responsive character.

Some features of critical pragmatism

Critical social theory

There are two aspects of a critical social theory (Benhabib 1986). The first is the explanatory-diagnostic one. The social sciences are appropriated in such a way as to develop an analysis of the crisis potential of the present.

Part two of this book, and the theory of cumulative bounding of rationality, represent this side of a critical theory of planning. The second aspect is anticipatory-utopian and constitutes the normative aspect of critique. Part one and the recommendation of flexibility, responsiveness, and reflection-in-action represent this properly normative side. 'When explicating the dysfunctionalities of the present, a critical social theory should always do so in the name of a better future and a more humane society' (ibid.226).

Habermas (1987) distinguishes system and lifeworld, and in keeping with the rationale and paradigms for planning set forth in Part one, I take it as the task for planning to rationalize each. We take a systems perspective on society as observers, viewing social life as a quasi-purposive whole. Here the unintended consequences of social actions come together to yield functional interdependencies. The rationalization of systems of action means specialization, development of self-steering capacity, adaptability to the environment, and improved problem-solving (Benhabib 1986:245). As argued in previous chapters, flexibility and reflection-in-action are required from planning contributing to this rationalization process.

The lifeworld perspective on society is reserved for the acting individual taking part in the events rather than observing them. The lifeworld signifies both a context of reference and a repository of intuitive knowledge and know-how for social actors. 'By the rationalization of the lifeworld is meant ... the increase in argumentative practices within the everyday world in the three crucial domains of action coordination, the reproduction of cultural tradition, and socialization' (ibid.242). The concept of lifeworld is the correlate of the concept of communicative action. The rationalization of communicative action entails 'a decreasing degree of repressiveness and rigidity, increasing role distance, and the flexible application of norms; in short, socialization without repression' (ibid.229). Thus, the rationalization of the lifeworld contains an emancipatory potential that public planning should seek to realize. Forester (1989) offers an excellent analysis of how planners can contribute by questioning in order to reveal and correct communicative distortions, and by anticipating organizational power and conflict. Again, I put more emphasis on flexibility and responsiveness, and the analysis of distortions is developed further in the chapter on parapraxis in planning.

Questioning vs legitimate secrecy

While questioning is an important part of a critical planning approach, one should aim at a balanced view of its possibilities. Questioning is a power strategy as well as an emancipatory procedure. There is a close relationship between questioning and secrecy, and because secrecy has positive aspects, questioning can have negative ones. By questioning we want to gain control over secrecy and openness. Then we can influence the information balance and thus power relations. The questioning theme confirms the significance of knowledge in planning. 'Questioning and shaping attention' is a critical theory version of the knowledge/action focus of mainstream planning theory.

One task for questioning in planning is to disclose opportunism and rigidity and the power relations backing these anomalies. The case for questioning in public planning is strong, because secrecy, like other kinds of power practice, can corrupt. 'Because it bypasses inspection and eludes interference, secrecy is central to the planning of every form of injury to human beings' (Bok 1982:26). All deceit relies on keeping something secret.

Questioning in the public planning process is also appropriate because 'secrecy can hamper the exercise of rational choice at every step: by preventing people from adequately understanding a threatening situation, from seeing the relevant alternatives clearly, from assessing the consequences of each, and from arriving at preferences with respect to them' (ibid.26). Secrecy counteracts democracy since it diminishes the sense of personal responsibility for joint decisions and facilitates all forms of biased or careless judgement, including that exhibited in taking needless risks. The moral principles supporting a choice should be capable of open statement and defence. Questioning helps to check if they are.

On the other hand, even if it enhances every form of abuse, secrecy is needed for human survival. 'To the extent that it is possible to strip people of their capacity for secrecy about their intentions and their actions, their lives become more transparent and predictable; they can then the more easily be subjected to pressure and defeated' (ibid.23).

> With no capacity for keeping secrets and for choosing when to reveal them, human beings would lose their sense of identity and every shred of autonomy. Their plans would be endangered and their creativity stifled; they could not count on retaining even the most fundamental belongings. (Bok 1982:282)

This indicates that limits should be set on questioning; as a planning strategy it is not intended to approach interrogation. We should consider if some things are better left private rather than being made public by our questioning. Universal transparency may not be unproblematic. There is also the drawbacks of too much information to be considered. Would we be able to cope with the impact upon us of all that we might learn about one another in such a society? 'And if secrecy were no longer possible, would brute force turn out to be the only means of self-defense and of gaining the upper hand?' (ibid.18). Questioning does not in itself bring us to dialogue. It may just as well express an authority relation, analogical to the repressive role it often plays in teaching situations (Dillon 1982).

When dialogue is the ideal, planning needs to be 'answering and organizing solutions' as well as 'questioning and organizing attention'. The issue is not only to wield power by *shaping* attention, but to empower by *paying* attention and being responsive. This corresponds to the listening-theme in Forester's approach.

Etzioni (1968) linked responsiveness to a critical aspect of his theory of the active society. He holds that a relationship, an institution, or a society is unauthentic if it provides the appearance of responsiveness while the underlying condition is alienating. 'Authenticity exists where responsiveness exists and is experienced as such' (ibid.620). Responsiveness is a requisite for his active society.

Contingency planning

I now turn from the critical side to the pragmatic side of critical pragmatism. The pragmatic approach is in evidence at all stages of such planning. I comment first on the initial phases where pragmatics comes through as the choice of a contingency approach. Planning depends on the context in which it takes place, so procedure and product should match types of problems and organizational settings. There are at least three starting points for classifying the contingencies. One can assume that planning procedures vary according to

(a)   what is being planned   (the substance of planning),
(b)   the kind of organization   (the planning system itself),
(c)   the demands of the political
        and economic system   (the planning environment).

The set of contingencies can be established by combining points (a), (b), and (c). An idea of what is meant by a contingency approach can be acquired from McCaskey (1974), Burrell and Morgan (1979:164-81), and from the work of John Bryson, who focuses directly on planning (Bryson and Delbecq 1979, Bryson 1983, Bryson, Bromiley and Jung 1990, Bryson and Bromiley 1993).

Referring to point (a), the communicative contents of the planning process and the need for public debate vary with the task being solved. The demands may be low when planning the winter maintenance of classified roads and high when planning the long term development of a city centre. With reference to point (b), the procedures for managing planning conflicts will vary between a typical Weberian bureaucracy and a private consultant engaged to plan the environmental restoration of a neighbourhood in close contact with its inhabitants.

The remarks below deal with point (c). The planning environment (Faludi 1987:52) is the societal context producing the norms and values determining the society's view of public planning and how it should be conducted. The demands of the planning environment can be derived in an 'informal' way, e.g., from a list of the positions of prominent politicians on important planning issues. The planning environment can also be described by using a more theoretical and institutional approach. Modern society is replete with political institutions, a substantial part of them administering and controlling the large public sector of the economy. By studying the political, economic, and legal institutions of a society, one can indicate what types of planning are most likely to succeed. It might be possible to give the procedural planning theories a more solid social foundation in this way.

Contingencies of type (c) can also be formulated in more abstract categories. Planners should respond differently depending on, e.g., which kinds of power relations are accepted for various problem-solving tasks, which outcomes of conflict management are satisfactory, the accepted ways of making collective decisions, and the communicative qualities of the public sphere (Habermas 1989, Calhoun 1992). Power and conflict are the two contextual variables dealt with at length in this book. I discuss three axes along which reactions to impulses from the political environment can be located. The efforts of the planners can (1) emphasize participation and dialogue or calculation and analytic technique, (2) reflect the peculiarities of a more or less synoptic or a more or less incremental process, and (3) be flexible and responsive or hold rigidly on to earlier ideas and decisions. With this approach the anchoring in an actually existing society becomes less explicit, but the ties between planning theories and theories of the other social sciences are strengthened. Consistency is thus improved in theorizing about planning. Such a contingency approach to critical pragmatism is more fully and explicitly outlined in Sager (1990a).

In his 1973-book on *Planning Theory*, Faludi wanted to construct a positive theory of planning on the basis of a contingency approach. He was hoping this would enable him to predict changes in planning style as related to anticipated changes in the planning environment (Faludi 1984:195). This presupposes that the planners adopt a passive and adaptive attitude, however. As soon as they actively try to influence the planning environment, as both Faludi and I think they should, the contingency approach becomes problematic as a foundation for a positive planning theory. Anyway, Faludi's recent work on planning doctrine seems to open a promising line of research on how planners anchor their everyday work in principles varying with the social and political environment (Faludi 1989, Alexander and Faludi 1990).

Adaptivizing

For a specific set of contingencies the planning should be flexible, as argued in the last chapter. Critical pragmatism might benefit from Ackoff's (1970) proposal for an 'adaptivizing' planning strategy as an alternative to optimizing and satisficing. Adaptivizing is an error-correcting process, and as such it is open for revisions of goals as well as courses of action. It does not necessarily imply lower ambitions than in the optimizing synoptic case, as the satisficing of disjointed incrementalism does. However, it is realized that uncertainty is likely to prevent one from staking out the right course towards the target from the outset, so a resilient process is prepared. Thus, adaptivizing is a flexible approach applicable in situations where it can be foreseen that multiple distortions of instrumental and communicative rationality will strongly affect the plan-making in unknown ways and make optimizing inexpedient.

In contrast to disjointed incrementalism, adaptivizing proceeds towards explicit goals. We cannot expect to approach the ends by following the path of least political resistance recommended by incrementalism. Neither do we have the knowledge and calculating capacity to follow the optimal synoptic route. There are constraints on our choice of a middle way, though, as we should always be able to adjust the course as the target moves. Often, there will not be absolute constraints, but rather thresholds that are difficult and expensive to force in order to recover the right course. This line of thinking seems suitable for environmental planning and the search for sustainable solutions (Kozlowski and Hill 1993). For example, directions of development should be chosen that avoid irreversible encroachment and discharge of pollutants which accumulate in nature and affect the ecological circulations in unanticipated causal chains that are hard to sever.

In synoptic planning there is a sequence of prefigured acts leading to a specific goal. Satisficing breaks with the optimizing procedure of strategical rationalism by relinquishing the goal. Adaptivizing breaks with optimizing by substituting the sequence of prefigured acts by a set of constraints on behaviour (Richards 1977).

There are unnecessary constraints on public and private problem-solving that are neither planned nor desirable. Here is where the critical and the flexible sides of critical pragmatism meet. In this mode of planning one aims to relax and remove constraints or distortions that unnecessarily limit the possibility of actors to reach attractive outcomes. One scans for problem areas in need of attention, and investigates these closer by further questioning. The attention-part locates the tensions, and the questioning-part contributes to the conflict-analysis. The questions implicitly criticize illegitimate use of force, reveal the real motives of the contenders, and disclose system-determined causes of conflict. In Forester's words, critical planning theory is 'pragmatics with vision'. It reveals true alternatives, corrects false expectations, counters cynicism, fosters inquiry, spreads political responsibility, engagement, and action (Forester 1989:162).

The view of the interpretation of plans as a possibility for keeping emancipatory strategies open, may be seen as an additional feature of the flexibility-side of critical pragmatism. It nevertheless warrants the special treatment given in the next section.

Interpretation and flexibility

The section explains how the possibility for interpretation creates opportunities for flexibility. The interpretation may aim at understanding the text (the plan) as an account of the intention of the author or the decision-makers passing the plan. I shall mainly be preoccupied with another kind of interpretation shifting the attention from original intention to future action. This approach can be particularly useful when the planning context changes rapidly, and when plans are to be revised by new planners and decision-makers. The crucial point is to grasp the action potential opened up by the plan in the new setting. The latter interpretation makes the plan a more elastic tool in new situations, and enhances the potential for emancipation.

Even a participatory and admirably dialogical planning process requires a text in addition to the conversation itself. The results of the process will be written down in a planning document, and I will call this document the plan. The plan seen as a text is an interpretation of intentions expressed and negotiation results reached in the planning process, and is itself always liable to interpretations. As March (1982:32) observes, 'a plan can often be more effective as an interpretation of past decisions than as a blueprint for future ones'. It may reflect the planners' interpretation of how the preferences of the various diverging interests can be adapted and possibly interfered with in order to reach a least common multiple. At the same time it may be acknowledged that the agreement does not necessarily go far enough to guide effective future action. The plan is then likely to gather dust on a shelf for some time, awaiting expanded agreement and opportunity for more effective action. This is certainly no rare event.

Interpretation is affiliated with a number of the concepts addressed in the previous chapters. It is an ex post activity, and it is part of posterior reasoning. When the process lives up to the dictum 'implementation shapes policy', one interprets what happens during the attempts at effectuation and reflects on it while it is still possible to influence the result. The interpretation inherent in this 'conversation with the materials of the situation' is part of reflection-in-action. Interpretation is also needed to perform the judgement required to distinguish opportunism from flexibility.

Flexibility renders the plan useful even if the pre-conditions change significantly. The question is now whether there is any relationship between flexibility and the possibilities for interpretation. There is no general and tidy one-to-one connection assuring that possibilities for interpretation will give flexibility. The plan may be infeasible in all interpretations. Imprecise and ambiguous plans are, indeed, no guarantee for usefulness under varying conditions. If, however, reinterpretations enable us to apply the plan to altered circumstances, they have led to flexibility.

Whitehead (1974:32) points out that flexibility has often been associated with plans concentrating on broad strategy, avoiding too much detail, particularly in the longer term. As a definition this is - as he says - far from satisfactory. A plan concentrating on broad strategy may be diffuse instead of flexible. Sillince (1986) has noted the connection between ambiguity and flexibility. Ambiguity is useful in many cases, but so is specificity. This points to a dilemma: on the one hand specificity increases the chances of the plan becoming inappropriate, and it makes it more easy for opponents to criticize it for not meeting their particular requirements (ibid.169). On the other hand 'ambiguity reduces the intended influence of a plan. The problem is that either the plan becomes so bland that it proposes little or nothing, or ... its ambivalence can be manipulated by its opponents to their own ends' (ibid.170). There is, therefore, a delicate balance between inviting a wide range of interpretations through ambiguity in planning, and the need for specific instructions ensuring efficiency when everything goes as expected. There are planning contexts in which the problems caused by ambiguity of some variables may be offset by the ability to be specific on others. For instance, one of Lindblom's (1967:227) maxims says that: 'In collective decision-making, do not try to clarify values if the parties concerned can agree on policies ...'. In such cases surplus meaning, the redundancy of ambiguity, permits values to overlap the parties in dispute, providing some common ground for agreement and thereby flexibility (Landau 1969:356).

Interpretation is crucial on at least two levels concerning planning. First, messages from the planning environment are not transmitted as unequivocal commands. Second, the planning document needs to be interpreted before the plan can be implemented. As regards the first level, some additional comments are in order to associate it with critical pragmatism. The planners can question the importance and the legitimacy of the signals from the environment. They do not have to pay equal attention to all messages received. The need to interpret grants degrees of freedom in forming the planning process and designing the plan. The planning process can be made more or less communicative or calculative, more or less synoptic or incremental, and more or less flexible or rigid. A certain organizing of our attention leads to a particular interpretation of what is going on. In turn, the interpretation of what has happened in the planning process so far occasions subsequent questions.

Turning to the second level, I comment on the interpretation of the planning document in the spirit of Ricoeur (1976). Interpretation is always present where one has to act on the basis of a text. The possibility for immediate questioning and explanation is absent. One has to search for the underlying meaning: hermeneutics starts where dialogue ends. Interpretation is all the more important because years may elapse before a plan is finally implemented (if it is at all). An 'incubation time' of six to eight years is not unusual for master-plans concerning classified roads. Other kinds of plans, like comprehensive plans for city centres, are not meant to be implemented in any detail. They are input in a continuous debate and may be used as guide-lines for action for years until they are replaced by new ones or simply regarded as outdated.

When the circumstances in which we consider making use of the plan deviate significantly from the situation at the time it was written, it is mandatory that 'the intentional fallacy' is avoided (Wimsatt and Beardsley 1946). This is to say that the major aim of our interpretative efforts should not be to identify and clarify the intentions of the authors. It is more fertile to ask what the text itself has to offer today. What counts as a virtue is not being true to the interests once expressed in the text, but to take responsibility for the future partly formed by the plan. The salient question is what scenarios the plan (the text) opens the way for. Ricoeur (1976) pushes the point to the extreme by stating that the hermeneutical task is to acknowledge the substance of the text and not the psychology of the author.

The interpretation should actualize the meaning of the text to the present user. The meaning of the text or plan resides in its suggestions for future action. Meaning emanates from the plan's ability to disclose new ways to act in the situation at hand, whether these alternatives were previously unknown or just not substantiated. Hence, meaning lies in the effectiveness of the plan as a tool for creating flexibility and new opportunities. '(W)hat we want to understand is not something hidden behind the text, but something disclosed in front of it. What has to be understood is not the initial situation of discourse but what points toward a possible world' (Ricoeur 1991:165). When plans are interpreted in this manner, the correct exegesis will no longer be given as the original intention of the author. This does not mean that planning approaches opportunism. The interpreters will have principles of their own regarding the way planning should be conducted and the contents of the plan. As long as the interpreting and implementing planner sticks to his principles, he is not opportunistic, even though he may deviate from the intention of the original author.

This approach to the interpretation of texts can be applied both to the plan as reflection and interpretation of external messages, and to the interpretation of a planning document. It is anti-authoritarian and can be seen as a clue to planning in accordance with the emancipatory interest. As interpreters we free ourselves from the intentions and the preferences of the authors and their employers, and therefore apply their product without necessarily confirming their power.

The critical hermeneutics of Ricoeur is often called 'hermeneutic phenomenology' (Thompson 1981). There is also a phenomenologic-hermeneutic side of critical pragmatism (Lim and Albrecht 1987). Studies in this vein usually include a detailed description of fragments of actual everyday conversations, negotiations, documents, etc. that are part of a planning process. The phenomenological account is followed by an interpretation and analysis of the communicative interaction. This aims to show how the intentions and motives of planners, politicians, entrepreneurs, and local inhabitants are expressed in more or less distorted ways. The misrepresentations leave their imprint on the whole communication and hamper the development towards mutual understanding. The analysis can tell the critical pragmatist much about the background for sympathies and antipathies, the history and social context of planning conflict, the local power relations, the potential for future coalitions, and the possibilities for planned action. Recent studies are carried out by Forester (1988, 1990b, 1992), Healey (1992a, 1993), and Hillier (1993).

To sum up: the communicative model of planning as questioning and organizing attention can be combined with a recognition of the need felt by those using a plan (e.g., being affected by it) to shift the focus from the intentions of the plan-makers to the problem-solving capacities of the text itself. We reformulate the questioning from 'how to implement what was once figured out', to 'how to figure out what is now implementable'. Accommodating the plan to a communicative process approaching the qualities of dialogue, we ask for flexibility instead of control. The approach to interpretation advocated here furthers the responsiveness of critical pragmatism.

Conclusion

Among the challenges confronting social scientists is the demand for relevance. For some, this demand is a curse because it precludes the justification of total abstraction. The inevitable question in social science is always: 'So what? What difference does this make to the real world?' The social scientist may respond by making his or her work directly applicable to meaningful empirical questions. Another approach, that I think is equally relevant, does not aim to change the real world directly but rather to alter our conception of it by defying the prevailing theoretical paradigm among scholars. In other words, one approach is to directly theorize about the real world, whereas the other is to theorize about the theories available for describing the real world. This book offers some of the first approach but most of the latter.

Planning theory could be a richer and more interesting field contributing far more to planning practice, if the theory was more closely interwoven with central social science concepts. It would then become more obvious that the interpretations of planning practice need to be contingent upon the social and political features of the planning environment. Furthermore, a clearer picture would emerge of what can and what cannot be expected to be achieved by planning. Interdisciplinary conceptual research is called for because the literature on planning abounds with notions and theoretical elements adopted from other social sciences.

The book links planning theory more firmly to the other social sciences by explaining how different demands related to the concepts of communication, power, conflict, and responsiveness require conditional theorizing on how to plan. It shows that practical planning, dealing with controversial issues, is a compromise between instrumental and communicative rationality. The compound rationale of planning relates the various concepts of legitimation to planning as integration, politics, and production.

In both research and teaching I have long missed a more solid and easily identifiable theoretical core in planning theory. For analytical reasons, there is a need for theoretical archetypes that remain unaffected by trends in planning practice. An analogy is found in economics, where central parts of the theory construction are built on such a platform. The perfectly competitive market has proved to be a well-suited starting point for analysis, although it is obvious that no actual market satisfies all the theoretical assumptions. The model continues to be helpful as a reference point even if there is a tendency in modern economies towards large corporations and co-operation within industries. However, the usefulness of the competitive model is greatly enhanced due to the fact that there is also a contrasting theoretical model. This model of pure monopoly scarcely finds an equivalent in the real world. Nevertheless, by comparing the actually observed intermediate forms of market organization with the two contrasting theoretical models, one is often able to derive conclusions about the functioning of existing markets. This experience from economics has influenced my reformulation of the synoptic/incremental planning dichotomy.

In research one should be able to distinguish rational and irrational behaviour. The planning profession has long been familiar with models of instrumentally rational action, reflected in the synoptic planning theory. However, planners are well aware that the model does not cover all the behaviour one would consider reasonable. This creates a need for models that are contrasts to the synoptic one. By this I mean models based on different types of rationality. When such models are lacking, too much planning behaviour appears irrational. As such it is arbitrary and scientifically unknowable, and the residual noninstrumental categories remain useless. The synoptic paradigm is too restricted as a normative model for all that public planning is expected to be. To bring about a rewarding discussion of planning based on the conceptual pair rational/irrational, our notions of rationality should cover more of the behaviour approved by common sense. I move in this direction by introducing a revised type of incrementalism as the contrast to synoptic planning, and basing the revision on a claim for dialogue.

Concerning the above theme, the main achievements of the book are the following: it reformulates and gives more depth to the principal planning theoretical distinction between synoptic and incremental theory. It specifies dialogical incrementalism as a communicatively fully rational planning mode and thus opens for considering planning practice as rational even if it deviates from the synoptic ideal.

Local planning is a close companion to local politics, and it is faced with constantly recurring claims for democracy. This does not only imply majority decisions on planning matters. The interested parties demand to be kept informed and to have the opportunity to argue their case throughout the planning process. Two-way communication is the key word. On the other hand the division of labour develops, and the specialized tool-kit at the disposal of each branch of the planning profession is expanding. This is the case for analytic techniques as well as for technical equipment. A planner having a good command of the analytic aids might easily feel that he can find solutions to planning problems without being in touch with those affected. Hence the need to stress the close connection between planning and politics. The plans are not only to function well as technical solutions but even as political ones. For this reason, a study of the relationship between communication and technique in public planning is of interest (Sager 1990a). My contribution here is to specify synoptic planning as analytic technique and incrementalism as dialogue and study the relationship between these theoretical modes of planning.

In this area the main achievement of the book is that it demonstrates how opposite problem-solving procedures, dialogue and analytic technique, can be incorporated into main conceptualizations of planning and form a fruitful perspective for the analysis of planning theories.

There is a continuous tension between plan and market. Among producers and consumers alike, public planning seems to have earned a reputation as a contrivance which is difficult to handle, and which is an obstacle to smooth adjustment to emerging opportunities. To what degree should it be possible to change planning decisions that prove to be inexpedient or unprofitable judged from a private business point of view? What is the role of public planning in the political system: restraining or arranging for private enterprise? What should planners aim at: security or profit, equity or efficiency, control or democracy? Flexibility/rigidity is a dimension of planning that is often just beneath the surface of this public debate. The flexibility concept is a key to several affiliated notions which are helpful in characterizing planning theories and illuminating their struggle with the well-known but intriguing questions above. In general, the main planning categories applied throughout underline the close connection between planning and politics. The questions 'how responsive?', 'how dialogical?', and 'how small and safe steps?' do all reflect consideration for democracy and the need to obtain political support.

With regard to flexibility, the main achievement of the book is the following: it underpins theoretically that the contrast between flexibility and rigidity is important to planning theory, one reason being the emphasis given to the unavoidable trade-offs between reliability and efficiency and between future opportunities and commitment.

Critical social theory has inspired the book, and it informs the discussion throughout without entering the centre stage. Therefore, it feels all the more natural to round off by epitomizing from a critical theory perspective. Part one shows how communicative rationality provides the basis for a dialogical and incremental ideal, that (better than Lindblom's model) avoids lack of direction and systematic support of the powerful. Furthermore, the ideal of communication undistorted by power relations is integrated with the rationale and paradigm of planning. Part two offers a critique of instrumental power in planning. It examines which types of power relations and conflict management procedures preserve possibilities for dialogue-like communication. It is shown that there are limits on instrumental power when the aim is to convert emancipation into freedom. Part three argues that people cannot feel safe under planning approaching opportunism, and that they can hardly feel free being faced with rigid planning. Flexibility is thus an aspect of planning that is of interest to critical theory. I introduce 'responsiveness' in order to link flexibility to a notion that is more explicitly political. In the typical case where the powerful people plan and the less powerful are affected, responsive planning is an aim of critical theory. Both answering and questioning are required to approach fair communication in planning and to counter domination and destructive conflict. Part three does not only outline - under the heading of 'critical pragmatism' - what a critical theory of planning could be like. It is also explained how distortions can arise and accumulate. I argue that the theory of parapraxis which is set forth, helps us take a step towards a critical theory of irrationality in planning.

To put it in a nutshell: I hope to have outlined the main features of a critical and pragmatic planning theory founded on the concept of communicative rationality and on a commitment to responsiveness and flexibility.

Bibliography

Ackoff, R.L. (1970), *A Concept of Corporate Planning*, Wiley, New York.

Ainslie, G. (1975), 'Specious reward: a behavioral theory of impulsiveness and impulse control', *Psychological Bulletin*, 82 (4) 463-96.

Akerlof, G.A. & W.T. Dickens (1982), 'The economic consequences of cognitive dissonance', *American Economic Review*, 72 (3) 307-19.

Albrecht, J. & G.-C. Lim (1986), 'A search for alternative planning theory. Use of critical theory', *Journal of Architectural and Planning Research*, 3 (2) 117-31.

Alexander, E.R. (1977), 'Communication and conflict resolution', pp. 287-304 in Huseman, R.C.; C.M. Logue & D.L. Freshley (eds), *Readings in Interpersonal and Organizational Communication*, Allyn & Bacon.

Alexander, E.R. (1984), 'After rationality, what?', *American Planning Association Journal*, 50 (Winter) 62-9.

Alexander, E.R. (1988), 'After rationality', *Society*, 26 (1) 15-19.

Alexander, E.R. (1992), 'A transaction cost theory of planning', *Journal of the American Planning Association*, 58 (2) 190-200.

Alexander, E.R. & A. Faludi (1990), *Planning Doctrine: Its Uses and Implications*, Working paper 120, Planologisch Demografisch Instituut, University of Amsterdam.

Amir, S. (1972), 'Highway location and public opposition', *Environment and Behavior*, 4 (Dec.) 414-36.

Amy, D.J. (1987), *The Politics of Environmental Mediation*, Columbia University Press, New York.

Arendt, H. (1961), *Between Past and Future. Six Exercises in Political Thought*, Viking Press, New York.

Arendt, H. (1970), *On Violence*, Harcourt, Brace & World, New York.

Arrow, K.J. (1963) [1951], *Social Choice and Individual Values*, Wiley, New York.

Arrow, K.J. (1987), 'Rationality of self and others in an economic system', pp. 201-15 in Hogarth, R.M. & M.W. Reder (eds), *Rational Choice. The Contrast between Economics and Psychology*, University of Chicago Press, Chicago.

Bachrach, P. & M.S. Baratz (1962), 'Two faces of power', *American Political Science Review*, 56 (Nov.) 947-52.

Bachrach, P. & M.S. Baratz (1963), 'Decisions and non-decisions: an analytical framework', *American Political Science Review*, 57 (Sept.) 632-42.

Bailey, F.G. (1983), *The Tactical Uses of Passion. An Essay on Power, Reason, and Reality*, Cornell University Press, Ithaca.

Baker Miller, J. (1992), 'Women and power', pp. 240-48 in Wartenberg, T. (ed.), *Rethinking Power*, State University of New York Press, Albany.

Bales, R.F. (1953), 'The equilibrium problem in small groups', pp. 111-61 in Parsons, T.; R.F. Bales & E.A. Shils (eds), *Working Papers in the Theory of Action*, Free Press, New York.

Ball, T. (1975), 'Power, causation and explanation', *Polity*, 8 (2) 189-214.

Ball, T. (1992), 'New faces of power', pp. 14-31 and 289-94 in Wartenberg, T. (ed.), *Rethinking Power*, State University of New York Press, Albany.

Banfield, E.C. (1959), 'Ends and means in planning', *International Social Science Journal*, 11 (3) 361-8.

Banham, R.; P. Barker; P. Hall & C. Price (1969), 'Non-plan: an experiment in freedom', *New Society*, 20 (March) 435-43.

Barnes, B. (1982), *T.S. Kuhn and Social Science*, Macmillan, London.

Bartlett, R.V. (1986), 'Ecological rationality: reason and environmental policy', *Environmental Ethics*, 8 (Fall) 221-39.

Batty, M. (1974), 'Social power in plan-generation', *Town Planning Review*, 5 (3) 291-310.

Baudrillard, J. (1985), *Forførelse (Seduction)*, Sjakalen, Århus. In French 1979 as De la séduction, Éditions galilee, Paris.

Baum, H.S. (1983), 'Autonomy, shame, and doubt. Power in the bureaucratic lives of planners', *Administration and Society*, 15 (2) 147-84.

Baum, H.S. (1987), *The Invisible Bureaucracy. The Unconscious in Organizational Problem Solving*, Oxford University Press, New York.

Beesley, M.E. & P.B. Kettle (1979), 'The Leitch Committee's recommendations and the management of the road programme', *Regional Studies*, 13 (6) 513-29.

Benditt, T.M. (1973), 'The public interest', *Philosophy and Public Affairs*, 2 (3) 291-311.

Benhabib, S. (1986), *Critique, Norm, and Utopia. A Study of the Foundations of Critical Theory*, Columbia University Press, New York.

Benton, T. (1981), '"Objective" interests and the sociology of power', *Sociology*, 15 (2) 161-84.

Benton, T. (1982), 'Realism, power and objective interests', pp. 7-33 in Graham, K. (ed.), *Contemporary Political Philosophy, Radical Studies*, Cambridge University Press, Cambridge.

Benyon, J. (1978), 'Some political implications of airport location: the case of Edinburgh Airport', *Public Administration*, 56 (Winter) 439-56.

Bergh, T. (ed.) (1983), *Deltaker-demokratiet (The Participative Democracy)*, Universitetsforlaget, Oslo.

Bernard, T.J. (1983), *The Consensus-Conflict Debate*, Columbia University Press, New York.

Bernstein, R.J. (1971), *Praxis and Action*, University of Pennsylvania Press, Philadelphia.

Bierstedt, R. (1974), *Power and Progress: Essays on Sociological Theory*, McGraw-Hill, New York.

Bloom, C. (1986), 'Strategic planning in the public sector', *Journal of Planning Literature*, 1 (2) 253-9.

Boelen, B.J. (1978), *Personal Maturity. The Existential Dimension*, Seabury Press, New York.

Bok, S. (1982), *Secrets. On the Ethics of Concealment and Revelation*, Pantheon Books, New York.

Bolan, R.S. (1983), 'The structure of ethical choice in planning practice', *Journal of Planning Education and Research*, 3 (1) 23-34.

Boudon, R. (1982), *The Unintended Consequences of Social Action*, St. Martin's Press, New York.

Boulding, K. (1962), *Conflict and Defence*, Harper & Row, New York.

Boulding, K. (1964), 'Review of "A Strategy of Decision"', *American Sociological Review*, 29 (6) 930-31.

Bowles, S. & H. Gintis (1986), *Democracy and Capitalism: Property, Community, and the Contradictions of Modern Social Thought*, Basic Books, New York.

Boyer, M.C. (1983), *Dreaming the Rational City. The Myth of American City Planning*, MIT Press, Cambridge.

Bratman, M. (1983), 'Taking plans seriously', *Social Theory and Practice* 9 (2-3) 271-87.

Braybrooke, D. & C.E. Lindblom (1963), *A Strategy of Decision*, Free Press, New York.

Breheny, M. & A. Hooper (eds) (1985), *Rationality in Planning*, Pion, London.

Brehmer, B. & K.R. Hammond (1977), 'Cognitive factors in interpersonal conflict', pp. 79-103 in Druckman, D. (ed.), *Negotiations. Social-Psychological Perspectives*, Sage, Beverly Hills.

Brickman, P. & D.T. Campbell (1971), 'Hedonic relativism and planning the good society', pp. 287-302 in Appley, M.H. (ed.), *Adaption-Level Theory*, Academic Press, New York.

Brown, J.A.C. (1963), *Techniques of Persuasion*, Penguin, Harmondsworth, Middlesex.

Brubaker, R. (1984), *The Limits of Rationality. An Essay on the Social and Moral Thought of Max Weber*, George Allen & Unwin, London.

Bruton, M.J. (1980), 'Public participation, local planning and conflicts of interests', *Policy and Politics*, 8 (4) 423-42.

Bryson, J.M. (1983), 'Representing and testing procedural planning methods', pp. 245-68 in Masser, I. (ed.), *Evaluating Urban Planning Efforts*, Gower, Aldershot, Hampshire.

Bryson, J.M. (1988), *Strategic Planning for Public and Nonprofit Organizations*, Jossey-Bass, San Francisco.

Bryson, J.M. & P. Bromiley (1993), 'Critical factors affecting the planning and implementation of major projects', *Strategic Management Journal*, 14 (5) 319-37.

Bryson, J.M.; P. Bromiley & Y.S. Jung (1990), 'Influences of context and process on project planning success', *Journal of Planning Education and Research*, 9 (3) 183-95.

Bryson, J.M. & A.L. Delbecq (1979), 'A contingent approach to strategy and tactics in project planning', *American Institute of Planners Journal*, 45 (2) 167-79.

Bryson, J.M. & P. Smith Ring (1990), 'A transaction-based approach to policy intervention', *Policy Sciences*, 23 (3) 205-29.

Bråten, S. (1973), 'Model monopoly and communications: systems theoretical notes on democratization', *Acta Sociologica*, 2 (16) 98-107.

Buchanan, J.M. (1975), *The Limits of Liberty. Between Anarchy and Leviathan*, University of Chicago Press, Chicago.

Burger, T. (1987) [1976], *Max Weber's Theory of Concept Formation. History, Laws, and Ideal Types*, Duke University Press, Durham.

Burrell, G. & G. Morgan (1979), *Sociological Paradigms and Organisational Analysis*, Gower, Aldershot, Hampshire.

Calhoun, C. (ed.) (1992), *Habermas and the Public Sphere*, MIT Press, Cambridge.

Camic, C. (1986), 'The matter of habit', *American Journal of Sociology*, 91 (5) 1039-87.

Caplin, D. & J. Kornbluth (1975), 'Multiobjective investment planning under uncertainty', *Omega*, 3 (4) 423-41.

Carey, J.W. (1975), 'A cultural approach to communication', *Communication*, 2 (1) 1-22.

Castells, M. (1978), 'The social function of urban planning: state action in the urban-industrial development of the French northern coastline', pp. 62-92 in Castells, M., *City, Class and Power*, Macmillan, London.

Castells, M. (1983), *The City and the Grassroots. A Cross-Cultural Theory of Urban Social Movements*, Edward Arnold, London.

Cenzatti, M. (1987), 'Marxism and planning theory', pp. 437-47 in Friedmann, J., *Planning in the Public Domain: From Knowledge to Action*, Princeton University Press, Princeton.

Chadwick, G.F. (1971), *A Systems View of Planning: Towards a Theory of the Urban and Regional Planning Process*, Pergamon Press, Oxford.

Chan, J. & D. Miller (1991), 'Elster on self-realization in politics: a critical note', *Ethics*, 102 (1) 96-102.

Cherniak, C. (1986), *Minimal Rationality*, MIT Press, Cambridge.

Churchman, C.W. (1961), *Prediction and Optimal Decision*, Prentice-Hall, Englewood Cliffs.

Clegg, S.R. (1989), *Frameworks of Power*, Sage, Newbury Park.

Coan, R.W. (1974), *The Optimal Personality. An Empirical and Theoretical Analysis*, Routledge & Kegan Paul, London.

Cohen, L.J. & D.C. Paris (1982), 'Ethical issues in goal conflict: a continuing problem for policy analysis', *Western Political Quarterly*, 35 (1) 65-80.

Cohen, M.D. & R. Axelrod (1984), 'Coping with complexity: the adaptive value of changing utility', *American Economic Review*, 74 (1) 30-42.

Cohen, M.D.; J.G. March & J.P. Olsen (1972), 'A garbage can model of organizational choice', *Administrative Science Quarterly*, 117 (1) 1-25.

Coombs, C.H. & G.S. Avrunin (1988), *The Structure of Conflict*, Lawrence Erlbaum, Hillsdale.

Cormick, G.W. (1982), 'Intervention and self-determination in environmental disputes: a mediator's perspective', *Resolve*, (Winter) 1-7.

Cormick, G.W. (1985), 'Introduction. Negotiation and mediation in planning disputes'. Paper presented at the seminar *Negotiation and Mediation in Social Planning* at the Institute of Urban and Regional Planning, Norwegian Institute of Technology, Trondheim.

Coser, L.A. (1956), *The Functions of Social Conflict*, Free Press, New York.

Coser, L.A. (1967), *Continuities in the Study of Social Conflict*, Free Press, New York.

Cotta, S. (1985), *Why Violence? A Philosophical Interpretation*, University of Florida Press, Gainesville.

Cowan, P. (1963), *Studies in the Growth, Change and Aging of Buildings*, University College, London.

Cowan, P. (1969), 'On irreversibility', *Architectural Design*, 39 (Sept.) 485-6.

Cyert, R.M. & J.G. March (1963), *A Behavioral Theory of the Firm*, Prentice-Hall, Englewood Cliffs.

Dalton, L. (1990), 'Planners in conflict: experience and perceptions in California', *Journal of Architectural and Planning Research*, 7 (4) 284-302.

Davidoff, P. (1965), 'Advocacy and pluralism in planning', *Journal of the American Institute of Planners*, 31 (Nov.) 596-615.

Davidoff, P. & T.A. Reiner (1962), 'A choice theory of planning', *Journal of the American Institute of Planners*, 28 (May) 103-15.

De Neufville, J.I. (1987), 'Knowledge and action: making the link', *Journal of Planning Education and Research*, 6 (2) 86-92.

De Wolfe, I. (1963), *The Italian Townscape*, Architectural Press, London.

Delbecq, A.L.; A.H. Van de Ven & D.H. Gustafson (1975), *Group Techniques for Program Planning: A Guide to Nominal Group and Delphi Processes*, Scott-Foresman, Glenview.

Deutsch, K.W. (1966), *The Nerves of Government. Models of Political Communication and Control*, Free Press, New York.

Deutsch, M. (1973), *The Resolution of Conflict*, Yale University Press, New Haven.

Diamond, M.A. (1984), 'Bureaucracy as externalized self-system', *Administration and Society*, 16 (2) 195-214.

Diamond, M.A. (1986), 'Resistance to change: a psychoanalytic critique of Argyris and Schön's contributions to organization theory and intervention', *Journal of Management Studies*, 23 (5) 543-62.

Diesing, P. (1950), 'The nature and limitations of economic rationality', *Ethics*, 61 (1) 12-26.

Diesing, P. (1955), 'Noneconomic decision-making', *Ethics*, 66 (1) 18-35.

Diesing, P. (1958), 'Socioeconomic decisions', *Ethics*, 69 (1) 1-18.

Diesing, P. (1962), *Reason in Society: Five Types of Decisions and Their Social Conditions*, University of Illinois Press, Urbana.

Dillon, J.T. (1982), 'The effect of questions in education and other enterprises', *Journal of Curriculum Studies*, 14 (2) 127-52.

Downs, A. (1957), *An Economic Theory of Democracy*, Harper & Row, New York.

Dreyfus, H.L. & P. Rabinow (1982), *Michel Foucault: Beyond Structuralism and Hermeneutics*, University of Chicago Press, Chicago.

Dryzek, J.S. (1982), 'Policy analysis as a hermeneutic activity', *Policy Sciences*, 14 (4) 309-29.

Dryzek, J.S. (1983), 'Ecological rationality', *International Journal of Environmental Studies*, 21 (1) 5-10.

Dryzek, J.S. (1990), *Discursive Democracy*, Cambridge University Press, Cambridge.

Dworkin, G. (1971), 'Paternalism', pp. 107-26 in Wasserstrom, R.A. (ed.), *Morality and the Law*, Wadsworth, Belmont.

Dworkin, R. (1977), *Taking Rights Seriously*, Duckworth, London.

Eadie, D.C. (1983), 'Putting a powerful tool to practical use: the application of strategic planning in the public sector', *Public Administration Review*, 43 (5) 447-52.

Ehnmark, A. (1986), *Maktens hemligheter. En essä om Machiavelli (The Secrets of Power. An Essay on Machiavelli)*, Norstedts, Stockholm.

Elkin, S.L. (1985), 'Economic and political rationality', *Polity*, 18 (2) 253-71.

Ellul, J. (1973) [1962], *Propaganda. The Formation of Men's Attitudes*, Vintage Books, New York.

Elmore, R.F. (1979-80), 'Backward mapping: implementation research and policy decisions', *Political Science Quarterly*, 94 (4) 601-16.

Elmore, R.F. (1985), 'Forward and backward mapping: reversible logic in the analysis of public policy', pp. 33-70 in Hanf, K. & T.A.J. Toonen (eds), *Policy Implementation in Federal and Unitary Systems*, D. Reidel, Dordrecht.

Elster, J. (1978), *Logic and Society*, Wiley, Chichester.

Elster, J. (1982), *Explaining Technical Change*, Cambridge University Press, Cambridge.

Elster, J. (1983), *Sour Grapes*, Cambridge University Press, Cambridge.

Elster, J. (1984), *Ulysses and the Sirens*, Cambridge University Press, Cambridge.

Elster, J. (1987), 'The possibility of rational politics', *Archives Européennes de Sociologie*, 28 (1) 67-103.

Elster, J. (1988), 'From here to there; or, if cooperative ownership is so desirable, why are there so few cooperatives?', *Social Philosophy and Policy*, 6 (2) 93-111.

Elster, J. (1989), *The Cement of Society. A Study of Social Order*, Cambridge University Press, Cambridge.

Elster, J. (1992), 'Argumenter og forhandlinger. Om strategisk bruk av kommunikativ atferd' (Arguments and negotiations. On the strategical use of communicative behaviour), *Tidsskrift for samfunnsforskning*, 33 (2) 115-32.

Emerson, R.M. (1970), 'Power-dependence relations', pp. 44-53 in Olsen, M. (ed.), *Power in Societies*, Macmillan, New York.

Etzioni, A. (1967), 'Mixed-scanning: a "third" approach to decision-making', *Public Administration Review*, 27 (Dec.) 385-92.

Etzioni, A. (1968), *The Active Society. A Theory of Societal and Political Processes*, Free Press, New York.

Etzioni, A. (1986), 'Mixed scanning revisited', *Public Administration Review*, 46 (1) 8-14.

Eulau, H. & P.D. Karps (1977), 'The puzzle of representation: specifying components of responsiveness', *Legislative Studies Quarterly*, 2 (3) 233-54.

Fadiman, J. & R. Frager (1976), *Personality and Personal Growth*, Harper & Row, New York.

Fainstein, S.S. (1987), 'The politics of criteria: planning for the redevelopment of Times Square', pp. 232-47 in Fischer, F. & J. Forester (eds), *Confronting Values in Policy Analysis*, Sage, Beverly Hills.

Faludi, A. (ed.) (1973), *A Reader in Planning Theory*, Pergamon Press, Oxford.

Faludi, A. (1984) [1973], *Planning Theory*, Pergamon Press, Oxford.

Faludi, A. (1986), *Critical Rationalism and Planning Methodology*, Pion, London.

Faludi, A. (1987), *A Decision-Centred View of Environmental Planning*, Pergamon Press, Oxford.

Faludi, A. (1989), 'Perspectives on planning doctrine', *Built Environment*, 15 (1) 57-64.

Faludi, A. & J.M. Mastop (1982), 'The IOR School - the development of a planning methodology', *Environment and Planning B: Planning and Design*, 9 (3) 241-56.

Fanon, F. (1967), *The Wretched of the Earth*, Penguin, Harmondsworth, Middlesex.

Fay, B. (1987), *Critical Social Theory*, Polity Press, Cambridge.

Feiveson, H.A.; F.W. Sinden & R.H. Socolow (eds) (1976), *Boundaries of Analysis. An Inquiry into the Tocks Island Dam Controversy*, Ballinger, Cambridge.

Fink, C.F. (1968), 'Some conceptual difficulties in the theory of social conflict', *Conflict Resolution*, 12 (4) 412-60.

Fischer, F. (1990), *Technocracy and the Politics of Expertise*, Sage, Newbury Park.

Fisher, B.A. (1980), *Small Group Decision Making. Communication and the Group Process*, McGraw-Hill, New York.

Fisher, R. & S. Brown (1988), *Getting Together. Building a Relationship That Gets to Yes*, Houghton Mifflin, Boston.

Fisher, R. & W. Ury (1981), *Getting to YES. Negotiating Agreement Without Giving In*, Hutchinson, London.

Fishman, R. (1980), 'The anti-planners: the contemporary revolt against planning and its significance for planning history', pp. 243-52 in Cherry, G.E. (ed.), *Shaping an Urban World*, Mansell, London.

Flyvbjerg, B. (1991), *Rationalitet og magt* (Rationality and Power, Volumes 1 and 2), Akademisk Forlag, Copenhagen.

Forester, J. (1977), *Questioning and Shaping Attention as Planning Strategy: Toward a Critical Theory of Analysis and Design*, PhD-dissertation, University of California, Berkeley.

Forester, J. (1981), 'Questioning and organizing attention. Toward a critical theory of planning and administrative practice', *Administration and Society*, 13 (2) 161-205.

Forester, J. (1982a), 'Critical reason and political power in project review activity: serving freedom in planning and public administration', *Policy and Politics*, 10 (1) 65-83.

Forester, J. (1982b), 'Understanding planning practice: an empirical, practical and normative account', *Journal of Planning Education and Research*, 1 (2) 59-72.

Forester, J. (1985a), 'Practical rationality in planmaking', pp. 48-59 in Breheny, M. & A. Hooper (eds), *Rationality in Planning*, Pion, London.

Forester, J. (ed.) (1985b), *Critical Theory and Public Life*, MIT Press, Cambridge.

Forester, J. (1988), 'Sources of influence in planning practice and their implications for development negotiations', pp. 208-35 in Knox, P.L. (ed.), *The Design Professions and the Built Environment*, Croom Helm, London.

Forester, J. (1989), *Planning in the Face of Power*, University of California Press, Berkeley.

Forester, J. (1990a), 'Reply to my critics ...', *Planning Theory Newsletter*, no. 4, 43-60.

Forester, J. (1990b), 'No planning or administration without phenomeno-logy?', *Public Administration Quarterly*, 14 (1) 56-65.

Forester, J. (1992), 'Critical ethnography: on fieldwork in a Habermasian way', pp. 46-65 in Alvesson, M. & H. Wilmott (eds), *Critical Management Studies*, Sage, Beverly Hills.

Foucault, M. (1980), *Power/Knowledge*, Harvester Press, Brighton.

Foucault, M. (1982), 'The subject and power', pp. 208-26 in Dreyfus, H.L. & P. Rabinow, *Michel Foucault: Beyond Structuralism and Hermeneutics*, University of Chicago Press, Chicago.

Foucault, M. (1987), 'The ethic of care for the self as a practice of freedom' (interview 1984), pp. 1-20 in Bernauer, J. & D. Rasmussen (eds), *The Final Foucault*, MIT Press, Cambridge.

Freire, P. (1972), *Pedagogy of the Oppressed*, Penguin, Harmondsworth, Middlesex.

Friedmann, J. (1969), 'Notes on societal action', *Journal of the American Institute of Planners*, 35 (Sept.) 311-18.

Friedmann, J. (1973), *Retracking America. A Theory of Transactive Planning*, Anchor Press/Doubleday, Garden City, New York.

Friedmann, J. (1978), 'Innovation, flexible response and social learning: a problem in the theory of meta-planning', pp. 163-77 in Burchell, R.W. & G. Sternlieb (eds), *Planning Theory in the 1980's*, Center for Urban Policy Research, Rutgers University Press, New Brunswick.

Friedmann, J. (1979), *The Good Society*, MIT Press, Cambridge.

Friedmann, J. (1987), *Planning in the Public Domain. From Knowledge to Action*, Princeton University Press, Princeton.

Friedmann, J. (1989), 'Another development: possibilities of a counter-hegemonic planning', *Berkeley Planning Journal*, 4 (1) 5-18.

Friedmann, J. & G. Abonyi (1976), 'Social learning: a model for policy research', *Environment and Planning A*, 8 (8) 927-40.

Friedmann, J. & B. Hudson (1974), 'Knowledge and action: a guide to planning theory', *American Institute of Planners Journal*, 40 (1) 2-16.

Friedrich, C.J. (1972), *Tradition and Authority*, Macmillan, London.

Friend, J.K. (1983), 'Reflections on rationality in strategic choice', *Environment and Planning B: Planning and Design*, 10 (1) 63-9.

Friend, J.K. & A. Hickling (1987), *Planning under Pressure. The Strategic Choice Approach*, Pergamon Press, Oxford.

Friend, J.K. & W.N. Jessop (1969), *Local Government and Strategic Choice: An Operational Research Approach to the Processes of Public Planning*, Tavistock Publications, London.

Friend, J.K.; J.M. Power & C.J.L. Yewlett (1974), *Public Planning: The Inter-Corporate Dimension*, Tavistock Publications, London.

Galtung, J. (1969), 'Violence, peace, and peace research', *Journal of Peace Research*, 6 (3) 167-91.

Gaventa, J. (1980), *Power and Powerlessness. Quiescence and Rebellion in an Appalachian Valley*, University of Illinois Press, Urbana.

Geertz, C. (1975), 'Common sense as a cultural system', *Antioch Review*, 33 (1) 5-27.

Gert, B. & C.M. Culver (1976), 'Paternalistic behavior', *Philosophy and Public Affairs*, 6 (1) 45-57.

Getter, R.W. & P.D. Schumaker (1978), 'Contextual bases of responsiveness to citizen preferences and group demands', *Policy and Politics*, 6 (2) 249-78.

Giddens, A. (1984), *The Constitution of Society*, Polity Press, Cambridge.

Gill, S.P. (1986), 'The paradox of prediction', *Daedalus*, 115 (3) 17-48.

Goodin, R.E. (1982), *Political Theory and Public Policy*, University of Chicago Press, Chicago.

Goodin, R.E. & I. Waldner (1979), 'Thinking big, thinking small, and not thinking at all', *Public Policy*, 27 (1) 1-24.

Gordon, C. (1980), 'Afterword', pp. 229-59 in Foucault, M., *Power/Knowledge*, Harvester Press, Brighton.

Grauhan, R.-R. & W. Strubelt (1971), 'Political rationality reconsidered: notes on an integrated evaluative scheme for policy choices', *Policy Sciences*, 2 (3) 249-70.

Greenson, R.R. (1967), *The Technique and Practice of Psychoanalysis*, International Universities Press, New York.

Griffin, J. (1985), 'Towards a substantive theory of rights', pp. 137-60 in Frey, R.G. (ed.), *Utility and Rights*, Basil Blackwell, Oxford.

Grunberg, E. & F. Modigliani (1954), 'The predictability of social events', *Journal of Political Economy*, 62 (6) 465-78.

Gupta, S.K. & J. Rosenhead (1968), 'Robustness in sequential investment decisions', *Management Science*, 15 (2) B18-B29.

Gustafson, J.P. & L. Cooper (1979), 'Unconscious planning in small groups', *Human Relations*, 32 (12) 1039-64.

Habermas, J. (1970), 'On systematically distorted communication', *Inquiry*, 13 (3) 205-18.

Habermas, J. (1971a), *Knowledge and Human Interest*, Beacon Press, Boston.

Habermas, J. (1971b), *Towards a Rational Society*, Heinemann, London.

Habermas, J. (1977), 'Hannah Arendt's communications concept of power', *Social Research*, 44 (1) 3-24.

Habermas, J. (1984), *The Theory of Communicative Action. Volume 1: Reason and the Rationalization of Society*, Heinemann, London.

Habermas, J. (1987), *The Theory of Communicative Action. Volume 2: Lifeworld and System: A Critique of Functionalist Reason*, Beacon Press, Boston.

Habermas, J. (1989) [1962], *The Structural Transformation of the Public Sphere*, MIT Press, Cambridge.

Habermas, J. (1990), *Moral Consciousness and Communicative Action*, Polity Press, Cambridge.

Habermas, J. (1991), 'A reply', pp. 214-64 and 287-94 in Honneth, A. & H. Joas (eds), *Communicative Action*, Polity Press, Cambridge.

Hajer, M.A. (1989), *City Politics*, Avebury, Aldershot.

't Hart, P. (1990), *Groupthink in Government. A Study of Small Groups and Policy Failure*, Dissertation, Rijksuniversiteit, Leiden.

Hashimoto, T.; J.R. Stedinger & D.P. Loucks (1982), 'Reliability, resiliency, and vulnerability criteria for water resource system performance evaluation', *Water Resources Research*, 18 (1) 14-20.

Hawes, L. & D. Smith (1973), 'A critique of assumptions underlying the study of communication in conflict', *Quarterly Journal of Speech*, 59 (4) 423-35.

Haworth, L. (1984), 'Orwell, the planning profession, and autonomy', *Environments*, 16 (2) 10-15.

Hayek, F.A. (1944), *The Road to Serfdom*, Routledge & Kegan Paul, London.

Healey, P. (1992a), 'A planner's day. Knowledge and action in communicative practice', *American Planning Association Journal*, 58 (1) 9-20.

Healey, P. (1992b), 'Planning through debate. The communicative turn in planning theory', *Town Planning Review*, 63 (2) 143-62.

Healey, P. (1993), 'The communicative work of development plans', *Environment and Planning B: Planning and Design*, 20 (1) 83-104.

Heiner, R.A. (1983), 'The origin of predictable behavior', *American Economic Review*, 73 (4) 560-95.

Heiner, R.A. (1985), 'Origin of predictable behavior: further modeling and applications', *American Economic Review*, 75 (May) 391-6.

Heiner, R.A. (1988), 'Imperfect decisions in organizations. Towards a theory of internal structure', *Journal of Economic Behavior and Organization*, 9 (1) 25-44.

Held, D. (1987), *Models of Democracy*, Polity Press, Cambridge.

Henshel, R.L. (1978), 'Self-altering predictions', pp. 99-123 in Fowles, J. (ed.), *Handbook of Futures Research*, Greenwood Press, Westport.

Heskin, A.D. (1980), 'Crisis and response. A historical perspective on advocacy planning', *American Planning Association Journal*, 46 (1) 50-63.

Hiley, D.R. (1984), 'Foucault and the analysis of power: political engagement without liberal hope or comfort', *Praxis International*, 4 (2) 192-207.

Hillier, J. (1993), 'Discursive democracy in action', *AESOP Congress Paper Lodz*, Lodz.

Hirschhorn, L. & J. Krantz (1982), 'Unconscious planning in a natural work group: a case study in process consultation', *Human Relations*, 35 (10) 805-44.

Hirschman, A.O. (1967), 'The principle of the hiding hand', *Public Interest*, 6 (Winter) 10-23.

Hirschman, A.O. & C. Lindblom (1962), 'Economic development, research and development, policy making: some converging views', *Behavioral Sciences*, 7 (2) 211-22.

Hoch, C. (1988), 'Conflict at large: a national survey of planners and political conflict', *Journal of Planning Education and Research*, 8 (1) 25-34.

Hoch, C. & A. Cibulskis (1987), 'Planning threatened: a preliminary report of planners and political conflict', *Journal of Planning Education and Research*, 6 (2) 99-107.

Hodson, J.D. (1977), 'The principle of paternalism', *American Philosophical Quarterly*, 14 (1) 61-9.

Hogarth, R.M. (1980), *Judgment and Choice. The Psychology of Decisions*, Wiley, New York.

Hogarth, R.M. & M.W. Reder (eds) (1987), *Rational Choice: The Contrast between Economics and Psychology*, University of Chicago Press, Chicago.

Hoy, D.C. (1986), 'Power, repression, progress: Foucault, Lukes, and the Frankfurt School', pp. 123-47 in Hoy, D.C. (ed.), *Foucault: A Critical Reader*, Basil Blackwell, Oxford.

Hubin, D.C. (1986-87), 'Of bindings and by-products: Elster on rationality', *Philosophy and Public Affairs*, 15 (1) 82-95.

Hudson, B.M. (1979), 'Comparison of current planning theories: counterparts and contradictions', *American Planning Association Journal*, 45 (4) 387-98.

Husak, D.N. (1980), 'Paternalism and autonomy', *Philosophy and Public Affairs*, 10 (1) 27-46.

Ingram, D. (1987), *Habermas and the Dialectic of Reason*, Yale University Press, New Haven.

Irland, L.C. (1975), 'Citizen participation - a tool for conflict management on the public lands', *Public Administration Review*, 35 (May/June) 263-9.

Jacobs, J. (1965) [1961], *The Death and Life of Great American Cities. The Failure of Town Planning*, Penguin, Harmondsworth, Middlesex.

Janis, I.L. (1982), *Groupthink. Psychological Studies of Policy Decisions and Fiascoes*, Houghton Mifflin, Boston.

Janis, I.L. & L. Mann (1977), *Decision Making. A Psychological Analysis of Conflict, Choice, and Commitment*, Free Press, New York.

Johansen, L. (1977), *Lectures on Macroeconomic Planning. Volume 1*, North-Holland, Amsterdam.

Karlsson, G. (1962), 'Some aspects of power in small groups', pp. 193-202 in Criswell, J.H; H. Salomon & P. Suppes (eds), *Mathematical Methods in Small Group Processes*, Stanford University Press, Stanford.

Kartez, J.D. (1984), 'Crisis response planning. Toward a contingent analysis', *American Planning Association Journal*, 50 (1) 9-21.

Kartez, J.D. (1989), 'Rational arguments and irrational audiences. Psychology, planning, and public judgment', *American Planning Association Journal*, 55 (4) 445-56.

Kaufman, J.L. (1978), 'The planner as interventionist in public policy issues', pp. 179-200 in Burchell, R.W. & G. Sternlieb, *Planning Theory in the 1980's*, Center for Urban Policy Research, Rutgers University Press, New Brunswick.

Kaufman, J.L. & H.M. Jacobs (1987), 'A public planning perspective on strategic planning', *Journal of the American Planning Association*, 53 (1) 21-31.

Kemp, R. (1980), 'Planning, legitimation, and the development of nuclear energy: a critical theoretic analysis of the Windscale inquiry', *International Journal of Urban and Regional Research*, 4 (3) 350-71.

Kemp, R. (1985), 'Planning, public hearings, and the politics of discourse', pp. 177-201 in Forester, J. (ed.), *Critical Theory and Public Life*, MIT Press, Cambridge.

Kets de Vries, M.F.R. & D. Miller (1989), *The Neurotic Organization*, Jossey-Bass, San Francisco.

Kierkegaard, S. (1971) [1843], *Either/Or. Volume 1*, Princeton University Press, Princeton.

Klosterman, R.E. (1985), 'Arguments for and against planning', *Town Planning Review*, 56 (1) 5-20.

Kozlowski, J. & G. Hill (eds) (1993), *Towards Planning for Sustainable Development. A Guide for the Ultimate Environmental Threshold Method (UET)*, Avebury, Aldershot.

Kraushaar, R. (1988), 'Outside the whale: progressive planning and the dilemmas of radical reform', *American Planning Association Journal*, 54 (1) 91-100.

Kravitz, A.S. (1970), 'Mandarinism: planning as handmaiden to conservative politics', pp. 240-67 in Beyle, T.L. & G.T. Lathrop (eds), *Planning and Politics: Uneasy Partnership*, Odyssey Press, New York.

Krippendorff, K. (1991), 'The power of communication and the communication of power: toward an emancipatory theory of communication', *Communication*, 12 (3) 175-96.

Kuhn, T.S. (1970), *The Structure of Scientific Revolutions*, University of Chicago Press, Chicago.

Lakatos, I. & A. Musgrave (eds) (1974), *Criticism and the Growth of Knowledge*, Cambridge University Press, London.

Landau, M. (1969), 'Redundancy, rationality, and the problem of duplication and overlap', *Public Administration Review*, 29 (July/Aug.) 346-358.

Lasswell, H.D.L. & A. Kaplan (1950), *Power and Society*, Yale University Press, New Haven.

Leibenstein, H. (1976), *Beyond Economic Man. A New Foundation for Microeconomics*, Harvard University Press, Cambridge.

Leonard, S.T. (1990), *Critical Theory in Political Practice*, Princeton University Press, Princeton.

Levi, A.M. & A. Benjamin (1977), 'Focus and flexibility in a model of conflict resolution', *Journal of Conflict Resolution*, 21 (3) 405-25.

Levi, I. (1986), *Hard Choices. Decision Making under Unresolved Conflict*, Cambridge University Press, Cambridge.

Lewis, N.C. (1993), *Road Pricing. Theory and Practice*, Thomas Telford, London.

Lilja, E. (1988), *The Modern Planner - a Symbol of Instrumental Reason*, Meddelande 1988:2, Nordic Institute for Studies in Urban and Regional Planning, Stockholm.

Lim, G.-C. & J. Albrecht (1987), 'A search for an alternative planning theory: use of phenomenology', *Journal of Architectural and Planning Research*, 4 (1) 14-30.

Lindblom, C. (1959), 'The science of "muddling through"', *Public Administration Review*, 19 (2) 79-88.

Lindblom, C. (1965), *The Intelligence of Democracy. Decision Making Through Mutual Adjustment*, Free Press, New York.

Lindblom, C. (1967), 'Some limitations on rationality: a comment', pp. 224-8 in Friedrich, C.J. (ed.), *Rational Decision (Nomos VII)*, Atherton Press, New York.

Lindblom, C. (1968), *The Policy-Making Process*, Prentice-Hall, Englewood Cliffs.

Lindblom, C. (1977), *Politics and Markets*, Basic Books, New York.

Lindblom, C. (1979), 'Still muddling, not yet through', *Public Administration Review*, 39 (6) 517-26.

Lindblom, C. (1990), *Inquiry and Change*, Yale University Press, New Haven.

Lindblom, C. & D.K. Cohen (1979), *Usable Knowledge*, Yale University Press, New Haven.

Lorange, E. (1986), 'Formelle byplaner og selvgrodde byer' (Formal town plans and self-grown towns), pp. 36-51 in Olsen, A. & A. Selfors (eds), *Fysisk planlegging (Physical Planning)*, Fagbokforlaget, Oslo.

Luban, D. (1985), 'Bargaining and compromise: recent work on negotiation and informal justice', *Philosophy and Public Affairs*, 14 (4) 397-416.

Luft, H.S. (1976), 'Benefit-cost analysis and public policy implementation', *Public Policy*, 24 (Fall) 437-62.

Lukes, S. (1974), *Power. A Radical View*, Macmillan, London.

Lynch, K. (1981), *A Theory of Good City Form*, MIT Press, Cambridge.

McAllister, D. (1980), *Evaluation in Environmental Planning*, MIT Press, Cambridge.

McCarthy, T. (1992), 'The critique of impure reason: Foucault and the Frankfurt School', pp. 121-48 and 304-13 in Wartenberg, T. (ed.), *Rethinking Power*, State University of New York Press, Albany.

McCarthy, W. (1985), 'The role of power and principle in "Getting to YES"', *Negotiation Journal*, 1 (Jan.) 59-66.

McCaskey, M.B. (1974), 'A contingency approach to planning: planning with goals and planning without goals', *Academy of Management Journal*, 17 (2) 281-91.

McDougall, G. (1982), 'Theory and practice: a critique of the political economy approach to planning', pp. 258-71 in Healey, P.; G. McDougall & M.J. Thomas (eds), *Planning Theory. Prospects for the 1980s*, Pergamon Press, Oxford.

Machiavelli, N. (1984) [ca 1515], *The Discourses*, Penguin, Harmondsworth, Middlesex.

McLoughlin, J.B. (1969), *Urban and Regional Planning. A Systems Approach*, Faber & Faber, London.

Macmillan, C.J.B. (1983), '"On Certainty" and indoctrination', *Synthese*, 56 (3) 363-72.

Majone, G. & A. Wildavsky (1978), 'Implementation as evaluation', pp. 103-17 in Freeman, H.E. (ed.), *Policy Studies Review Annual Volume 2*, Sage, Beverly Hills.

Mannheim, K. (1940), *Man and Society in an Age of Reconstruction*, Routledge & Kegan Paul, London.

March, J.G. (1971), 'The technology of foolishness', *Civiløkonomen*, 8, 7-12.

March, J.G. (1978), 'Bounded rationality, ambiguity, and the engineering of choice', *Bell Journal of Economics*, 9 (2) 587-608.

March, J.G. (1982), 'Theories of choice and making decisions', *Society*, 20 (1) 29-39.

March, J.G. & J.P. Olsen (1986), 'Garbage can models of decision making in organizations', pp. 11-35 in March, J.G. & R. Weissinger-Baylon (eds), *Ambiguity and Command. Organizational Perspectives on Military Decision Making*, Pitman Publishing, Marshfield.

March, J.G. & J.P. Olsen (1989), *Rediscovering Institutions. The Organizational Basis of Politics*, Free Press, New York.

Masser, I.; O. Svidén & M. Wegener (1992), 'From growth to equity and sustainability. Paradigm shift in transport planning?', *Futures*, 24 (6) 539-58.

Masuch, M. (1986), 'The planning paradox', pp. 89-99 in Geyer, F. & J. van der Zouwen (eds), *Sociocybernetic Paradoxes*, Sage, Beverly Hills.

May, A.D. (1991), 'Integrated transport strategies: a new approach to urban transport policy formulation in the U.K.', *Transport Reviews*, 11 (3) 223-47.

Meier, R.L. (1985), 'The coming paradigm for planners: community ecology', *Berkeley Planning Journal*, 1 (2) 69-93.

Merton, R.K. (1936), 'The unanticipated consequences of purposive social action', *American Sociological Review*, 1 (6) 894-904.

Merton, R.K. (1957) [1949], *Social Theory and Social Structure*, Free Press, London.

Miller, C.R. (1990), 'The rhetoric of decision science, or Herbert A. Simon says', pp. 162-84 in Simons, H.W. (ed.), *The Rhetorical Turn. Invention and Persuasion in the Conduct of Inquiry*, University of Chicago Press, Chicago.

Minnery, J.R. (1985), *Conflict Management in Urban Planning*, Gower, Aldershot, Hampshire.

Mischel, W. (1986), *Introduction to Personality. A New Look* (Fourth edition), Holt, Rinehart & Winston, New York.

Moore, C. (1986), *The Mediation Process*, Jossey-Bass, San Francisco.

Moore, C.M. (1987), *Group Techniques for Idea Building*, Sage, Newbury Park.

Mueller, C. (1973), *The Politics of Communication*, Oxford University Press, New York.

Nagel, J.H. (1975), *The Descriptive Analysis of Power*, Yale University Press, New Haven.

Nimmo, D. (1978), *Political Communication and Public Opinion in America*, Goodyear, Santa Monica.

Noelle-Neumann, E. (1974), 'The spiral of silence. A theory of public opinion', *Journal of Communication*, 24 (1) 43-51.

Norgaard, R.B. & J.A. Dixon (1986), 'Pluralistic project design', *Policy Sciences*, 19 (3) 297-317.

O'Neill, J. (1985), 'Decolonization and the ideal speech community: some issues in the theory and practice of communicative competence', pp. 57-76 in Forester, J. (ed.), *Critical Theory and Public Life*, MIT Press, Cambridge.

Olsen, S.A. (ed.) (1982), *Group Planning and Problem-Solving Methods in Engineering Management*, Wiley, New York.

Olsson, G. (1991), *Lines of Power. Limits of Language*, University of Minnesota Press, Minneapolis.

Ordeshook, P.C. (1986), *Game Theory and Political Theory: An Introduction*, Cambridge University Press, Cambridge.

Parsons, T. (1967), *Sociological Theory and Modern Society*, Free Press, New York.

Parsons, T. (1977), *Social Systems and the Evolution of Action Theory*, Free Press, New York.

Pearman, A.D. (1985), 'Uncertainty in planning: characterisation, evaluation, and feedback', *Environment and Planning B: Planning and Design*, 12 (3) 313-20.

Peleg, B. & M.E. Yaari (1973), 'On the existence of a consistent course of action when tastes are changing', *Review of Economic Studies*, 40 (Jan.) 391-401.

Piven, F.F. (1970), 'Whom does the advocacy planner serve?', *Social Policy*, 1 (May-June) 32-7.

Pollak, R.A. (1976), 'Habit formation and long-run utility formation', *Journal of Economic Theory*, 13 (Oct.) 272-97.

Pondy, L.R. (1967), 'Organizational conflict: concepts and models', *Administrative Science Quarterly*, 12 (2) 296-320.

Popper, K. (1966a) [1945], *The Open Society and Its Enemies. Volume 1. Plato*, Routledge & Kegan Paul, London.

Popper, K. (1966b) [1945], *The Open Society and Its Enemies. Volume 2: Hegel and Marx*, Routledge & Kegan Paul, London.

Popper, K. (1972) [1962], *Conjectures and Refutations* (Fourth edition), Routledge & Kegan Paul, London.

Popper, K. (1986) [1957], *The Poverty of Historicism*, Routledge & Kegan Paul, London.

Pressman, J.L. & A. Wildavsky (1973), *Implementation*, University of California Press, Berkeley.

Priscoli, J.D. (1975), 'Citizen advisory groups and conflict resolution in regional water resources planning', *Water Resources Bulletin*, 11 (6) 1233-43.

Pye, R. (1978), 'A formal, decision-theoretic approach to flexibility and robustness', *Journal of the Operational Research Society*, 29 (3) 215-27.

Quinn, J.B. (1980), *Strategies for Change: Logical Incrementalism*, Irwin, Homewood.

Raiffa, H. (1982), *The Art and Science of Negotiation*, Belknap Press, Cambridge.

Rapoport, A. (1960), *Fights, Games, and Debates*, University of Michigan Press, Ann Arbor.

Rapoport, A. (1966), *Two-Person Game Theory: The Essential Ideas*, University of Michigan Press, Ann Arbor.

Rapoport, A. (1974), *Conflict in Man-Made Environment*, Penguin, Harmondsworth, Middlesex.

Rawls, J. (1972), *A Theory of Justice*, Oxford University Press, Oxford.

Read, J.H. (1989), 'Nietzsche: power as oppression', *Praxis International*, 9 (1/2) 72-87.

Richards, L.D. (1977), 'Beyond planning: controllability vs predictability', pp. 314-23 in Society for General Systems Research, *The General Systems Paradigm: Science of Change and Change of Science*, SGSR, Washington.

Ricoeur, P. (1976), *Interpretation Theory*, Texas Christian University Press, Fort Worth.

Ricoeur, P. (1981), *Hermeneutics and the Human Sciences*, Cambridge University Press, Cambridge.

Ricoeur, P. (1991) [1971], 'The model of the text: meaningful action considered as a text', pp.144-67 in Ricoeur, P., *From Text to Action. Essays in Hermeneutics, Volume 2*, Northwestern University Press, Evanston.

Rittel, H.W.J. & M.M. Webber (1973), 'Dilemmas in a general theory of planning', *Policy Sciences*, 4 (2) 155-69.

Robertson, K.A. (1978), 'Political impact analysis in transportation planning', *Journal of Community Development Society of America*, 9 (1) 112-23.

Rodrik, D. & R. Zeckhauser (1988), 'The dilemma of government responsiveness', *Journal of Policy Analysis and Management*, 7 (4) 601-20.

Rogers, C.R. (1961), *On Becoming a Person*, Houghton Mifflin, Boston.

Rogers, C.R. (1977), *Carl Rogers on Personal Power*, Delacorte Press, New York.

Rohrbaugh, J.W. (1976), *Conflict Management in Decision-Making Groups: A Comparison of Social Judgment Analysis and the Delphi Technique*, PhD-dissertation, Faculty of the Graduate School of the University of Colorado.

Rorty, R. (1989), *Contingency, Irony, and Solidarity*, Cambridge University Press, Cambridge.

Rosenhead, J. (1980), 'Planning under uncertainty: 1. The inflexibility of methodologies', *Journal of the Operational Research Society*, 31 (3) 209-16.

Rosenhead, J. (1989), 'Robustness analysis: keeping your options open', pp. 193-218 in Rosenhead, J. (ed.), *Rational Analysis for a Problematic World*, Wiley, Chichester.

Rosenhead, J.; M. Elton & S.K. Gupta (1972), 'Robustness and optimality as criteria for strategic decisions', *Operational Research Quarterly*, 23 (4) 413-31.

Rouse, J. (1987), *Knowledge and Power. Toward a Political Philosophy of Science*, Cornell University Press, Ithaca.

Rousseau, J.-J. (1968) [1762], *The Social Contract*, Penguin, Harmondsworth, Middlesex.

Roweis, S.T. (1988), 'Knowledge-power and professional practice', pp. 175-207 in Knox, P.L. (ed.), *The Design Professions and the Built Environment*, Croom Helm, London.

Runciman, W.G. & A.K. Sen (1965), 'Games, justice and the general will', *Mind*, 74 (Oct.) 554-62.

Saaty, T.L. & K.P. Kearns (1985), *Analytical Planning. The Organization of Systems*, Pergamon Press, Oxford.

Sager, T. (1990a), *Communicate or Calculate. Planning Theory and Social Science Concepts in a Contingency Perspective*, Dissertation 11. Nordic Institute for Studies in Urban and Regional Planning, Stockholm.

Sager, T. (1990b), *Notions of Flexibility in Planning-Related Literature*, Meddelande 1990:5, Nordic Institute for Studies in Urban and Regional Planning, Stockholm.

Sager, T. (1992), 'Why plan? A multi-rationality foundation for planning', *Scandinavian Housing and Planning Research*, 9 (2) 129-47.

Sager, T. (1993a), 'Paradigms for planning: a rationality-based classification' *Planning Theory Newsletter*, no. 9, 1-38.

Sager, T. (1993b), 'From impact assessment to recommendation: presentation and use of IA-results in urban transportation planning', *Research Note*, Department of Transportation Engineering, Norwegian Institute of Technology, Trondheim.

Sager, T. (1994), 'Dialogical incrementalism', *Journal of Architectural and Planning Research*, (forthcoming).

Saltzstein, G. (1985), 'Conceptualizing bureaucratic responsiveness', *Administration and Society*, 17 (3) 283-306.

Sanders, K.R.; L.L. Kaid & D. Nimmo (eds) (1985), *Political Communication Yearbook 1984*, Southern Illinois University Press, Carbondale and Edwardsville.

Sartre, J.-P. (1982) [1960], *Critique of Dialectical Reason*, Verso, London.

Schattschneider, E.E. (1975) [1960], *The Semisovereign People*, Dryden Press, Hinsdale.

Schön, D. (1983), *The Reflective Practitioner. How Professionals Think in Action*, Temple Smith, London.

Schön, D. (1986), 'Toward a new epistemology of practice', pp. 231-50 in Checkoway, B. (ed.), *Strategic Perspectives of Planning Practice*, Lexington Books, Lexington.

Schön, D. (1987), *Educating the Reflective Practitioner*, Jossey-Bass, San Francisco.

Schramm, W. (1971), 'The nature of communication between humans', pp. 1-53 in Schramm, W. & D.F. Roberts (eds), *The Process and Effects of Mass Communication*, University of Illinois Press, Urbana.

Schumaker, P.D. (1981), 'Citizen preferences and policy responsiveness', pp. 227-43 in Nichols Clark, T. (ed.), *Urban Policy Analysis. Directions for Future Research*, Sage, Beverly Hills.

Scott, A.J. (1980), *The Urban Land Nexus and the State*, Pion, London.

Seel, M. (1991), 'The two meanings of "communicative" rationality: remarks on Habermas's critique of a plural concept of reason', pp. 36-48 and 267-9 in Honneth, A. & H. Joas (eds), *Communicative Action*, Polity Press, Cambridge.

Sennett, R. (1970), *The Uses of Disorder. Personal Identity and City Life*, Alfred A. Knopf, New York.

Sennett, R. (1981), *Authority*, Vintage Books, New York.

Shapley, L.S. & M. Shubik (1954), 'A method for evaluating the distribution of power in a committee system', *American Political Science Review*, 48 (3) 787-92.

Sieber, S.D. (1981), *Fatal Remedies. The Ironies of Social Intervention*, Plenum Press, New York.

Sillince, J. (1986), *A Theory of Planning*, Gower, Aldershot, Hampshire.

Simon, H.A. (1954), 'Bandwagon and underdog effects and the possibility of election predictions', *Public Opinion Quarterly*, 18 (Fall) 245-53.

Simon, H.A. (1957) [1945], *Administrative Behavior* (Second edition), Macmillan, New York.

Simon, H.A.; M. Egidi; R. Viale & R. Marris (1992), *Economics, Bounded Rationality and the Cognitive Revolution*, Edward Elgar, Aldershot, Hampshire.

Skjei, S.S. (1976), 'Urban problems and the theoretical justification of urban planning', *Urban Affairs Quarterly*, 11 (3) 323-44.

Slote, M. (1989), *Beyond Optimizing: A Study of Rational Choice*, Harvard University Press, Cambridge.

Smith, J.G. (ed.) (1984), *Strategic Planning in Nationalised Industries*, Macmillan Press, London.

Sorensen, A.D. & R.A. Day (1981), 'Libertarian planning', *Town Planning Review*, 52 (4) 390-402.

Stone, C.N. (1980), 'Systemic power in community decision making: a restatement of stratification theory', *American Political Science Review*, 74 (4) 978-90.

Strotz, R.H. (1955-56), 'Myopia and inconsistency in dynamic utility maximization', *Review of Economic Studies*, 23 (Winter) 165-80.

Sullivan, T. (1984), *Resolving Development Disputes Through Negotiation*, Plenum Press, New York.

Susskind, L. (1983), 'The uses of negotiation and mediation in environmental impact assessment', pp. 154-67 in Rossini, F.A. & A.L. Porter (eds), *Integrated Impact Assessment*, Westview Press, Boulder.

Susskind, L. & J. Cruikshank (1987), *Breaking the Impasse. Consensual Approaches to Resolving Public Disputes*, Basic Books, New York.

Taylor, M. (1982), *Community, Anarchy and Liberty*, Cambridge University Press, Cambridge.

Taylor, R.N. (1975), 'Psychological determinants of bounded rationality: implications for decision-making strategies', *Decision Sciences*, 6 (3) 409-29.

Tett, A. & J.M. Wolfe (1991), 'Discourse analysis and city plans' *Journal of Planning Education and Research*, 10 (3) 195-200.

Thompson, J.B. (1981), *Critical Hermeneutics. A Study in the Thought of Paul Ricoeur and Jürgen Habermas*, Cambridge University Press, Cambridge.

Tretvik, T. (1992), 'The Trondheim toll ring: applied technology and public opinion, pp. 69-78 in Frey, R.L. & P.M. Langloh (eds), *The Use of Economic Instruments in Urban Travel Management*, WWZ-Report no. 37, Wirtschaftswissenschaftliches Zentrum der Universität Basel, Basel.

Turner, J.H. (1982), *The Structure of Sociological Theory*, Dorsey Press, Homewood.

Uhlaner, C.J. (1989), '"Relational goods" and participation: incorporating sociability into a theory of rational action', *Public Choice*, 62 (3) 253-85.

Ury, W. (1991), *Getting Past No. Negotiating with Difficult People*, Century Business, London.

Van Witteloostuijn, A. (1988), 'Maximising and satisficing: opposite or equivalent concepts?', *Journal of Economic Psychology*, 9 (3) 289-313.

Vernon, R. (1979), 'Unintended consequences', *Political Theory*, 7 (1) 57-73.

Wachs, M. (1982), 'Ethical dilemmas in forecasting for public policy', *Public Administration Review*, 42 (Nov./Dec.) 562-7.

Wachs, M. (1990), 'Ethics and advocacy in forecasting for public policy', *Business and Professional Ethics Journal*, 9 (1/2) 141-57.

Warren, M. (1992), 'Democratic theory and self-transformation', *American Political Science Review*, 86 (1) 8-23.

Warren, M. (1993), 'Can participatory democracy produce better selves? Psychological dimensions of Habermas's discursive model of democracy', *Political Psychology*, 14 (2) 209-34.

Wartenberg, T.E. (1988), 'The concept of power in feminist theory', *Praxis International*, 8 (3) 301-16.

Watts, T.J. (1987), *Arbitration, Mediation, and Other Forms of Alternative Dispute Resolution: A Selected Bibliography*, Public Administration Series P-2255, Vance Bibliographies, Monticello.

Weizsäcker, C.C. von (1971), 'Notes on endogenous changes of tastes', *Journal of Economic Theory*, 3 (Dec.) 345-72.

Wenk, E. Jr. (1979), 'The political limits to forecasting', pp. 289-322 in Whiston, T. (ed.), *The Uses and Abuses of Forecasting*, Macmillan, London.

West, D. (1987), 'Power and formation: new foundations for a radical concept of power', *Inquiry*, 30 (1-2) 137-54.

Whitehead, P. (1974), 'Flexibility in structure plans', *Planning Outlook*, 14 (Spring) 31-42.

Wiberg, H. (1975), *Konfliktteori och fredsforskning (Conflict Theory and Peace Research)*, Scandinavian University Books, Esselte, Stockholm.

Wildavsky, A. (1973), 'If planning is everything, maybe it's nothing', *Policy Sciences*, 4 (2) 127-53.

Wilkins, L.T. & T. Gitchoff (1969), 'Trends and projections in social control systems', *Annals of the American Academy of Political and Social Science*, no. 381, 125-36.

Williamson, O.E. (1975), *Markets and Hierarchies: Analysis and Antitrust Implications. A Study in the Economics of Internal Organization*, Free Press, New York.

Williamson, O.E. (1981), 'The economics of organization: the transaction cost approach', *American Journal of Sociology*, 87 (3) 548-77.

Wimsatt, W.K. Jr. & M.C. Beardsley (1946), 'The intentional fallacy', *Sewanee Review*, no. 54, 468-88.

Wolff, R.P. (1970), *In Defense of Anarchism*, Harper & Row, New York.

Wrong, D.H. (1979), *Power. Its Forms, Bases and Uses*, Harper & Row, New York.

Yewlett, C.J.L. (1985), 'Rationality in planmaking: a professional perspective', pp. 209-228 in Breheny, M. & A. Hooper (eds), *Rationality in Planning*, Pion, London.

Index

Rosenhead, J. 224-5, 230, 236-7, 244

Rousseau, J.-J. 133, 140-1

Sartre, J.-P. 187-8

satisficing 13-14, 56, 114, 236-8, 251

Schattschneider, E.E. 34, 55, 118

Schön, D. 174, 176, 178, 181-2, 192-3

secrecy 208, 247-9

seduction 67, 70-2, 75, 92-3, 135, 155

self-altering forecasts 113, 121-6

Sennett, R. 51, 78, 93, 126-7, 192-3

SITAR package 26-8, 45, 49-53, 56

social science 9, 22-3, 43, 61, 76, 82-3, 122, 188, 227, 246, 250, 256

spiral of silence 106

staging 227, 231, 244

strategic choice approach 42, 46-7, 50

strategic planning 42-3, 46, 50

strategical rationalism, see synoptic planning

structured group process 82, 165

structural influence 60, 63-6, 91, 130, 132, 135, 138, 148, 152-3

synoptic planning 8-10
    concept 8-10
    and conflict 158-9
    and flexibility 236
    and power 88-9, 114-7
    and responsiveness 185

technocracy 43, 76, 78, 129, 162-3, 209

threat 18, 67, 75, 101-2, 116, 119, 126, 155, 166

transactive planning 5, 22, 24-7, 32, 39, 42-3, 47, 50, 53, 89, 136, 157

transportation 80, 224-7, 231-3, 238
    and land use planning 195-220
    toll ring 95-112, 177-8

unanticipated consequences 33, 90-1, 130, 181, 187-9, 194, 226-7, 240, 247

uncertainty 47, 73, 135-7, 144, 185, 192, 202, 205, 223, 231, 235-40, 251

undistorted communication, see dialogue

validity claims 6, 97-8, 106, 201

Wachs, M. 122, 139, 205, 207

Wildavsky, A. 190, 194